PRAISE FOR *THE WAY OF THE DRAGON OR THE WAY OF THE LAMB*

"Jamin and Kyle have a finger on the pulse of something significant here. I have often been concerned with the current view of strength and power as it is currently understood and embraced in our culture. The church must see power for what it is and where it's found. True Holy Spirit power is found in weakness, not brazen human strength and skill. It is imperative for us to understand and embrace this truth. *The Way of the Dragon or the Way of the Lamb* will help us all along the path to pursuing the way of the Lamb."

—MATT CHANDLER, LEAD PASTOR OF THE VILLAGE CHURCH AND PRESIDENT OF THE ACTS 29 CHURCH PLANTING NETWORK

"This is a book every Christian leader needs to read and soon. Nuanced, wise, pastoral, and yet challenging, *The Way of the Dragon or the Way of the Lamb* will shape more than your leadership and your ministry, it will shape your soul and reorient you to following Jesus. In our day and age, this is a message we need desperately."

—SARAH BESSEY, AUTHOR OF *OUT OF SORTS* AND *JESUS FEMINIST*

"I was both encouraged and humbled by this book. The authors' openness to the sages in the generation before them is in shining contrast to the 'generationalism' that is so common today. But the combined weight of their analysis is a sobering reminder of the seductive coils of power in which we are all so easily entangled."

—OS GUINNESS, AUTHOR OF *IMPOSSIBLE PEOPLE* AND *FOOL'S TALK*

"*The Way of the Dragon or the Way of the Lamb* is possibly one of the most unique, yet profound books I've read in years. The wisdom packed into its pages is so remarkable, I felt like I was standing on holy ground with each page, needing to take off my shoes. What a monumental book. A must-read."

—NISH WEISETH, AUTHOR OF *SPEAK*

"Insightful, humbling, and worshipful, this book is a necessary call for the church to seek its power in the Spirit, not in the celebrity culture of a lost world. *The Way of the Dragon or the Way of the Lamb* will encourage pastors and church members to look at themselves and their fellowships through the lens of the gospel."

—RUSSELL MOORE, PRESIDENT OF THE ETHICS & RELIGIOUS LIBERTY COMMISSION OF THE SOUTHERN BAPTIST CONVENTION

P9-DMT-593

"These two young men have done it right: they've listened to some of the greats in the church today, some great leaders noted not by power, but by humility and by a cruciform existence. *The Way of the Dragon or the Way of the Lamb* charts a path for today's young leaders—the way of listening to the wisdom of the wise."

—SCOT MCKNIGHT, JULIUS R. MANTEY PROFESSOR OF NEW TESTAMENT, NORTHERN SEMINARY

"You need this book, I need this book. We all need this book, probably a lot more than we imagine. Too many of these lessons I've learned the hard way. I can only pray that a rising generation of Christian leaders will learn from Jamin and Kyle's journey and realize that the path to true glory passes through the way of the Lamb."

—COLLIN HANSEN, EDITORIAL DIRECTOR OF THE GOSPEL COALITION AND AUTHOR OF BLIND SPOTS

"American Evangelicalism needs Jesus. These pages testify to the reality that an exodus from celebrity to humility, certainty to maturity, toxic leadership to simple discipleship, successful to faithful, isn't through the way of self-righteous rants, power plays, or smug condemnation. Instead, this is the confession of two brothers seeking the way of the Lamb by surrendering to the wisdom of elders. Leaders whose lives look like Christ. When these elders are listened to, a culture that proclaims 'Jesus is the Way' will join them in 'The Way of Jesus.'"

—JARROD MCKENNA, TEACHING PASTOR AT WESTCITY CHURCH AND COFOUNDER OF FIRST HOME PROJECT

"Absolutely brilliant! *The Way of the Dragon or the Way of the Lamb* is a counter-cultural roadmap for life in God's kingdom. The lust for power doesn't escape any of us, even those who are stewards of God's church. This book provides a gripping diagnosis, as well as a cure for those who desire it. Read this book!"

—ALBERT TATE, LEAD PASTOR OF FELLOWSHIP MONROVIA

"Our culture—and our churches—often associate power and relevance with youth and self-exaltation. Fortunately, Jamin and Kyle have confronted this distortion and many corruptions of power today. You're invited to join them and discover afresh that as astounding as it may be, the way of the Dragon is ultimately over-come by the way of the Lamb."

—JOSHUA RYAN BUTLER, PASTOR OF LOCAL AND GLOBAL OUTREACH AT IMAGO DEI COMMUNITY AND AUTHOR OF THE SKELETONS IN GOD'S CLOSET AND THE PURSUING GOD

"What if our idea of success is all wrong? What if the church has glorified the wrong things? For many pastors the overwhelming desire for success and celebrity is a constant temptation, leading to an obsession with numbers and notoriety. In *The Way of the Dragon or the Way of the Lamb*, Jamin Goggin and Kyle Strobel embark on a pilgrimage to show us a different way, spending time with men and women who have eschewed the way of the Dragon for a life marked by kingdom depth, lasting influence, and the wisdom of weakness. Sharing the lives and wisdom of their mentors, this book is a tonic for the twenty-first century church, showing Christians that the wisdom of the cross is the path to lasting meaning, deep joy in the midst of suffering, and powerful influence—in short, the recipe for renewal, both personal and corporate. I hope this book is read widely."

—JIM BELCHER, AUTHOR OF *IN SEARCH OF DEEP FAITH* AND COAUTHOR OF *DEEP CHURCH*

"The question of power is the most momentous issue facing Christians today. Whenever and wherever Christianity runs off the rails, in toxic and destructive ways, it is because we stumble at this point, opting for the way of the Dragon. I encourage you to join Jamin Goggin and Kyle Strobel on their journey to discover the way of the Lamb. This is a wise, urgent, and prophetic book."

—RICHARD BECK, PROFESSOR OF PSYCHOLOGY AT ABILENE CHRISTIAN UNIVERSITY, BLOGGER, AND AUTHOR OF *REVIVING OLD SCRATCH* AND *UNCLEAN*

"A fresh perspective on the search for power. Jamin and Kyle explore the notion of power found in weakness and what they discover—through personal experience and in conversation with others—is that this is the power which sets us free. Lay down your wearying notions of what it means to embrace and pursue power and accept the invitation here, to so much more."

—DEIDRA RIGGS, AUTHOR OF *ONE: UNITY IN A DIVIDED WORLD*

"Goggin and Strobel effectively wrestle with the tension of power versus weakness by leaning on the Scriptures and the wisdom of fellow believers. Power is alluring for some and repulsive for others. Weakness is difficult, but in it the Lord works wonders. This book helps the Christian think correctly on these things."

—ED STETZER, EXECUTIVE DIRECTOR OF THE BILLY GRAHAM CENTER FOR EVANGELISM AND AUTHOR OF *PLANTING NEW CHURCHES IN A POSTMODERN AGE* AND COAUTHOR OF *TRANSFORMATIONAL CHURCH*

"There are plenty of reasons to question what the modern church has become and there are many critical voices eager to expose her failures. Goggin and Strobel are not among them. Like expert physicians, they dissect and diagnose the church's maladies. They consult with brilliant and wise experts and show how the pathogen of worldly power enters the church and corrupts it. Like good doctors, Goggin and Strobel pursue their work with both precision and compassion and their genuine love for the church is evident on every page. But what makes the book a must-read for every leader is the revelation that Goggin and Strobel aren't ultimately trying to heal the church, but themselves."

—Skye Jethani, author of *With: Reimagining the Way You Relate to God* and cohost of the Phil Vischer Podcast

"I have personally witnessed the destructive effects of leading a church in the way of the Dragon. Jamin and Kyle have provided a humble and much needed prophetic exhortation, both exposing their own brokenness, while drawing from the wisdom of godly leaders who have learned to lead in the way of the Lamb. The church and her leaders desperately need to hear this message and heed its call to follow the Lamb so that we might humbly, gently, and lovingly lead the bride of Christ."

—Jeff Vanderstelt, visionary leader of Soma and Saturate, lead teaching pastor of Doxa Church, and author of *Saturate*

"What happens when Christians embody a worldly approach to power and try to use that to advance Christ's kingdom? This is the question that drove Goggin and Strobel on their quest to gain wisdom about a Christ-shaped understanding of power. Along the way we are allowed to eavesdrop on their conversations with remarkable men and women who not only understand where power comes from, what it is for, and how it should be expressed, but whose lives have faithfully embodied the way of the Lamb. As skilled curators, Goggin and Strobel provide profound reflections that draw out the beauty and wisdom of these sages. The result is a trail of gems, glistening in the night, leading Christians today to recover an ancient and forgotten path."

—Glenn Packiam, lead pastor of New Life Downtown and author of *Discover the Mystery of Faith* and *Secondhand Jesus*

THE WAY OF THE DRAGON
OR THE WAY OF THE LAMB

THE WAY OF THE DRAGON OR THE WAY OF THE LAMB

SEARCHING FOR JESUS' PATH OF POWER IN A CHURCH THAT HAS ABANDONED IT

JAMIN GOGGIN AND KYLE STROBEL

NELSON BOOKS

An Imprint of Thomas Nelson

Published in Nashville, Tennessee, by Nelson Books, an imprint of Thomas Nelson. Nelson Books and Thomas Nelson are registered trademarks of HarperCollins Christian Publishing, Inc.

Published in association with the literary agency of D. C. Jacobson & Associates, LLC, an Author Management Company, www.dcjacobson.com.

Thomas Nelson titles may be purchased in bulk for educational, business, fund-raising, or sales promotional use. For information, please e-mail SpecialMarkets@ThomasNelson.com.

Unless otherwise noted, Scripture quotations are taken from the ESV® Bible (The Holy Bible, English Standard Version®). Copyright © 2001 by Crossway, a publishing ministry of Good News Publishers. Used by permission. All rights reserved.

Scripture quotations marked KJV are from the King James Version. Public domain.

Scripture quotations marked CEV are from the Contemporary English Version. Copyright © 1991, 1992, 1995 by American Bible Society. Used by permission.

Scripture quotations marked NASB are from New American Standard Bible®. Copyright © 1960, 1962, 1963, 1968, 1971, 1972, 1973, 1975, 1977, 1995 by The Lockman Foundation. Used by permission. (www.Lockman.org)

Scripture quotations marked NLT are from the Holy Bible, New Living Translation. © 1996, 2004, 2007, 2013 by Tyndale House Foundation. Used by permission of Tyndale House Publishers, Inc., Carol Stream, Illinois 60188. All rights reserved.

ISBN 978-0-7180-2236-5 (eBook)

Library of Congress Cataloging-in-Publication Data
ISBN 978-0-7180-2235-8

Names: Goggin, Jamin, 1982- author. | Strobel, Kyle, 1978- author.
Title: The way of the dragon or the way of the lamb : searching for Jesus' path of power in a church that has abandoned it / Jamin Goggin and Kyle Strobel.
Description: Nashville : Thomas Nelson, 2017. | Includes bibliographical references.
Identifiers: LCCN 2016024877 | ISBN 9780718022358
Subjects: LCSH: Power (Christian theology)
Classification: LCC BT738.25 .G64 2017 | DDC 261--dc23 LC record available at https://lccn.loc.gov/2016024877

Printed in the United States of America

18 19 20 21   RRD   10 9 8 7 6 5 4

"There were giants in the earth in those days."
Genesis 6:4 KJV

We dedicate this book to the giants we
met with on our pilgrimage:

To Marva Dawn: *Your prophetic courage, tender heart, and humble life are signs of a deeper way. Thank you for your guidance. Thank you for your faithful and steady ministry. Thank you for your continued devotion to "the unseen way." You helped us see the powers and the kind of power needed to stand firm against them.*

To J. I. Packer: *Your pastorally conscious academic ministry has been a model of faithful theology to us. Thank you for sharing your heart and mind with us. Thank you for your continued witness to the way from above as you embrace ever further that "weakness is the way."*

To James Houston: *Your generous spirit and depth of love witness to a day in which there will be no more tears. Thank you for the wisdom you shared in personal mentoring. Thank you for taking us into your life. Thank you for the long conversations over the phone. Thank you for showing us what it truly means to be human.*

To John Perkins: *You have gazed evil in the face and responded in love. Your witness to the way of Jesus is so humbling. Thank you for that witness. Thank you for your commitment to a gospel that can save racists too. You are blessed.*

To Jean Vanier: *Your towering gentle love, beaming joy, and extravagant hospitality are a fragrant aroma of the way of Christ. Thank you for teaching and displaying the way of love to us. Thank you for modeling vulnerability and weakness. Thank you for reminding us of all the precious ones whom God loves.*

To Eugene Peterson: *Your wit, humor, and pastor's heart are outdone only by your devotion to Christ's way, your love of Scripture, and your life of faithfulness. Thank you for your letters. Thank you for exposing us to a deeper life of ministry and opening your home to us. Watch out for the trolls.*

To Dallas Willard: *You, Dallas, are missed. Your own ministry has influenced ours deeply, but your life continues to proclaim the kingdom of God even beyond death. Thank you for a life marked by running the race to win the prize. Surely an imperishable wreath rests upon your head now. Thank you for your witness and for the hope you shared with us. Thank you for giving us time when you had so little left.*

Saints have their power, their brilliance, their victory, their attraction, and have no need of carnal or intellectual greatness, where these have no place since they neither add nor subtract anything. They are recognized by God and the angels, and not by bodies nor curious minds. God is enough for them.

BLAISE PASCAL

CONTENTS

CONTENTS

We choose: we follow the dragon and his beasts along their parade route, conspicuous with the worship of splendid images, elaborated in mysterious symbols, fond of statistics, taking on whatever role is necessary to make a good show and get the applause of the crowds in order to get access to power and become self-important. Or we follow the Lamb along a farmyard route, worshipping the invisible, listening to the foolishness of preaching, practicing a holy life that involves heroically difficult acts that no one will ever notice, in order to become, simply, our eternal selves in an eternal city. It is the difference, politically, between wanting to use the people around us to become powerful (or, if unskilled, getting used by them), and entering into covenants with the people around us so that the power of salvation extends into every part of the neighborhood, the society, and the world that God loves.

—EUGENE PETERSON

INTRODUCTION:
SEEKING THE WAY

THE STREET WAS BUSIER THAN USUAL, BUT I (KYLE) DIDN'T think much of it. Our ministry team shouldered through the crowds as only American high school students do, oblivious to the signs that all was not well. It was in the midst of laughter that my eyes slammed closed and tears cascaded down my face. Screams and shouts seemed to come from every possible direction. As I felt shoulders rubbing against mine, I ran—attempting to keep contact with the mob that was rushing somewhere. But as quickly as the running started, it stopped, and suddenly I was alone. I tried opening my eyes but experienced a deep burning and acidic tears that seemed to worsen the pain. I stood still, convinced that no movement was better than blind movement.

My eyes were on fire. I bent over and pressed my palms to my face. Even though rubbing hurt, I hoped tears might wash away the feeling. The voices I recognized were now distant, moving to my left, and I heard more screams behind me. Then there was another noise, a much more ominous one. *Click . . . Clack . . . Click.*

I stood up, still rubbing my eyes. Some light came through the tears. As I pressed my forearm to my face, I still heard the *click, clack, click*ing all around me mixed with screams and muffled yells from my friends. I finally squinted my eyes open. The tears abated slightly as the burning subsided. I could finally make out the source of the ominous noise. Rocks flew through the air toward me, *click*, *clack*, *click*ing to my right and left, in front and behind. A mob of people walked toward me, just past a bus that lay on its side in flames. I didn't move. The scene felt familiar from images I'd seen on television, but I wasn't safe on a couch thousands of miles away; I was twenty yards from an angry mob with bats and rocks.

I had been hit with a cloud of tear gas, but it was only the edge of the cloud. Our group had run headlong into a mob, which had been driven to riot by conditions in the poorest neighborhood of the Dominican Republic. As I stood frozen in place in the middle of the street, I saw a man throw a rock over houses, trying to hit my friends as they fled down the side street. Then I saw a man pick up a bottle without ever unlocking his eyes from mine. He cocked back his arm to throw, and I ran. I ran until the *click*, *clack*, *click*ing stopped.

When our team eventually found its way back to our camp, we sat in silence at picnic tables under a metal awning, replaying the day in our minds. The street where the riot occurred was just over the wall, no fewer than fifty feet away, but by now the sounds of the mob were well in the distance. The pride, arrogance, and bravado normally displayed by my high school buddies were gone, and in their place was a shell-shocked perplexity.

Up to that point, the mission trip had been a typical one. A bunch of upper-middle-class kids traveled to a place with real poverty, did some hard labor (but not very well), and spent a lot of money on useless trinkets to bring home. Everything had followed the script, but the day's events jolted our comfort and shook our confidence. The day also revealed something about me: My weakness had been exposed. I sat on a picnic bench, staring off in the darkness, and thought about that man whose eyes locked with mine. The fear I had felt at that moment remained with me. But as much as I felt my own impotence, I could also imagine that man's helplessness. There was a desperation in his face and his actions that I could feel, and it was far beyond anything that my privileged self had known. As I considered the pain that drove him to pick up that bottle, I felt small. The evil embedded in his circumstances was great, and my prepackaged solutions seemed silly in the face of such despair.

DESIRING POWER

I have had several moments like this in my life, epiphanies that burst my bubble of self-assurance and control and revealed the truth of my frailty. These moments are always invitations from God to walk in a different way, one of dependence on him. In truth, my heart has not always accepted such invitations, but instead has grasped for power and control.

This hunger for power was reinforced by four years of high school athletics, playing for a team that didn't lose much. I had learned to equate winning with work ethic. If you put in the hard work, you should win. Winning, of course, was the goal. What was the point of playing if you weren't focused on winning? As I started Bible college, I quickly discovered that I could apply the approach I learned from sports to academics and receive the very accolades and praise I was so desperate for.

I had healthy intentions to be faithful and grow in Christ. But my desire for power was stronger than those intentions, and my desire came to the surface quickly. The words of Jesus were thorns piercing open my flesh. At every turn, my grandiosity was exposed. I wanted to control reality, to create a self that would thrive in the world, while Jesus said, "Take up your cross and follow me" (Matt. 16:24 CEV). I wanted to be cutting-edge and savvy, knowing the right people and being accepted in the right circles, while Jesus said, "The last will be first, and the first last" (Matt. 20:16), and warned against imitating the Pharisees who "love the place of honor at feasts and the best seats" (Matt. 23:6). I wanted to come up with a way to prove my value to people who doubted me, to prove my worth to people who thought I had nothing to offer, while Jesus said, "Apart from me you can do nothing" (John 15:5). I wanted to do something big. I wanted to create a name and a legacy. I wanted to make a difference. In the midst of this Jesus said, "One who is faithful in a very little is also faithful in much, and one who is dishonest in a very little is also dishonest in much" (Luke 16:10).

Both Jamin and I were confronted with this tension in our early years of seminary and ministry life. We excelled academically and professionally and were touted as young, up-and-coming voices in the church. We were invited into places of leadership beyond our emotional or spiritual maturity. And yet we were continuously confronted by the biblical understanding of power. The Bible's vision of power in weakness and suffering for the sake of the gospel didn't harmonize very well with our quest for power, influence, and ministerial acclaim, yet somehow we managed to avoid facing this tension. We overlooked truths despite staring right at them. Too busy basking in the glow of success, we failed to consider the biblical vision of power as a viable option.

Then came a season when we both experienced failure rather than success. Instead of being in the right circles, we felt the sting of rejection and isolation. Our work ethic and willpower couldn't change our circumstances. Our résumés and talents—where we had placed our hope—didn't deliver. We believed we were following a genuine calling from God into ministry, and we believed we were being faithful to that call: going to seminary, taking our time, and growing in maturity. But God revealed clearly that beneath the surface we were desperate for power. God led us into the truth of our hearts, revealing how deeply and pervasively pride drove our lives and how much we relied upon our own strength.

We are both grateful for this season. It was a gift. The grace of God saved us from ourselves. Jesus' words echoed ominously in our hearts: "For what does it profit a man to gain the whole world and forfeit his soul?" (Mark 8:36). We saw friends who were thrust into positions of leadership too early, only to fall hard and lose their families, jobs, and dreams of ministering. We saw the foolishness of youth—a foolishness we shared—ruin lives, devastate churches, and fracture relationships. The Lord saved us from this. It was not our cunning or our strategic life plans that led us through this particular wilderness. It was the mercy of God.

CHRISTIAN POWER

Over time we have come to see that the way of power commended in Scripture is not the way of power we have seen in evangelicalism. Our initial question was simple. *What does Christian power look like?* But as we moved deeper into our inquiry, more disturbing questions rose to the surface. *What happens if the church rejects the power of Christ? What happens when Christians embody a worldly approach to power and try to use that to advance Christ's kingdom? What happens when believers live their lives according to a power that is antagonistic to Christ?*

Two decades removed from my trip to the Dominican Republic, I saw the complexity concerning power increasing rather than decreasing. The mob scene that engulfed me for but a few minutes gave me a glimpse into deep, complex, and dark elements of dehumanization and oppression the people of that country have long experienced. What still overwhelmed me was the sense of helplessness I felt in the face of such evil. The riot I experienced was the fruit of corrupt and oppressive systems of power that had impacted the people on the ground. What could I possibly do to help?

What became clear is that I did not know how to stand firm amid the stark realities of this present evil age (Eph. 6:12). I began to realize that our view of power is an issue undergirding all that we do as Christians. We are called to be a people of power, certainly, but ours is a kind of power antithetical to the power of the world. So what does it mean to employ the power of Christ? What happens when the power of Christ comes head-to-head with the powers of evil? What happens when we feel this conflict, even within our churches? These became the driving questions for Jamin and me as we embarked on a journey of discovery for which neither of us was prepared.

PART 1
DISCOVERING THE WAY

CHAPTER 1

THE WAYS OF POWER

I (JAMIN) HAD BEEN IN MINISTRY LONG ENOUGH TO HEAR the stories. It's a familiar narrative these days: pastors disqualified from ministry due to moral failure. For years I had listened to devastating tales of infidelity and broken families in the lives of fellow pastors. My immediate reaction, in all honesty, was typically swift judgment. I mentally distanced myself from such pastors, believing I was cut from a different sort of spiritual cloth than such sinners. *How on earth could this happen? How could anyone, let alone a pastor, ever do such a thing?* These stories, while far too commonplace, were quite removed from my immediate life and church world. I couldn't imagine any of my pastoral peers ever experiencing such a fall from grace.

Then it happened. I remember the phone call vividly. A dear friend, a fellow pastor, called me to confess his infidelity and ask for prayer amid the consequences he was going to face from the leadership of his church. As he talked I felt numb. The shock of the moment gripped me in a way I had never experienced. I knew this man. I thought I knew him well. All of a sudden, I found myself living in one of those distant stories.

A few days later we met. My friend shared his grief, his pain, and his overwhelming sense of guilt and shame. I listened. As he continued to share his heart, I grew increasingly uncomfortable with the conversation. Not uncomfortable in the way you might imagine. I didn't squirm at the details of his sin. Rather, something in what he shared struck a chord in my own heart. I couldn't conveniently distance myself from his sin.

As he talked about the dynamics that contributed to his infidelity, at the forefront were pride, status, and grandiosity. While there were unhealthy dynamics in his relationship with his wife, his hunger for power had played a large part in this painful and tragic saga. He recently had been promoted to a significant leadership position and was being showered with the affirmation and accolades that went along with it. The recognition and status he had received emboldened an already unhealthy desire for power and a vision for pastoral life informed by his own grandiosity and quest for significance. In recent months he had incrementally given himself over to such things, and as a result was doing ministry apart from dependence upon Christ. As he invited me into these deeper channels of his heart, I found myself all too familiar with the current. I knew the temptations of status and recognition. I was well acquainted with the hunger for power he spoke of and the temptation to craft a false self worthy of praise. I could not distance myself from such a "horrible sinner" because I could see the ingredients of such behavior in my own heart.

For years Kyle and I had no trouble looking critically upon others in their quest for power. We bemoaned the rock-star pastors who were in the spotlight, whose churches appeared to be more concerned with growing their brand than proclaiming the gospel. This is the first temptation of power: We view the problem as "out there." We recognize it in other churches, pastors, fellow Christians, or political and cultural leaders, but we ignore the problem in our own hearts. For Kyle and me personally, this remains a strong temptation. As men with a calling to teach and lead, we can often default to analyzing the error of others without honestly assessing the truth about ourselves.

Accordingly, it is easy to allow the word *power* to trigger a mental list of tyrannical and narcissistic leaders. Likewise, it can be much harder to find examples of those who have embraced power properly. Mother Teresas are rare. In a fallen world, this is reality. In contrast, our first inclination should not be to identify the problem of power as somewhere "out there," but as "in here," within our own hearts. Jesus says, "You hypocrite, first take the log out of your own eye, and then you will see clearly to take out the speck that is in your brother's eye" (Luke 6:42). We find it much easier to become burdened and angered by sins that are not our own. When those sins are committed by those in leadership, we find it even easier. Notice, Jesus is not saying the solution is to ignore the sins of others. We should name sins, just as Jesus did. However, we must recognize that only after naming the truth of our own sin can we come in grace and truth to name the sins of others. Only when we see the truth of ourselves can we have mercy to address others in God's grace. As those forgiven by God, we pray, "Forgive us our sins, as we have forgiven those who sin against us" (Matt. 6:12 NLT).

During my tenure as a pastor in the last decade, I have had a front row seat to witness the beauty in the church. I have seen lives transformed, relationships healed, and the outcasts of society loved. However, my years in the church have also given me enough time to see abuse. I have seen leaders in the church destroy the careers of other staff members because they viewed them as threats to their authority. I have known pastors who focus their energy on the members of the church with money and influence while neglecting the rest of the congregation. More importantly, I have felt the weight of the log in my own eye. I have seen my thirst for power driving my ministry. I have viewed other pastors as competition and the church as a means of self-glory. I have acted in ways that place me alongside the powermongers I so readily critiqued.

Paradoxically, as I began to acknowledge my longing for power, another temptation appeared in my heart. I became tempted to reject power altogether. It simplifies things quite a bit if we can reject power wholesale, viewing any position of influence as intrinsically evil. For our generation—which is drowning in a sea of political, social, and religious examples of power gone awry—this is an alluring temptation. The abuse of power seems pervasive, committed even by the people we expect to love us and care for us the most. Some of us have been abused, misled, and manipulated by "shepherds" who turned out to be wolves. Abuses have caused some to leave the church altogether. It is difficult to return to the house where you were abused.

As painful as our experiences in the church may have been, we must avoid the temptation of viewing power itself as bad. From the moment of creation God intended for people to have power. Adam and Eve were given rule and dominion over creation by God himself (Gen. 1:28). Part of being created in God's image is having the power to shape the world around us.[1] Power is a grace of God. And as a grace, it is not generic, but a part of God's self-giving. Grace is God's giving of himself to his people, and in Christ, we come to receive the kind of power God offers: the power of the cross.[2] This is a power known through death and resurrection—moving through our weakness to a new kind of strength—strength in abiding in, submitting to, and resting in God alone.

Power is *the capacity to affect reality*. We human beings have the capacity to physically, emotionally, and spiritually influence the world around us. God has given us this capacity for good—to glorify him and bless the world. But as Christians, our primary interest is not simply in affecting reality. Our primary interest is to bear fruit of the kingdom—the fruit of the Spirit (Gal. 5:22–23). We were not created to pursue power as an end in itself, but rather to pursue God, the powerful one, and abide in his power to bless the world. But because of our sin, our ability to use power is disordered and is damaging the world around us. Just as Adam and Eve grasped for power apart from God, so do we. Just as Cain wielded his power to destroy his perceived competition, so do we. A way of power exists that is good, true, and beautiful; but there is also a way of power that is evil, false, and ugly. After the fall, two ways of power are always before us. Even those of us who are followers of Jesus will be tempted to embrace the sinful way of power rather than the way of power embodied on the cross. We may happily receive the good news of Jesus' cross, but we often shy away from his call to pick up our own.

THE WAYS OF POWER

"You are so wise and powerful. Will you not take the Ring?"

"No!" cried Gandalf, springing to his feet. "With that power I should have power too great and terrible. And over me the Ring would gain a power still greater and more deadly." His eyes flashed and his face was lit as by a fire within. "Do not tempt me! For I do not wish to become like the Dark Lord himself. Yet the way of the Ring to my heart is by pity, pity for weakness and the desire of strength to do good. Do not tempt me! I dare not take it, not even to keep it safe, unused."[3]

In J. R. R. Tolkien's *The Lord of the Rings*, the wizard Gandalf is the embodiment of true wisdom, but his wisdom may appear foolish—as when he refuses to take the ring of power. Gandalf is powerful, yet his is a power found in weakness.[4] Other characters reject Gandalf's way, believing that the only way to truly defeat the enemy is by wielding the ring. But in the end they are unmasked as fools. Their eyes can see worldly power, but they are blind to the power of wisdom.

As with Middle Earth, so with our world. Two ways of power are presented to us. Only one is the true path of wisdom. James unfolds these opposing ways:

> Who is wise and understanding among you? By his good conduct let him show his works in the meekness of wisdom. But if you have bitter jealousy and selfish ambition in your hearts, do not boast and be false to the truth. This is not the wisdom that comes down from above, but is earthly, unspiritual, demonic. For where jealousy and selfish ambition exist, there will be disorder and every vile practice. But the wisdom from above is first pure, then peaceable, gentle, open to reason, full of mercy and good fruits, impartial and sincere. And a harvest of righteousness is sown in peace by those who make peace. (James 3:13–18)

James draws here from a long biblical tradition of wisdom literature. Earlier in the letter, James says that wisdom is to be desired and that it has one source, God, who gives wisdom and delights in doing so (James 1:5). As with all good gifts, wisdom comes from above (James 1:17). Godly wisdom is not achieved, but is received. This way from above has descended in the person of Christ, who is *the* power and wisdom of God (1 Cor. 1:24). Wisdom is not essentially about making right decisions, but about living by the power of God in Christ Jesus. Wisdom and folly are right and wrong ways not only of thinking, but also of living in the world. There are two paths, but only one is the path of true wisdom and power.

According to James these two paths are *the way from above and the way from below.* They are two opposing ways of power in the world. These ways of power are distinguished first by their source. The way from above is power from God. The way from above is embracing God's power and depending upon him. As we will see in the next chapter, embracing God's power involves embracing our own weakness and abiding in Christ (John 15:1–5). Conversely, the way from below is a rejection of God's power and a dependence upon ourselves in sinful autonomy. The way from below rejects abiding in God in favor of our own willpower, turning to the power of the self to make a difference in the world. Ultimately the source of this power, as we will see in chapter 4, is the world, the flesh, and the devil.

As important as our source of power is, we cannot simply ask where power is from. We also have to ask, *What is power for?* These are two sides of the same coin, even as they are distinct questions. The way from above and the way from below are distinguished not only by the *source* of power, but also by the *fruit* or results of power. The way from above is power for love. As we walk the way from above, our lives are "pure, then peaceable, gentle, open to reason, full of mercy and good fruits, impartial and sincere" (James 3:17). By contrast, the way from below is power for the sake of being powerful, for the sake of control. As we walk the way from below, our hearts grow full of "jealousy and selfish ambition"; and the fruit we produce is "disorder and every vile practice" (James 3:16). James builds upon the Old Testament wisdom literature, which also couches wisdom in journey imagery.

> Hear, my son, and accept my words, that the years of your life may be many. I have taught you the way of wisdom; I have led you in the paths of uprightness. When you walk, your step will not be hampered, and if you run, you will not stumble. Keep hold of instruction; do not let go; guard her, for she is your life. Do not enter the path of the wicked, and do not walk in the way of the evil. Avoid it; do not go on it; turn away from it and pass on. (Prov. 4:10–15)

We are constantly confronted by these two ways, and we can easily delude ourselves into believing that we are walking the way from above when in fact we are walking the way from below. I (Jamin) have seen this in my own journey. In my early years of ministry I was convinced that my quest for power was merely a fervent commitment to the important work of the kingdom. My grandiose fantasy of success was excused as an embrace of God's big plan for my life. I had big dreams because I had "bold faith." My emphasis on building a strong résumé and winning the approval of others was about making the most of my talents and abilities for God's glory. I found it surprisingly easy to adorn the way from below in the platitudes of Christian leadership, magically transforming evil into good.

James warns us of this very reality. He tells us that the way from below masquerades as the way from above. This is worldliness pretending to be wisdom. False wisdom deludes us into believing it is the truth (James 3:14): "There is a way that seems right to a man, but its end is the way to death" (Prov. 14:12). In Christ we have been born anew into the way from above (John 3:3), but there are places in our hearts that still long for the old path of Adam and Eve's quest to be like God. The question we must face is whether we will abide in the way of Jesus—continuing to trust in him—or return to the way of Adam. Whereas the way of Adam will feel right, and often will give us the results we desire, the Scriptures are clear: *The way from below is the way of death, and the way from above is the way of life* (Matt. 7:13–14). These paths lead to drastically different places.

Jesus offers us an invitation into the way from above in John 15:5: "I am the vine; you are the branches. Whoever abides in me and I in him, he it is that bears much fruit, for apart from me you can do nothing." The power from abiding in Christ produces kingdom fruit. We can only embrace the way from above by embracing the one who descended from above and is now seated above (Col. 3:3). It is only as we depend upon Christ, by the Spirit, that we can hope to produce kingdom fruit (Gal. 5:22–23). Jesus simplifies things even more a few verses later in John 15 when he says, "Abide in my love" (v. 9). And so we see that the way from above is power *from* love and *for* love. Love here is not sentimental—a romantic comedy kind of love; love directs our attention to God himself, the all-powerful Creator of the universe (1 John 4:8). As Martin Luther King Jr. noted, love and power are not mutually exclusive:

> One of the great problems of history is that the concepts of love and power have usually been contrasted as opposites, polar opposites, so that love is identified with a resignation of power, and power with a denial of love . . . What is needed is a realization that power without love is reckless and abusive and that love without power is sentimental and anemic. Power at its best is love, implementing the demands of justice, and justice at its best is love correcting everything that stands against love.[5]

BAD TREES WITH GOOD FRUIT?

What Martin Luther King Jr. recognized is that the way of Jesus is power in love: "By this all people will know that you are my disciples, if you have love for one another" (John 13:35). Such love is not self-generated or merely external, but comes from an abiding relationship with Jesus and is first and foremost an issue of the heart (John 15). To produce kingdom fruit, both internally and externally, fruit that is *from* God and *for* God's glory, we must abide in Christ by the Holy Spirit. But the flip side to this is that kingdom fruit can seemingly be produced by those who reject the way from above.[6] Outward fruit is not a guarantee that a heart is truly abiding in God. And such fruit does us no good at all (1 Cor. 13:1–3).

We see this in the life of Moses. While the Israelites wandered in the wilderness, God called Moses to speak to a rock to produce water for the needs of his people (Num. 20:1–13). Instead Moses chose to strike the rock, the same course of action he had earlier performed successfully—giving him the sense that *he* was making something happen (Ex. 17:1–7). The result of Moses' disobedience was judgment: Moses was forbidden from entering the promised land. Despite the judgment, however, water still poured from the rock. The same act that brought judgment upon Moses quenched the thirst of the people. God's power to act is not contingent upon our obedience.

God can move in his grace to produce kingdom fruit despite our pride, but the call for followers of Jesus is to have hearts congruent with his work. True kingdom fruit is both internal and external. God seeks to make good trees that produce good fruit. To use the language from James 3 again, we can do things in bitter jealousy and selfish ambition, and despite our motives God can still bring about good results. But this is not all that God desires. God calls us to produce fruit from the heart and to participate genuinely in his work in the world.

God wants us to embrace his way of power from the heart, a power that is never depersonalized. Often we have a notion of God's power as a kind of pixie dust. God has the most power and is able to do special and amazing things, so he sends his magic fairy (aka the Holy Spirit) to sprinkle some magic dust on us so we can do special and amazing things too. God's power, in this view, is stuff God gives out. When Scripture talks about God's power in the Christian life, however, the assumption is of the presence of the Holy Spirit working in and through us. A. W. Tozer reminds us, "The power of God, then, is not something God has; it is something God is."[7] God's power is God's very presence in our hearts, which is why *self-control* is understood as a fruit *of the Spirit* (Gal. 5:22–23).

The way from above is power *from* God and power *for* God; it is a power known in our weakness and expressed in love. The other way of power, the way from below, seeks power from within and pursues power as an end in itself. As we will discover in chapter 4, this way from below has its propagators and its own schemes of discipleship. It is not merely the absence of the right way; it is the way of evil.

Scripture offers us an image of a dragon and of a lamb in describing these two ways. The way of the dragon is the way from below, but the way of the lamb, Jesus, is from above and is revealed through his own life. But if we are honest, this title for Jesus— "lamb of God"—feels powerlessly docile. "Who has any desire to be a lamb?"[8]

CAPITULATING TO WORLDLY POWER

When we embrace the way from below, we embrace the way of Adam, which is the way of death. We, too, become captivated by the tree in the garden we believe will provide true wisdom. Instead, false wisdom lies there waiting, masquerading as truth; this is the sin "crouching at the door" (see Gen. 4:7) that desires to take us captive. God has called us to embrace a different way, the way of life in Christ by the Spirit. This call is to follow the footsteps of Christ leading from the Garden of Gethsemane to the tree upon the hill. It is this tree, the cross, where true wisdom is found.

The challenge, of course, is that the way from below appears so wise. The path is wide, the companions are many, and the destination seems desirable. The road less traveled is less traveled for a reason. Our feet are trained to find paths of self-achievement and self-glorification. We use our vocations to build significance. We use our relationships to get ahead. We spend our money and our time trying to gain more power. Because we are prone to waywardness, prone to walk the path of pride, self-sufficiency, and power, we need the church to ground us in Christ and his way. We cannot live in Christ's way on our own. This likely sounds right, but many of us functionally doubt our need for the church. Pursuing the way of Christ seems like a "me and Jesus" kind of endeavor. But our focus on ourselves unearths a deep foolishness that owes more to our culture and worldliness than it does to Scripture. We have no hope of pursuing the way from above apart from the church.[9]

The church is called to be the "pillar and buttress of the truth" (1 Tim. 3:15). When we enter the household of God, we are all still planted in the way from below, but the church is called to mirror the truth of our hearts and to witness to the true path in Christ. In every facet of its mission, the church is called to strip us bare of our deep-seated desire to self-fulfill, to call us to repentance, and to invite us to die so that we may have eternal life in Christ alone. Sadly, rather than calling us to walk the way from above, the church has affirmed and even propagated the way from below.

In a culture drunk on power and in need of an intervention, the church has too often become an enabler. In many places, churches openly affirm the way from below. Instead of being told how desperately I am in need of God, I am repeatedly told how much God needs me. Instead of being exhorted to pick up my cross and follow Christ, I am told that Jesus wants to be my partner in the plan I have to rid my life of all struggles and challenges. We hear gospels of moralism, centering on my power to become a better person, and we hear sermons offering up God as merely another resource along my journey for successful and happy living. Sermons become pep talks amid a quest for power and significance. Instead of worship being an invitation to come before God in humble awe and reverence, worship becomes an experience meant to lift us above the travails of everyday life and give us a sense of transcendence.

Instead of hearing God's vision of redeeming all things in Christ by the power of his Holy Spirit, we hear of the pastor's vision to grow an even bigger church that does bigger things so that he can be powerful and we can be powerful with him.

The church is called to rest in the grace of God, whose power is perfected in weakness (2 Cor. 12:9).[10] Unfortunately, the church has often capitulated to the way from below. It has embraced the way of power to control. This must be addressed head-on. If we ignore the deep vices of the church by pointing to signs of success on the surface, we are in grave danger. The Lord, we are told, "weighs the spirit" (Prov. 16:2). When we embrace the way from below for ministry, we develop a superficial spirit. We can build buildings, programs, and services of power that are, in the end, weightless. What might it look like to become weighty churches? Who are the brothers and sisters in Christ we can look to who have embraced the way from above? Who are the voices crying out in the wilderness that there is a different way?

IN THE FOOTSTEPS OF OUR FOREBEARS

Kyle and I have committed to a journey to discover what it looks like to walk in the way from above. We long to see kingdom power and to unmask the temptations of the way from below. As we do so, our own failures are continually revealed, and our own temptations are more and more apparent. At times we curve inward looking for power rather than seeking the ways and power of God. At times we seek control, dominance, and success instead of love. We still feel the pull to walk the easy way of the world and reject the way of Jesus. Yet following our season of failure discussed in the introduction, we can no longer deny the truth that the way from below is the way of death. We've tasted the fruit of this way and know it to be poisoned. But we've also tasted the life that is in Christ, and have come to know its savory goodness. In short, we are on a pilgrimage of the kingdom defined by the cross, seeking to discover what it means to walk the way from above in our world today.

This is the journey we are inviting you to take with us. What you will find in the pages ahead is something like a travelogue of this pilgrimage. In our pursuit of wisdom we realized we had to seek living examples of Jesus' kingdom vision. So we set out looking for wisdom from sages in the faith who embodied power in weakness.[11] We spent several years seeking these people out and discerning who would help us in our quest. We didn't turn to the in-vogue power players in Christianity. We sought out people whose power and influence, if they had any, were not treasured for their own sake. We looked for those who had embraced their weakness, depended upon God's power, and lived a life of love for decades of fruitful ministry. When this journey began we had no idea it would take us to a lake house in Montana, a café in Vancouver, or a village in the French countryside. We spent time with men and women who have embodied the truth of life with Christ—the Christ who walked the way of the cross and who turns to wave us to his side to follow him.

In our mission to find wisdom, we wanted more than just successful people, but individuals with real kingdom depth. If you want depth, you don't talk to the youngest and the most "cutting-edge"; you turn to your elder. When Scripture uses the term *elder*, it means an older person. It wasn't just a title. We wanted to seek out our elders, trusting that their decades of faithfulness turned into wisdom. What we found were the holiest, wisest, and most powerful people we have ever met. These are people who had previously influenced us deeply through their writing, and in some cases, through phone calls and letters. They are mentors, and we hope that their faithfulness can be honored through this book.[12]

Through pain, disease, rejection, and the toil of ministering in an age when "old" is often synonymous with "out-of-touch," these mentors radiated incredible joy and a deep warmth of spirit. In our time with each of them, we knew we were loved, and we both hold on to that love even now.

CHAPTER 2

POWER IN WEAKNESS

HIS HOME WAS JUST A SHORT DISTANCE OUTSIDE THE city. I (Jamin) drove and Kyle served as navigator (since Kyle has always been better with directions). The Vancouver air was crisp this December morning. The faint trace of a rainbow across the skyline served as a reminder of the rain the night before. As we pulled up to the aqua-colored house, we saw a hint of Christmas hanging on the door in the form of a wreath. I glanced at Kyle as I rang the doorbell, unable to hold back the smile that betrayed my excitement. The door slowly opened and J. I. Packer greeted us with a brief hello, donning a beige trench coat to ward off the coming rain.

Jim took over as navigator as we drove into town, leading us to his favorite coffee shop just a few minutes down the road. After we ordered drinks we found a quiet corner table, seeking privacy in the bustling café. As we took off our coats and felt the warmth of the first sip of coffee, Jim recounted his recent hip surgery. This was one of his first ventures back into "normal" daily life. Getting out of the house, walking city streets, and getting a cup of coffee were all treated with deep gratitude.

As Kyle and I listened to Jim, we found ourselves both asking the same question: How did we end up here? We were humbled by this opportunity to talk with a theologian whose lifetime of ministry had meant so much to us over the years. We had started reading books by Dr. Packer in high school, never imagining that one day we would share a cup of coffee with him at Bean Brothers Café.

THE ROAD LESS TRAVELED

For me, the road leading to Jim Packer's doorstep began many years earlier in a moment of prayer. There was an uncommon purity about it, one of those moments in life that somehow feels sturdier than others. When you are twenty, those moments are few. I knew God was calling me to be a pastor. I had been wrestling with the possibility, toying around with the notion, but nothing felt firm until this moment. My calling felt certain. I suppose this is typically how pastors talk about "calling." There is always an air of certainty and purity attached to the story. In reality, it is never that clean. It wasn't until a couple of years later that I came to realize how messy it really was. I discovered that while my calling was true, my heart was anything but.

I accepted the call into ministry with a genuine desire to be faithful. I wanted to proclaim the gospel and shepherd God's people. But there were other desires at work in my heart as well. These were hidden desires, tucked deep away, but they were there—desires for significance, fame, and influence. While there are many different kinds of temptations, my central one was clear: a deep and abiding desire for power. The path to obtaining power is well-worn: Work hard, leverage talents, and capitalize on relationships. Power begets power, or so I thought.

The desires of our hearts don't simply lie dormant. They are dynamic. My desire for power was hard at work constructing a fantasy of me as a famous, powerful pastor. I had no fantasies about sitting in a hospital room, grieving with a church member who had just lost a loved one. I had no fantasies of long hours of study in my office, prayerfully preparing a sermon. Rather, my fantasy usually involved a big stage and a big audience. I had a clearly mapped-out strategy to accomplish this goal. After I'd spent a couple of years in ministry, my plan of becoming a powerful, famous pastor was well under way. The path isn't hard to find. Directions are laid out in numerous books, and workshops are readily available. I felt very secure and well supported in my endeavor.

Then, in an instant, it crumbled and my fantasy was exposed. "Jamin, we have to let you go." These were words I never thought I would hear, but the reality of the church's finances made it inevitable. More importantly, the loss of power revealed how much I longed for it. God highlighted my weakness to put to death my lust for power. He invited me into the wilderness of unemployment, which revealed how much more I wanted power and control than I even wanted God himself. I had succumbed to one of the most primal idolatries, using God as a tool to have life on my terms.

God took me on a journey to discover *the way from above.* During this time certain passages in Scripture became clear to me, perhaps none more powerfully than 2 Corinthians 12:7–10.

> So to keep me from becoming conceited because of the surpassing greatness of the revelations, a thorn was given me in the flesh, a messenger of Satan to harass me, to keep me from becoming conceited. Three times I pleaded with the Lord about this, that it should leave me. But he said to me, "My grace is sufficient for you, for my power is made perfect in weakness." Therefore I will boast all the more gladly of my weaknesses, so that the power of Christ may rest upon me. For the sake of Christ, then, I am content with weaknesses, insults, hardships, persecutions, and calamities. For when I am weak, then I am strong.

I began to see that grasping for power in those early years of ministry was a rejection of God's way. Followers of Christ are called to embrace their weakness and not deny it. The Christian life is one that requires dependence, humility, and weakness to know strength. This is the path set before us by Paul, and this was the path traveled by Christ as he marched to Golgotha.

God was gracious enough to expose the truth of my heart. Like a moment of group intervention after years of personal denial, it was painful and jarring at first, but it slowly became clear to me: This is necessary for real dependence on God. For Christians, the journey into true power begins with the realization of our desire for false power. This hunger for false power is not unique to the pastoral vocation, but is something we all are tempted by whether we are salespeople or stay-at-home moms. In our own ways, we long for validation, recognition, and significance. The Lord led me on a prayerful journey concerning my fantasy for power, and now God was charting a new course along this pilgrimage. It was a course that led right to J. I. Packer's doorstep.

WEAKNESS IS THE WAY

After chatting about his surgery, Jim looked at us both and said, "I know you had some things in mind for our conversation today, so why don't we get started." Questions flooded both our minds, but thankfully, Kyle had a good sense of where to begin.

"Jim, we are embarking on a pilgrimage to seek wisdom. We aren't sure where it will take us, really, but we know our meeting with you is one stop along the way. It's a journey to understand the way of true kingdom power." Kyle paused and continued, "In particular, we want to explore where power really comes from. As we search Scripture we find that strength is found in weakness, that we are called to embrace our limitations, and that the Christian life is one of utter dependence upon God. More specifically, we find this theme emphasized by the apostle Paul. He is the one who seems to crystallize and articulate this subversive approach to the Christian life more than anyone. Can you help us understand what Paul is getting at when he talks about the way of weakness?"

As Kyle talked it was evident that this question was already on Jim's mind. We later discovered that Jim had already begun to do research for his book *Weakness Is the Way*.

"In the Christian life and in ministry," he began, "weakness is the way. The way of weakness, as I understand it, has two basic aspects. One is that the watching world sees you as weak in the sense of being limited and inadequate. The second aspect is that you yourself are very conscious of being limited and inadequate. In that respect, we are all to walk in Paul's footsteps, knowing God's strength in the midst of our human weakness."

Jim's first point was key but could easily be overlooked: Power found in weakness is not only for monks, pastors, and missionaries, but rather is *the* way, the *only* truly Christian way of life. According to Paul, this is exactly right: "For the word of the cross is folly to those who are perishing, but to us who are being saved it is the power of God" (1 Cor. 1:18). To reject this path is to put oneself, rather than God, at the center of life. I (Jamin) found this self-centeredness disturbingly present in my life. In many ways, I functionally considered the way of weakness to be foolish, not only in ministry, but in my life as a whole. My power, my abilities, and my will were still very much at the center of my life. Rather than accept the truth of my limitations and inadequacies, I fought against them. When I was faced with challenges, my internal monologue was more shaped by "I can make it happen," "I have what it takes," and "I'll just try harder," than by "I need you, Lord," "I am lost without you," and "Apart from you I can do nothing." As Jim talked, it became clear to me that such an approach to the Christian life was not Christian at all.

THE SPECIAL CHURCH

The great danger, of course, is that even in the church we begin to see the way of weakness as foolish. We easily embrace the worldly way of power and call it God's way. Both Kyle and I have witnessed this, but we were curious if Jim saw this in the church as well. As he took another sip of coffee, I leaned in for the next question. "From our perspective, this way of weakness is not often embraced in the church today. Do you see this?"

He replied without hesitation. "Well, many churches today try to choose pastors who, in one way or another, are headline hitters and platform heroes. Eloquence, certain skills, personality, and force are the things that matter. They are looking for qualities that will make the pastor stand out in the larger Christian scene."

He spoke directly to my heart, to the deep desire for power I had discovered a few years earlier. This was precisely my fantasy. I wanted to be a "headline hitter" and a "platform hero." I had a plan to get there. Even now, I wrestle with that longing to be power-ful, to be known, to stand out "in the larger Christian scene." The scene he speaks of has also been called the Evangelical Industrial Complex—a grand machine with cultural and economic force that involves celebrity pastors, networks, conferences, and books.[1] In many ways, Kyle and I were oblivious to it because it was the air we breathed growing up in the church. When we wrote our first book together, we began to realize how pervasive and powerful this scene really is. We also began to see how much this scene imbibes the way from below. Building your platform, leveraging your relationships, and getting in with the right people are assumed to be the obvious approach to making a difference in the church. Making a name for yourself, hiding your weaknesses, and empha-sizing strengths are considered normal. How else would you get noticed? How else would people hear about your book? If you don't stake your claim in "the scene," nobody else will. The strength of this industrial complex and its normalization create a hidden pressure. I have felt its magnetic pull in my own life. Interestingly enough, this is exactly where Packer turned next.

"The thought is that such a pastor will, on the one hand, be attractive to those who are not yet members of the church and, on the other hand, be a leader to the members of the congregation." He briefly paused. "Which makes the congregational members themselves stand out as 'special.' That is the key phrase, I think. They get *special* wisdom from their *special* pastor. Being special is the Achilles' heel of many churches today. They want to stand out and be noticed. This passion to be seen as special is what drives the choice of pastor, and very often it works, at least on a surface level." Kyle and I sat back, exchanging glances, when Packer added as something of an afterthought, "Well, I must say, I am out of tune altogether with the emphasis on being special."

My mind meandered through all the different ways we see this playing out in the church. We celebrate what we have done, and continue to do, without talking about what God is doing. This reveals a subtle, yet evident, self-glorification within the church. We create metrics and tools for measuring our growth, our programs, and our ministry output because we need to feel as if we are doing something important. We locate our value and significance along the landscape of other churches, asking how we stack up in terms of size, influence, or pastoral notoriety.

The quest to be special and important, of course, plays out on a broader scale as well. Notoriety has become the centerpiece of evangelical culture as a whole. We see this in the yearly rankings of churches according to size. We want to know who is currently the largest and who is growing the fastest. What purpose could highlighting these institutions possibly serve other than the self-glorification of the churches that are big, the envy of those that are not, and the general culture of competition it breeds? We also see this longing to be important in our conferences, which promise to provide the secret formula to specialness and remind us that the special people ("the anointed") are the only ones worth listening to. That is why they are onstage in the first place. We see this in books and resources telling us that God wants to make us "winners." We see this in our functional sainting of cultural celebrities who happen to be Christians.

We all want to feel as if we are part of something important, something unique, something that is going somewhere. We want to be where the action is. We don't want to be part of something ordinary; we want to be part of something special. Being a part of God's kingdom just doesn't feel exciting and sexy enough. The day-to-day reality of being with God in our work, our home life, and our community lacks the power, the transcendence, the specialness we crave. We long for the validation of our importance.

With all of this churning around in my mind, I asked a follow-up question. "I'm curious if you think this emphasis on being special shows up in the life of the church in other ways. Perhaps, for example, in the way we worship?"

Jim began, again not needing much time to ponder. "Yes, well, what has replaced the focus on God and the radical, down-on-your-face spirit of worship in so many of our evangelical churches, is the sense that worship is something exuberant. It will command attention. It is something special. It will draw people in. It is a kind of exuberance that makes for shallowness because it makes for externality. People will say 'in praise of God' and 'for the glory of God,' but it's external. I think that in contemporary evangelical worship there is often an element of showing off, which is external. Pride is the disposition controlling the heart, but externally it looks like, it believes itself to be, the praise of God."

Jim was referring to an insidious self-deception. By co-opting the things of God and using them in our own quest for power, we render them impotent—or worse. For Packer, the nature of worship in churches today is a profound example. We can often approach worship for the purpose of something other than worship. It becomes a tool for our excitement, euphoria, and desire for a feeling of self-transcendence. Consequently the sights, sounds, and aesthetic of the "worship experience" become very important to us. Our churches seek to meet this "felt need" by investing in the right staging and lighting because the mood can determine the sense of importance and specialness. The focus is on the style of worship, and having a young, good-looking, talented musician is critical for this equation. Packer was right; we often focus more on external realities.

At this point both Kyle and I recognized Jim was tired. This was the longest he had been out of his home in quite some time. Our cups were empty. It was time to go. As we left Bean Brothers and headed toward our car, I walked behind Jim and Kyle as they chatted about Kyle's academic work on Jonathan Edwards. As they talked, I couldn't help but think about when Kyle and I would be eighty-five years old (Lord willing). Would we still be writing? Would we still be ministering? What would the Lord have for us in that season? I was brought back to something Jim had said in passing during our conversation: "You should have a fifty-year plan—a vision for growth over a long period of time as you embrace your weakness." Learning to walk the way from above takes a lifetime, and it doesn't happen by accident. The man we sat across from that day in the coffee shop was a sage of this way, something of a travel expert with GPS of the soul. In the land of kingdom power, he really was a giant. Even while his slightly hunched back and slowly shuffling feet strained to propel him down the sidewalk next to Kyle, I knew who the stronger, bigger man was. This was a man who had embraced the way of weakness and in so doing had embraced the way of true wisdom. It became clear to me that "the LORD sees not as man sees: man looks on the outward appearance, but the LORD looks on the heart" (I Sam. 16:7).

PAUL AND THE SUPER-APOSTLES

Throughout the course of our conversation with Jim, he continually referenced 2 Corinthians. This is base camp for any exploration of power in weakness. Here Paul develops the idea theologically, and here we see the confrontation between Paul's understanding of power and that of the church in Corinth.[2] Much of the impact of Paul's words comes from an understanding of the culture in Corinth at the time the letter was written.

Several years ago, I (Jamin) had the joy of vacationing in Greece. The drive from Athens to Corinth took about an hour. The drive is so beautiful you almost forget about your destination. The brilliant blue water of the Aegean Sea is visible nearly the entire way. The city of Corinth is strategically positioned as a byway from the Aegean Sea to the Ionian Sea, as well as from mainland Greece to the Peloponnese. As you arrive and see the ruins, it is easy to imagine how glorious this city must have been in the first century. When Julius Caesar reconstituted Corinth a century after its destruction in 146 BC, the city was repopulated with a large contingency of Roman freedmen (former slaves) along with Greeks, Jews, and others.[3] The Corinth that Paul visited in AD 50 was a cultural and economic hub with no solidified aristocracy, resulting in an open society with an unusual degree of freedom for upward mobility. This created an incredibly competitive environment. If you worked hard enough and were shrewd enough, you could ascend the ladder of status and power.[4] Once at the top, you were justified in boasting of such an accomplishment. As Tim Savage tells us, "In Corinth, perhaps more than anywhere else, social ascent was the goal, boasting and self-display the means, personal power and glory the reward."[5] The city's social landscape mirrored the competitive spirit of its famed Isthmian games.

When Paul first preached the gospel in Corinth he had success (Acts 18), but subsequently the Corinthians began to question Paul's authority as an apostle. They wanted proof that Christ was speaking through Paul (2 Cor. 13:3). The Corinthians were wrestling with the same question that Kyle and I were: What does Christian power really look like? More specifically in relationship to Paul was the question of what apostolic power ought to look like. The question had already caused a divide over which apostle/teacher Corinthian Christians thought was the most special—Paul, Apollos, Peter, or Jesus himself (1 Cor. 1:10–17). This question was at the heart of the tension between Paul and the "super-apostles" who had come into town challenging Paul's authority and vying for power (2 Cor. 11:5).

The problem confronting Paul was that he did not embody any of the marks of power the Corinthians valued. In many ways, he was the exact opposite of what they desired: He did not have an impressive physical presence, he lacked bravado and confidence, and he was meek and gentle in his leadership (2 Cor. 10:10). He did not speak with eloquence (2 Cor. 11:6), and he did not boast in money, intentionally refusing to take money for his "services," choosing to work a menial job that would have been socially dishonorable (2 Cor. 11:7). On top of all this, Paul experienced continual suffering and hardship (2 Cor. 11:21–30). Each of these things was a sign of weakness in the eyes of the Corinthians. The totality of Paul's weaknesses had become unpalatable to them. The Corinthians wanted a super-apostle, not an apostle of weakness.

MARKETING WEAKNESS

In the face of the Corinthians' critique of and open opposition to his authority, we might expect Paul to have marshalled a persuasive defense, silencing the Corinthians with an overwhelming display of his authority as an apostle of Christ. Or, at the very least, we might expect him to have hidden the weaknesses that were cause for criticism. He faced the potential of losing the Corinthian believers to a false gospel (2 Cor. 11:1–6), and the stability of the church at Corinth largely rested on how Paul would respond to the critiques of his apostolic authority. Rather than meeting the Corinthians' expectations, however, Paul shone a light on the very weaknesses that caused him criticism, putting his weakness front and center (2 Cor. 1:3–7; 6:2–10; 11:16–12:10). Radically, Paul embraced the very things that the Corinthians rejected, identifying these weaknesses as signs of his true apostleship. He argued that his weakness was actually verification of the power of God working through him, and he rejected the Corinthian view of power as worldly success, bravado, and status. For Paul, the power to dominate and win was antithetical to the nature of the gospel. This is not merely a question of what leadership "style" you like, but a question of whether you embrace the way of Jesus. The high point of Paul's defiant response to the Corinthians' lust for power is found in the passage we began with: "'My grace is sufficient for you, for my power is made perfect in weakness.' Therefore I will boast all the more gladly of my weaknesses, so that the power of Christ may rest upon me. For the sake of Christ, then, I am content with weaknesses, insults, hardships, persecutions, and calamities. For when I am weak, then I am strong" (2 Cor. 12:9–10).

For a culture so fixated on power, it is hard to imagine how paradigm-shifting these words were, and how difficult they would have been to hear. But, of course, our own cultural context mirrors the Corinthian context in nearly every way.[6] In a culture boasting of personal accomplishment and success, Paul's response was to boast in his weakness. Why did he do so? So that the power of Christ may rest upon him. Paul viewed an embrace of weakness as an embrace of strength, because in weakness he could depend upon the might of God. His weakness was the source of his power. Paul did not anchor his life as a follower of Jesus in his ability, talent, gifting, résumé, or strength, but in the grace of God alone. To marshal these skills or achievements in his flesh would have been to embrace power from below and thus reject the gospel. Paul wrote, "For Christ did not send me to baptize but to preach the gospel, and not with words of eloquent wisdom, lest the cross of Christ be emptied of its power" (1 Cor. 1:17). Incredibly, Paul argued that to embrace the Corinthian way—to put ourselves forward, emphasizing our strengths and seeking our own power—was to empty the cross of its power.

The way of life to which followers of Jesus are called entails discovering that power is found in weakness. As an apostle, Paul modeled what the Christian life should look like. The proclamation of the gospel is not only heard in his teaching, but is observed in his manner of living.[7] Following Paul's example is not simply mimicking certain ethical behavior, but is embracing his way of life. Paul makes this clear to the Corinthians, holding their way of life in contrast with the apostles' way:

> We are weak, but you are strong. You are held in honor, but we in disrepute. To the present hour we hunger and thirst, we are poorly dressed and buffeted and homeless, and we labor, working with our own hands. When reviled, we bless; when persecuted, we endure; when slandered, we entreat. We have become, and are still, like the scum of the world, the refuse of all things. I do not write these things to make you ashamed, but

to admonish you as my beloved children. For though you have countless guides in Christ, you do not have many fathers. For I became your father in Christ Jesus through the gospel. I urge you, then, be imitators of me. (1 Cor. 4:10–16)

Paul's exhortation follows on the heels of a discussion of his own weakness. Paul is not trying to create clones of himself but followers of Christ, exhorting them to "be imitators of me, as I am of Christ" (1 Cor. 11:1). This way of power found in weakness is not original to Paul, but is a sign that Paul has followed Christ faithfully: "For he was crucified in weakness, but lives by the power of God. For we also are weak in him, but in dealing with you we will live with him by the power of God" (2 Cor. 13:4). Embrace of weakness is patterned after the way of Christ, who took up his cross, wholly dependent upon the Father for life and strength.[8] Just as Jesus found his life in the Father by the Spirit, so now do we. We are those who gain our lives only when we lose them for Christ's sake (Matt. 16:25). We are called not to rely upon ourselves, "but on God who raises the dead" (2 Cor. 1:9). Power is found in dependence upon God in light of our weakness.

Importantly, embracing our weakness is not synonymous with self-loathing. We are not called to mope about like Eeyore from Winnie the Pooh, reciting a narrative of failure over our lives. An embrace of our weakness does not negate the truths that we are created in the image of God and are called beloved children of the Father. However, such truths do not override the existence of our weakness. Our weakness is seen in three aspects of our condition. First, as human beings we are created finite and temporal and therefore weak and limited. We are dust, even though we are God's beloved dust.[9] Second, each of us has unique areas of frailty, incapacity, and weakness, whether physical, emotional, or mental. Third, we are weak because of our sin. We have all sinned and fallen short of God's glory (Rom. 3:23), and we all continue to experience the "desires of the flesh" (Gal. 5:17–21). In all of this we are called to humbly acknowledge the totality of our weakness and rely wholly upon God for strength. Thus, confessing our weaknesses is not merely about pointing to our failure, but rather about magnifying God's power. In the words of Paul, "we have this treasure in jars of clay, to show that the surpassing power belongs to God and not to us" (2 Cor. 4:7).

This last point can easily be misunderstood. Because of sin, we are all drawn to autonomy—we are all oriented to independence rather than dependence upon God. Because of this, we will always be tempted to use our strengths (whether they are talents, abilities, or even spiritual gifts) in our own power rather than in reliance upon Christ. Even in our strengths, therefore, where we are most tempted, we need to rely upon God and abide in his love. It is in the areas of our lives where we are most able, the places we think we are strong, where we are most often called into weakness. It is in our strengths where we think we can avoid abiding in Christ, where we sow to the flesh rather than abide by the Spirit. It is in our strengths where we trust our own personal savvy rather than the calling of God. As those called, not in our power but in *God's* power, we are called to know our weakness amid our strengths, so that when we try to thrive in sinful autonomy, we turn instead to abiding in Christ and proclaiming to him, "Without you, we can do nothing" (see John 15:5). Power in the Christian life is found in one place and one place alone. In the words of Paul, "For this I toil, struggling with all his energy that he powerfully works within me" (Col. 1:29). It is *God's* energy at work within that we must come to embrace; but his energy is not the power to achieve, but the power of dependence and love.

Yet embracing weakness is not simply finding it in our strengths. We are often called into places where all we know is weakness.

Many of us parent from this place. The thought of another fight with our three-year-old or another sleepless night feels impossible. Parents confront their weaknesses when they yell at their children, knowing full well that this has more to do with their own hearts than it does with their child, and they are confronted with a deep sort of weakness. I (Kyle) have a job that is constantly pushing me into areas where I don't feel competent, whether it is a skill-based competence (for example, administration) or a knowledge-based competence (for example, a class topic I don't know much about). Whether I like it or not, I'm going to be in a meeting or standing in front of thirty graduate students, and I have to choose to rest in Christ's power or try to assert my own. In one way or another, we are called into weakness; and we are all called into our weakness in the church as well. Most of us don't feel fully equipped to do the kind of ministry and service we are called to—either in the church itself or when loving our neighbors, serving the poor, and so on. These are calls to embrace our weakness and know the presence and power of Christ.

As John Calvin reflected on Paul's idea of power being found in weakness, he was drawn toward an interesting image.

> For *then* do we make room for Christ's grace, when in true humility of mind, we feel and confess our own weakness. The *valleys* are watered with rain to make them fruitful, while in the mean time, the high summits of the lofty mountains remain dry. Let that man, therefore, become a *valley*, who is desirous to receive the heavenly rain of God's spiritual grace.[10]

In Calvin's image, the rain represents God's grace, poured out and given in power. It is not possessed, owned, or controlled. Only those who become like a valley can receive it. In other words, those who humble themselves and acknowledge their weakness will know the refreshing rainfall of God's power upon the soil of their hearts. Only those who become lowly will receive the nutrients necessary to truly produce fruit.

Conversely, if we do not become a valley and instead make ourselves to be high summits, we remain dry. As Scripture clearly proclaims, "God opposes the proud, but gives grace to the humble" (James 4:6). Our culture, in contrast, values the high summit. The Tower of Babel is in our hearts. Life is about how high you can get. We sacrifice good things for the sake of honor and praise. Like a sale-obsessed shopper on Black Friday, we knock down and stomp on people to grab the significance and notoriety we so covet. Perhaps we gossip about a coworker to get a leg up for a promotion. Or maybe we criticize the parenting style of others because we want to be viewed as the family that does it right. The goal of life becomes power. We want to be special. We use social media to create a significant self. Credit cards are used to maintain a certain perceived lifestyle. Our weaknesses are strategically hidden so that we can get ahead. Our culture proclaims that the mountaintop is the land of flourishing and is the place of life. But this is all a ruse. These mountaintops are dry, parched land. Mountaintops are lonely, windswept places where vegetation is dwarfed and gnarled. We ascend the mountain expecting to find the pinnacle of flourishing at the top, but instead we discover a place inhospitable for life.

God invites us into the valley. The question is whether we will accept the invitation. The valley will always be in the shadow of the mountains. The mountains, with their dramatic peaks and pillars to the clouds, will always appear more special to the world around you. Becoming a valley is truly humbling. And yet this is the place where the rain soaks deep and fruit is truly produced. The valley is the place of life. It is the place of kingdom power.

CHAPTER 3

BECOMING POWERFUL

WHEN I (JAMIN) WAS IN SEMINARY, I HAD A COUPLE OF influential mentors in my life, professors whose teaching dramatically impacted me. I was captivated by their knowledge. I wanted to be like them and thought, fantastically, I could do so by the end of seminary! I thought I would soak up their teaching and read the right books, and that would be enough. But these mentors were more than knowledgeable; they were wise. Their depth was not merely the result of having read more books than everyone else, but was the fruit of many years of deep communion with God. Their wisdom was the result of walking with God through suffering and hardship, such that they had learned to depend upon God in light of their weakness. Their power was not the fruit of shrewd self-engineering, but of abiding. Consequently, I wasn't quickly able to become like these men. I couldn't manufacture their depth by putting in a few devoted years of study in seminary. I couldn't gain their texture of soul by simply landing on the "right" answer.

Becoming like these men is a long-term endeavor. It requires decades of abiding in Christ. But behind my desire to be like them was something else: a desire for significance. Significance, unlike wisdom, does not take patience. I saw what these professors had, and I wanted to embody it without the trials, suffering, and time it took them. I wanted long-term fruit through short-term effort. I am, of course, not alone in this temptation. Impatience is a cultural epidemic. There is a widespread desperation for power, but an equally broad neglect of the patience it takes to bear kingdom fruit. We want the promised land without the testing of the wilderness; we want to have a voice that powerfully proclaims truth without first learning to be "slow to speak" (James 1:19). Jesus attacks our shortsighted impatience and calls us into the long way. He calls us to the way of power found in weakness that comes only from a long obedience in the same direction.[1]

As Kyle and I discussed the idea of power in weakness, we realized how enticing power without weakness really is. In moments of honest self-reflection, we thought the way of weakness sounded like a life void of power. Power and weakness seem completely antithetical to one another, the presence of one necessitating the absence of the other. Embracing our weakness certainly didn't sound like a flourishing human existence. Is this really the good, abundant, and full life Jesus talked about? The "way of weakness" sounds more like a depleted, insufficient, and irrelevant life. As we explored this tension in our hearts, we realized that much of our lingering skepticism was the result of a certain understanding of personhood. We still held beliefs about human identity and flourishing that could not digest this notion of power we were uncovering. Questions kept rising to the surface that we knew needed answering. Fortunately, we didn't have to go far to find wisdom.

While our time with Jim Packer had come to a close, our time in Vancouver was far from over. The next stop on our journey was in the heart of the city itself, to visit one of Packer's longest and dearest friends. The reason Jim had moved from Britain to Vancouver several decades earlier was because this man recruited him to teach at Regent College. Our surroundings changed significantly as we left the small-town feel of the suburbs for the high rises of the city. After riding the elevator up several floors, we walked the long hallway looking for the right apartment.

The warm face of James Houston greeted us at the door. The enthusiastic welcome from James was soon doubled by his wife, Rita. After hanging our coats in the closet, we rounded the corner leading into the living room and were immediately confronted by a panoramic view of Vancouver before our eyes. It is hard to imagine a more spectacular view of the city—the harbor in the foreground and the mountains in the back.

At the time of our trip, James was nearly ninety years old but looked as though he were seventy. His ever-beaming smile helped maintain his youthful appearance, and his astounding intellect hadn't slowed a bit. Now retired, James began his academic career at Oxford, only leaving to start Regent College in Vancouver. He has been a mentor to me over the years, but our conversations had always been on the phone, never in person. It was a joy to sit with him. In our previous conversations, I had shared with him the journey that Kyle and I were embarking on. He was delighted to hear about our time with his dear old friend Jim Packer, and he was eager to walk with us now on the next leg of our journey. As we took our seats, James pointed out a few of the more significant landmarks of the city out his window. Kyle and I briefly oriented ourselves to where we wanted to go in our conversation, got our pads and pens ready, and began.

"James, what Kyle and I are confronted with in Scripture is that power is found in weakness. As Christians, we are called to a radical dependence upon God. We want to grab hold of this vision and embody it, but what we are finding is that there remain places in our hearts that doubt this is truly the way of strength and abundant living. Can you begin by speaking into this fleshly desire for power? What is going on in our innate desire for the way of power?"

James sat forward with the enthusiasm I had grown familiar with. "The way of power, as you are talking about, is the way of self-redemption. We all have an Achilles' heel, and so we use our natural abilities to compensate for the limp it has caused. We compensate through self-improvement. A lot of what we think of as our strengths is really just the result of this compensation. Rather than looking to Christ to redeem, we have acted as our own redeemer. Twice over we neglect our Redeemer. We neglect him in our self-accomplishment, in our attempt to overcome our weaknesses with strengths. We also neglect him because we don't believe we need him where we are powerful; we only need him where we are failing or still poor. In this sense, operating from our strengths is practicing atheism. This is why there is a feeling in so many of our churches that we are role-playing. You can't expose your real self. If you are majoring in your strength, how can you ever live without a mask? You are always concealing things you don't want other people to see in you. Often, when our students graduate, they ask me, 'So what's going to be my ministry?' Your ministry, I tell them, is going to be dictated by your Achilles' heel. Where you limp is where you're directed."

Rather than viewing our strengths as the path to a meaningful and powerful life, James was calling us to view our weaknesses as the path of our calling. Seeking to live empowered by our strengths was, in his mind, a wholly unchristian way to live. The Christian way of life is living in dependence upon God, moving forward to embrace our weaknesses so that God's glory might be revealed. This has obvious implications for how we think about ministry and calling, but it also impacts our understanding of what it means to be a human being. On this understanding of life, part of what it means to mature as a person is to accept our weakness and abide within it.

This does not mean we reject our genuine God-given strengths and abilities. We are called to steward these things. If you are good with numbers, pursuing a career as a CPA may indeed be a wise decision. But it means that as we steward our strengths, we must do so from a posture of dependence upon God. We recognize these talents and gifts are from God and can be utilized for ultimate good only in dependence upon him. There is no calling in our lives that does not require a deep acceptance of our weakness. This may be harder to see in areas where we feel competent and capable, but in other areas our weakness is very much on the surface. Marriage, for instance, is a relational reality that calls us into our weakness, if, in fact, we are willing to grow in love. In marriage we are called into our brokenness, our inability to love another well, and our unhealthy desires. Whether we feel strong or weak, therefore, God invites us to walk forward in the truth of our weakness so we might know his power. The abundant, flourishing, and weighty life, therefore, is the life lived in weakness. Kyle and I quickly realized this had far-reaching implications, so we pressed a bit further.

"James, how does all of this impact the way we understand what it means to be a person? How does this redefine our understanding of identity?"

After pausing momentarily, James explained, "What we face in the world today is a self-achieved identity. As Christians, we believe in a given identity, not an achieved one. The Christian is found in Christ. The self-achieved identity is very fragile because we have to sustain it. Nobody else is going to sustain it for me when I have built it up myself. The result of this is a tendency toward narcissism, because there is a depleted sense of self. This is not what God ordained that we should have for an identity."

I (Kyle) immediately reflected on my own current vocational circumstances. I was in a kind of vocational limbo at the time. I had finished a PhD in systematic theology after five years of master's degrees and four years in my PhD program, and I was ready to find a position in a career I felt called to. I had worked hard for many, many years, and yet I was unable to find a job. I knew the fragility James talked about. I had done everything I could to succeed, yet it wasn't working out. In the academy, maybe even more than most areas, the way of power is king. You don't simply go to school; you go to the *right* school. You don't simply publish; you publish with the *right* publishers and in the *right* journals. As is often a temptation in our formation and growth as Christians, it is easy to think we can achieve our way out of our struggle. It is easy to think that if we do all the *right* things, everything will work out. I felt the temptation James spoke of, and knew my tendency to try to fix this myself. I knew what it looked like to try to reject my weakness and turn to power. I could see the ways in which I had bought into a self-achieved identity. The grasp for power is pervasive in my field, but is certainly not isolated to the academy. We want to buy the *right* house in the *right* neighborhood. We push our way into the *right* social circles. We obsess about having the *right* body. Our culture is dominated by the way of power.

We spent the next three days with James and Rita. We laughed a lot. Rita, a woman who pulls no punches in the best possible sense, has a wit that is unrivaled. They both peppered us with questions about our wives and children. We asked our share of questions as well. Rita told us tales of bird-watching vacations with John Stott, an old friend from her youth and a dear friend of her and James. James told us about the challenge of starting Regent with just four students and no real financial stability—walking away from the dream position at Oxford to start a fledgling school for *mere* Christians. He sarcastically reflected on his days of retirement, at one point saying, "You have to understand, I'm retired now. I'm no longer a person." We talked a great deal about this reality of being elderly and retired, since this had been a recent area of study and writing for him.[2]

When a culture has come to define itself by what you can achieve and what you do for a living—as ours has—the retired person ceases to be a real person. When a meaningful, powerful, and flourishing life is built on one's physical and mental capacities, what does that mean for the value and identity of those whose capacities are failing or nonexistent? As James spoke about the sad reality that Christians have followed the culture in this regard, focusing their attention on youth and ignoring the elders, I (Kyle) remembered our coffee shop conversation with Jim Packer. At one point during the discussion, I looked up and noticed that several older people were staring at us from other tables. They had a longing and curiosity in their eyes. Why would these two young men be listening so attentively to this elderly man?

After a day attending church, enjoying a delightful brunch, and taking a drive around town, we said our good-byes to the Houstons. It was now approaching dinnertime, and it was New Year's Eve. We headed downtown hoping, a bit nervously, that we might be able to find a restaurant with seats available. To our surprise there was a table available at a wonderful seafood restaurant right in the harbor. As we ate, we talked about our conversation with James, not merely what he had said, but who he was. He had a strong personality with an incredible academic background, and yet we didn't feel intimidated by him. We never felt as if we needed to prove ourselves to him or seek his validation. Rather, his power led us into honesty and vulnerability, not self-aggrandizement and posturing. Here was a powerful man who was truly flourishing, yet he was largely ignored by the world around him (even, often, by the church). He showed us that flourishing is not the absence of weakness, nor the absence of dependence or need, but that a genuinely human existence is discovered in relying fully on Christ.

HUMAN FLOURISHING

The source of our power always entails a reaction of some kind. Coal power, for instance, has the negative fallout of pollution. Nuclear power has the unfortunate effect of creating dangerous waste. The power we tap into is no different. The power from below radiates a certain waste product and pollution into our souls, shrinking our capacity for love and undermining our ability to really attend to others. The sad irony is that using this way helps us, in the short term, to get ahead in this world, but in the long term it undermines our ability to flourish as a human being.

When I (Kyle) landed my first teaching position at a university, I taught four classes a semester, each with a hundred students. My main class was Christian Worldview, the one course every student had to take. Our student body was composed of many Christians, but also many atheists, Buddhists, and Muslims, who all had to take my course. When I was hired, it was clear that this class had become despised on campus, and our new dean unfolded a vision for how we could turn the tide. We gutted the class and started from scratch, and it quickly became one of the favorite courses on campus. Everything seemed to be going well. There was a buzz about the class, my student evaluations were through the roof, and I had older students who weren't even in the class stopping in to hear lectures. But then I started really evaluating my own engagement with the students, and something else bubbled to the surface. I hadn't noticed, but in my attempt to make this class great (and by great, I mean popular), I forgot one of my main roles as a professor. I had learned how to "wow" my students, but I never got around to really educating them. It was a one-man play that was entertaining enough for applause, but it was something done *at* the audience and not done *with* them.

Amid the stress of a new job and the anxiety of trying to turn around a class with a bad reputation, I had turned to the power that was most natural to me—myself. I wielded the strength of my personality to try to captivate my students. The great evaluations and the buzz on campus validated my efforts and took my attention off of the really important questions. The fallout of this kind of power was a change in my own focus, from the student to myself. If I would have continued this long term, it would have affected the texture of my soul; my depth as a person would have been impacted, sliding further and further toward superficiality. When talking with James, I recognized someone who had given himself to power from above for decades. When talking with his past students, I was told that he was famous on campus because every time you would walk by his office, you would hear weeping. Students would come in, and James would unravel their souls by speaking directly into the deep places of their hearts. Students went in with all sorts of baggage, but in his office that fell away and they knew love. Whereas my students were entertained, James's students were given a vision for human flourishing as they met someone face-to-face who embodied love.

To understand what it means to flourish as a person, we first and foremost look to Jesus. To discover what it means to be human, we must fix our eyes on the incarnation of the Son of God. Here we get a front row seat to the long and developed story of human flourishing. Paradoxically, we don't discover what it means to be image-bearers by looking primarily at the first image-bearers (Adam and Eve); we discover what it means to be image-bearers by looking to the image of God himself, Jesus Christ. We read in Hebrews 1:3 that Jesus is the exact representation of God's nature. He is *the* image of God: an image that took on flesh as one of us. We are created *in* the image of God. He is the eternally begotten divine Son, and we are the adopted children, received by grace. We read in Colossians 1:15, "He is the image of the invisible God, the firstborn of all creation." We do, therefore, look to the firstborn of creation to discover the truth of the good life, but the firstborn is not Adam, but Christ. Jesus reveals the contours of human flourishing and defines our vocation as those made in *his* image.

In Jesus' ministry, therefore, we see the form of power in weakness. When Jesus faced extreme moments of weakness and rejection, he made the choice to embrace weakness instead of seeking to dominate it. In the words of Isaiah 53:7, "He was oppressed, and he was afflicted, yet he opened not his mouth; like a lamb that is led to the slaughter, and like a sheep that before its shearers is silent, so he opened not his mouth." Human flourishing is not about self-actualization, but about discovering our life in Christ. Flourishing entails discovering our insufficiency and coming to rest in the sufficiency of his grace. *The flourishing self is the abiding self, not the actualized self.* It is the self wholly dependent upon Jesus. This is what a genuinely human existence really looks like.[3]

SELF-ACTUALIZATION IN THE CHURCH

When Jesus' way of abundance is revealed to us, many of us assume he must have been speaking hyperbolically. *He couldn't have really meant, "Without me you can do nothing," right?* In the famous words of G. K. Chesterton, "The Christian ideal has not been tried and found wanting. It has been found difficult and left untried."[4] It is easy to read Jesus' call to embrace our weakness and treat it like a mind game that only needs to be tossed around in our brains rather than lived. We don't take Jesus seriously. In turn, we still view weakness as a problem to overcome. We take the quest of self-actualization through the grooming of talents and abilities as commonsensical—something that *must* be true—and then use that as a basic litmus test for understanding what it means to live a faithful and full human life.

One of the ways we mask our use of power in strength is to label it something different. This is self-deception at its finest. It is not unusual, therefore, to hear the call to fully realize our potential; to develop, build, and create selves in our own power; and to follow it up with, "for the glory of God." Similarly, the success stories I hear in ministry focus on those who get things done, who go on mission trips regularly, who preach with eloquence and profundity, or who give the most money (or maybe raise the most money). With increasing regularity I see the church championing and mimicking cultural elites, professional athletes, rock stars, or any and every aspect of Hollywood. These are the people who have "access" to a world so many are desperate for, so the church mirrors this reality in its own subcultures, dividing between those who are "someone" and those who aren't. As with my own teaching, it is easy to start believing in the effects of what we do and to equate success with the work of the kingdom. But Jesus not only undermined where we turn for power; he also recalibrated what flourishing looks like:

¤ In the kingdom, flourishing is found in serving others, not "lord[ing] it over them" (Matt. 20:25).

¤ In the kingdom, flourishing is discovered by being last, not being first (Mark 9:35).

¤ In the kingdom, flourishing is embracing the littleness of our roles and accepting that the "less honorable" parts of the body are more honored (1 Cor. 12:21–26).

¤ In the kingdom, flourishing is known in our weakness (2 Cor. 12:9).

We may look to find power in God, but is it for the sake of our own greatness rather than love? I made this mistake early on in my teaching. I was genuinely seeking to abide in Christ, but my goal was not aligned with his. I became so focused on what I wanted to make happen that I failed to recognize that my approach no longer mirrored the ways of Jesus. We will all be tempted along similar lines, to allow valuable ends to justify the means. As long as it will further what we believe is "good," we allow ourselves to do questionable things. Some pastors, for instance, have fallen into this temptation by using church funds to cheat the bestseller system so that their book will receive more attention. They believe in what they wrote, so they want an audience for it; but their means are unethical and antithetical to the way of Jesus.

Similarly, not only do we sometimes get the means wrong, but we often allow ourselves to invest in the wrong goals. It is easy, for instance, to define "kingdom power" in terms of what we find beautiful and unique, such that we assume that our creativity, by the very nature of its being creative, must be faithful to the way of Jesus. Furthermore, it is easy to embrace greatness without discernment, believing that greatness will always be characteristic of the kingdom. But Jesus champions not the great but the seemingly insignificant and irrelevant. As we see kingdom power in the church today, our starting question should not be "How can we be great?" but "What role do the weak, disabled, and elderly have in our midst?" When those who are obviously weak have no place in the church, we know that we have rejected the way from above and have embraced a power antagonistic to the gospel.

In this self-actualized account of human flourishing, the thrust of personhood is to achieve in my own power. The focus is on *my* ability, *my* creativity, and *my* potential. These become the pistons driving the engine of self (resulting, Jesus tells us, in the eternal loss of self). No place for weakness exists in this view of reality. More important, no place exists for God. We don't reject God outright, but we retain the god of Deism, who once did some powerful things but is generally detached from our day-to-day lives. So instead of abiding, we pray for God to give us some of his power. Instead of growing into him who is our head (Eph. 4:15), we ask him to give us some magic ("Just make me stop sinning," "Just make these temptations go away," and so on). Instead of entering into the way of weakness, we try to use God to become something powerful.

SPIRITUAL GIFTS

I (Jamin) remember the first time I took a spiritual gift test as an adult. I was new in pastoral ministry, eager to grow, and ready to maximize my potential. I remember finishing the test and feeling satisfied with the results. I won! At least that's how it felt. Pastor, teacher, leader—I had all the powerful and important gifts. It was confirmation of my grandiose vision for life in ministry. I quickly learned not everyone feels this way after they take a spiritual gift test. For some it is confusing, and for others it feels deflating. They think, *I feel called to do other things, but I guess I can't*, or even, *I don't have any gifts that really matter*. These are the kinds of things I have heard over the years from folks in the church. Spiritual gift tests are not always encouraging. You don't always feel like you won.

Maybe more than anywhere else in the church, spiritual gifts are entry points into the way from below. The way we understand it, spiritual gifts are unapologetically about power to control—where we assert our power in the service of the kingdom. These easily become devices for our self-actualization. We mistakenly believe these gifts are special abilities, almost like superpowers. This creates two problems. First, it establishes a hierarchy of value, where we come to see certain people as particularly important because of their gifts. We come to think about these "special abilities" in worldly terms, so naturally, we begin making worldly value judgments. The result is that we create a hierarchy of power within the church based on one's particular gift. Second, it tends toward self-reliance. If we tap into our superpower and cultivate it, we can do powerful things. Since we think these are *our* abilities, we come to believe we own them and therefore don't really need God. He may have given us the gifts, but now they are ours to actualize or to let atrophy. The results are up to us and our savvy.

In contrast, Paul's description of the spiritual gifts focuses on two key things: first, on the God who gives them, and second, on how the gifts we perceive to be weaker and less significant are actually more honorable in the kingdom. The first point is important, but here the second point is particularly helpful. A flourishing Christian existence is embracing what we are called to. Paul states explicitly, "But God has so composed the body, giving greater honor to the part that lacked it, that there may be no division in the body, but that the members may have the same care for one another. If one member suffers, all suffer together; if one member is honored, all rejoice together" (1 Cor. 12:24–26). The question we must ask ourselves is whether our church culture allows for this. Are our churches honoring the members of the family of God who are often ignored and overlooked? Or rather, have we succumbed to a worldly view of power and value that raises some figures to the top and ignores others? When flourishing is seen as "getting things done" or "achieving," we tend to reject the people Jesus sought out—the outcasts, those with disabilities, and the weak. When our goals become secularized, we turn to the young and exciting and we lose the wisdom and discernment that come only through age and faithfulness. Spiritual gifts are an interesting test case in how the church views power, because they are how we put our power into practice.

A MERE MORTAL

As Kyle and I reflected on strength and weakness, I was reminded of a conversation I had with James. As a younger man, James was mentored by C. S. Lewis. It feels odd even writing that. When I think of C. S. Lewis, I mentally put him so far back in history that no one alive could have known him. But James used to meet with him regularly. I was talking to James on the phone the first time he told me a story about Lewis. It was almost by accident. My ears perked up, as you may expect. It's not often you have a conversation with someone who was friends with C. S. Lewis! I could tell that Lewis had meant a great deal to him, that he had informed James's understanding of personhood and identity in Christ as well. So I asked him, "What do you feel you learned from Lewis the most?"

"In 1955 Lewis left to go to Cambridge," James said, "and that same spring I was getting married. I knew I wouldn't see him very much anymore and so I asked him, 'What is the most important message you want to communicate through your writing?' He responded, 'Against reductionism.' That was precisely what Lewis taught me most."

Against reductionism? It was not what I was expecting. But as I considered it, I began to see this theme throughout all of James's writings, and it became clear how profoundly Lewis's comment had resonated with him. In particular, James is concerned that our view of what it means to be human is reduced into something that is subhuman. James is worried that we are becoming less than what we are—that we have accepted categories of personhood that are dehumanizing and superficial. This is the great irony of seeking to define personhood through power. In our pursuit to be *more than*, to transcend our weaknesses and frailty, we are reduced. When we seek to create a self through our professional abilities and success, we are dehumanized, becoming less than God has called us to be. When we grasp for control of our identity to generate value and significance, we shrink our identity. We easily give in to the temptation to reduce our identities down to certain gifts, our professions, or the approval of others. The entire endeavor to create a self in our own power results in an empty, superficial self.

James's explanation of human flourishing recalls the reality that "the LORD weighs the spirit" (Prov. 16:2). When we come to see the Christian existence as a deepening of our spirits—making our deepest spiritual selves more substantial—then the way of the world seems to fade away. James is a living example of a weighty spirit, an ideal he inherited from Lewis. In his provocative book *The Great Divorce*, Lewis imagines what it would be like to venture into heaven when one is not a natural inhabitant of it. The narrator describes his fellow adventurers as "transparent" and ghostlike, not as real as the place they visited. They were lighter and less substantial beings than the heavenly realities.

> It was the light, the grass, the trees that were different; made of some different substance, so much solider than things in our country that men were ghosts by comparison. Moved by a sudden thought, I bent down and tried to pluck a daisy which was growing at my feet. The stalk wouldn't break. I tried to twist it, but it wouldn't twist. I tugged till the sweat stood out on my forehead and I had lost most of the skin off my hands. The little flower was hard, not like wood or even like iron, but like diamond. There was a leaf—a young tender beech-leaf, lying in the grass beside it. I tried to pick the leaf up: my heart almost cracked with the effort, and I believe I did just raise it. But I had to let it go at once; it was heavier than a sack of coal. As I stood, recovering my breath with great gasps and looking down at the daisy, I noticed that I could see the grass not only between my feet but *through* them. I also was a phantom.[5]

It is difficult for a person not of heaven to walk there, the narrator notes, because the grass was more real than he was. His weight could not bend the grass because it was "hard as diamonds to [his] unsubstantial feet," and made him "feel as if [he] were walking on wrinkled rock."[6] This image describes the Christian existence in this world. In our natural and unsubstantial state, we see the depth and weightiness of what God calls us to, and our initial inclination is to try to achieve it by means contrary to the kingdom (trying to break the diamond-hard daisy with the phantom hands of our flesh). What Scripture suggests is that the way that seems substantial to us is actually weightless and superficial, and that the way of God is the only way of wisdom and depth. While we are running around trying to create a life that matters, Jesus tells us that if we try to save our lives we will lose them, and if we try to be first we will be last.

A GENUINELY HUMAN EXPERIENCE

To embrace a genuinely human existence, we must live along the contours of the kingdom. When we give ourselves to sin, we are not simply doing bad things; we are becoming lighter beings. The fallout from the power of sin is a decrease in weightiness and an ever-pervasive superficiality. We lack a sturdiness of person and instead are easily "tossed to and fro by the waves" (Eph. 4:14). When we give ourselves to sin, our hearts and souls are being conformed to that reality, so that the world as it really is becomes foreign and God's kingdom becomes increasingly alien. For example, scientific studies have now shown that watching pornography rewires the brain, such that our sexuality becomes more and more distorted and subhuman. Pornography addiction is not more of the same, but is an addiction that needs more *and* different. What is different sexually turns violent and deviant quickly; it becomes

53

a dehumanizing act.[7] Our sexuality is designed for spiritual and physical union within the covenant of marriage—the self-giving and embracing of one another in love—but pornography is the practice of purely selfish sexual behavior. Pornography dehumanizes the person watching by reworking the contours of their sexuality in isolation, without a physical partner in covenantal union. The result is a shift of sexuality into the realm of power and control. It is not surprising that there has been a rise in the number of men who started watching pornography at a young age who now show no interest in real women. When sexuality is learned on your own terms—according to your own power—another person is just a bother.

Everything we do taps into a deeper reality of power: power from below for control, or power from God for love. Power for control gets things done quickly and is the easiest way to "make something of yourself." Even the way we respond to our sin, such as pornography, illustrates our turn to self-power. We feel shame, and so turn to self-help, self-condemnation, or willpower to defeat it, but it doesn't work. If we pray about it, we turn against ourselves, often praying through self-condemnation in an attempt to lessen the judgment of God. We quickly forget that it was in our sin that Christ died for us (Rom. 5:8), and that for those in him there is now no condemnation (Rom. 8:1). We think that a worldly sort of grief will make up for our sin, but in doing so we become more enslaved to it. As Paul says, "Godly grief produces a repentance that leads to salvation without regret, whereas worldly grief produces death" (2 Cor. 7:10). Becoming weighty, becoming a substantial and genuinely human person, requires that we take another path entirely. When we talked with James, it was clear that he had been on this path with Christ for decades, and the work of wisdom in his life was palpable. But the most profound aspect of our time with him wasn't his brilliant analysis of theology, his stories about Lewis, or even his pastoral counsel to us (and those were all profound). What was most profound was his love for Rita.

Since our conversation with James, Rita has passed away. At the time of our visit with the Houstons, she was struggling with dementia. Rita was an incredibly sharp and witty woman, chiding James for saying something "just because it sounded good," and holding her own in any conversation. So she was able to hide her sickness well. But when she left the room for a nap and returned, she would want to know why James hadn't told her he had people over. This happened a handful of times. When Rita went to rest, we asked James how they were doing, and his answer was somewhat shocking. James explained, "People will say to us, 'It is so tragic that this has happened.' But that isn't true." James smiled. "This is the best time of our lives together. Things have never been better. Why? Because never have things been more relational. I really mean it. It is the best time of life, because it is stripped of all the nonessentials."

James knew that their union of love was what held them together even as Rita's memory failed. Growing old may appear tragic, but it is a part of the rhythm of reality. The real tragedy is the person who has lived a lifetime in fantasy, trying to deny weakness, and is left with nothing because he or she failed to become weighty of soul. But when weakness is the way, these days are not tragedies but opportunities. James offered a picture of what it means to be deeply human, to truly flourish in marital relationship. What was needed most was not a skill set, mental capacity, or ability, but love. He saw a person in full, not in part, when he looked at his wife. This view is impossible if we continue to buy into the lie that human flourishing is about self-actualization. That lie, James explained, has affected the way we view the mind. We believe the truly flourishing person is bright, socially adept, and healthy. But what do we do with people who have dementia or Alzheimer's? Or what about those in our churches who have physical or mental disabilities? According to our cultural values of power, their lives have functionally ended. Yet if identity and personhood are defined not by earthly power but by God's grace, then we are in a different position. If we lose our mental or physical capacities, a thorn in the flesh remains; but we are still capable of flourishing in dependence upon God. In fact, it is here where we can be most open to the way of life God calls us to.

The sun was setting and we were about to leave. James and Rita sat side by side on the couch while Jamin and I listened intently to James talking about living in weakness. Our final question was only meant to put a period at the end of a profound couple of days with the Houstons, but the answer took us off guard. We asked, "Where have you learned most significantly that strength really does come in weakness?" As James leaned forward to answer, Rita muttered under her breath, "I could tell you after a few years." Jamin and I sat silently, knowing that this disease was the great trial of her life; but then James inserted his own thought.

"You see," he started, looking over at his bride, "Rita is worried that as she loses her memory, she will forget Jesus." James glanced at us but continued to talk to her. "So I remind her, what matters is not that you remember him, but that he remembers you."

There, in summary, is the flourishing human being. As James and Rita pressed into frailty and disability, they were shifting their identity and value more and more onto Jesus. This is not an ability that just comes to us. They were able to see the end of life as an opportunity because they had lived lives of dependence. Many years ago they left all the comforts and certainties of life in the UK and ventured into the unknown of starting a school in Canada, trusting in God the whole way through. That posture of trust had marked their journey from that point until now. They were weighty souls who were able to embrace the end as a gift of love.

James and Rita were free because they knew that their lives r̶
on Christ and not in themselves. "Your life is hidden with Christ
in God," Paul tells us (Col. 3:3). When we as Christians embrace
the way from below, we reject not only the way of Christ but also
the truth of ourselves. We are warping our souls and rewiring
our hearts to a world that isn't real. In doing so we embrace fantasy, and our hearts, souls, and minds recalibrate for a world that
doesn't exist. We had to find help distinguishing fantasy from reality, which meant that we needed to ask deeper questions about the
true nature of kingdom power and worldly power.

CHAPTER 4

STANDING AGAINST
THE POWERS

SEVERAL YEARS BEFORE WE HAD CHILDREN, MY WIFE, Kelli, and I (Kyle) decided to visit some friends out of state. On Sunday morning we attended church with them. It was a church known for being "biblical." As we waited for our friends to arrive, we noticed something odd at one end of the lobby: a huge model of an ancient ziggurat. A ziggurat was a pyramid-shaped building that increased in height with steps. Importantly, this is what the Tower of Babel probably was. "Why in the world do they have a huge Tower of Babel in the lobby?" I muttered to Kelli. Of all the images in Scripture to portray, especially in a church not often in the business of making images, the Tower of Babel seemed like a strange choice. Why portray a story about human arrogance in your church lobby?

The only thing I could imagine was that the children's ministry had created a huge model for their Sunday school classes, so we decided to check it out. I was wrong. It was a massive fountain. What was most shocking was not the exorbitant cost of erecting such a tower in their lobby, although that was certainly troubling. What was more disconcerting was its purpose. At the foundation of this edifice were huge boulders, and on each boulder was a plaque that named something the church had achieved. Let that sink in. Without realizing the implications, someone built the Tower of Babel in the lobby of a church with the foundation stones representing their own achievements. Someone built a model of the biblical portrayal of human arrogance as a physical representation of their own success.

The church, no doubt, believed God had been a part of these achievements. As we are all prone to do, they undoubtedly assumed whatever they did was for God. But the hubris undergirding these achievements was unveiled with the presence of this statue. If God really was the focus, why not include other churches or ministries? Presumably God is at work elsewhere, right? What could possibly be the goal of spending a fortune to erect such a monstrosity other than proving that they had something to be proud of? This is a perfect example of the idolatry of "specialness" that Packer had talked about. No matter how genuine the desire, the quest to win and feel powerful had seeped into the veins of this church.

Years later, I learned that some elders in this church began pointing out how little accountability there had been for the budget. Furthermore, they dared to name the culture of "fear and intimidation" in the leadership. The response? They were kicked out, rumors were spread about their character, congregants were urged to alienate them, and the elders were vilified by the rest of the board. Another elder even denounced them as satanic. Such are the devastating effects of the way from below. Jesus himself faced this when his own critics labeled his ministry demonic (Matt. 12:24). Giving ourselves to the way from below so warps the soul that we begin confusing God's way with the way of the demons. What had been exposed was a culture of domination, underhanded power plays, and fear-driven leadership. Jesus claimed that his people would be known by their love, yet this place—in its quest to be biblical—somehow sought out worldly power to win.

MINIMIZING THE PROBLEM

How could this happen in a conservative Bible church? What is going on when the quest to dominate and win becomes the lifeblood of the church, and anyone who gets in the way of that engine is attacked and tossed to the side? I wish this story were fictitious. I wish it were an anomaly. Sadly, we hear these kinds of stories regularly. It seems this has become a new norm in the evangelical world. It is increasingly rare to meet someone who has not experienced some kind of spiritual abuse within the church, or seen the church reject the way of Jesus for something else. It is not unusual to find pastors using their congregations as platforms to advance *their* influence and profile. It is not uncommon to find churches that relate to neighboring congregations as competition, rather than as family in the kingdom. It is not uncommon to discover scandals of power and abuse in the church that have been hidden to protect the "right people" from getting in trouble. This does not stop with pastors or church leaders; they are just the most visible. This desire to be special, to be significant and powerful, is endemic in our culture; and we bring those things to the body of Christ. We imbibe the social hierarchies of the world—with its focus on celebrity, material possessions, and status—and we bring these values into the Christian life. Then these values become our litmus test for spiritual wisdom and leadership.

We see the way from below embraced in evangelical Christianity all the time, and yet we are blind to the magnitude of the situation. Perhaps things like self-sufficiency and control have become such a part of the status quo that we don't recognize how devastating they are to the body of Christ. Or maybe the faint concern we do have about such things is swiftly mollified by the "successes" we observe in the church. We ignore narcissism, self-glorification, and domination as long as the number of conversions is up and more baptisms are happening.[1] Perhaps we believe these kinds of concerns are much ado about nothing, and we ought to simply focus on the positive. We cling to the notion that the "glass is half full," but we fail to notice that the glass is actually a broken cistern (Jer. 2:13). The problem is serious. In the words of Bernard of Clairvaux, "No poison or sword ought to terrify you as much as the lust for domination."[2]

As we return to James 3, we are faced with the harsh reality of how serious the problem is. As James talks about the way from below, he doesn't treat it as a minor concern but instead emphasizes the evil nature of this way. James tells us that the way from below is earthly, unspiritual, and, most provocatively, "demonic" (James 3:15). Yes, the way of selfish ambition is demonic. In other words, the way of power found in the self and for the self is evil. As we return to 2 Corinthians, we discover that Paul views the super-apostles' penchant for boasting, cultural honor, and power through this spiritual lens as well, saying, "Such men are false apostles, deceitful workmen, disguising themselves as apostles of Christ. And no wonder, for even Satan disguises himself as an angel of light. So it is no surprise if his servants, also, disguise themselves as servants of righteousness. Their end will correspond to their deeds" (11:13–15). We are dealing not merely with uncritical adoption of the cultural values around us, but with spiritual warfare.

This realization struck Jamin and me deeply. The true spiritual nature of the problem revealed a deeper issue in the church's accommodation to the way from below than we had expected. What are the implications if we come to accept this way in our churches, and how might we stand against it? This time we wouldn't have to travel far to find an answer to our questions.

A POWERFULLY WEAK WOMAN

She sat down and took a deep breath. I (Jamin) could tell she was physically exhausted. It had taken all of her strength to navigate the uneven terrain of Spanish pavers leading to my office. Without her husband's assistance, it would have been nearly impossible to maintain balance on her prosthetic leg. After glancing around the room to get a sense of her surroundings, she caught my eyes and smiled. The bright pink shirt she wore was a physical representation of the warmth she personally exuded. The ivory cross necklace draped around her neck seemed a fitting vestment for this beautiful saint. For someone facing an unending list of health maladies, she had an unusual strength and joy about her. As if the prosthetic leg didn't make life challenging enough, she had also battled cancer, lost eyesight and hearing, and faced a variety of other pervasive challenges to her body that had progressed (or, in fact, degenerated) through the years. Marva Dawn is a powerfully weak woman.

There is not a hint of pretense or pomp about Marva, yet she has her PhD from the University of Notre Dame and has written numerous books, both popular and academic. Marva is assuredly an expert on many topics. Indeed, it was tempting to explore a variety of subjects with her, but our goal was singular. We had sought out Marva to learn about the evil nature of the way from below, and the inherent danger in the Christian's capitulation to this way. As our tea bags steeped in mugs on the table, I began with the question that had soaked in my heart the longest. "Marva, as we think about the two ways of power, we are struck by the dangerous position the church finds itself in. We know that Jesus has defeated the powers of evil, Satan, and his demons, but we also know that they have not yet been destroyed. How does this impact the way the body of Christ responds to the evil at work in our world?"

Marva took a deep breath, as if to take in my question before responding. "It is crucial that Christ's victory over evil be realized not only by Christians in isolation, but by communities of believers. That is why the New Testament is so concerned that churches remain an alternative society, not fostering the parasitic growth of the powers of evil but maintaining purity and freedom. If churches took this stand, it would change the attitude of our congregations, so that rather than trying to be *powerful* in the world, we would be a *servant* in the world. We wouldn't try to be the strongest or most powerful or richest or most attractive or most popular churches, but we would be willing to be the servant, and therefore walk humbly with God."

The church is called to purity, to keep her heart "unstained from the world" (James 1:27). The church must be wary of the deceiving poison of the powers of evil. The "powers of evil" is not a part of our common vocabulary, but it is thoroughly biblical. Throughout the New Testament the forces of the way from below are referred to as principalities and powers.[3] What we wanted to know was how susceptible the church was to these forces of evil. So I continued along this line, asking, "Marva, how do you see these things infiltrating the church?"

"Many evil powers are tempting the church today. Number one is the power of personality. I call that an evil power because many pastors depend on their own personality to attract people. It's an evil power that pits personality against the force of the gospel in Jesus Christ alone." Marva paused briefly, then continued, "A great temptation is the principality and power of Mammon. I call it Mammon, which was an ancient Hebrew name for the god of money and wealth. When you call it the god Mammon, you know it is a principality and power, and that it's more than just money. It's the love of money. It's when we let money be a god in our lives. Whenever money pulls churches away from their God-given purposes, then it is functioning as Mammon. Too many churches rely on their money and their gadgetry. Too many people rely on their salaries to support them in the world, and they lose track of God's providing for them. He provides home, food, and drink. I don't mean drink as evil power; I mean, like water." Marva giggled, clearly amused at how she could have been misunderstood.

We talked a bit more about powers threatening the church. Marva shared concerns about the experience-based models of worship she saw in the church, and grieved the emphasis placed on popularity. Her words were heavy for my pastoral heart to take in. The North American culture has capitulated to these powers, and I could not deny how readily many churches have been seduced by them. We were so engrossed in conversation that we almost didn't notice lunchtime had arrived, but the grumbling of our stomachs finally interrupted us.

We decided to head into downtown San Juan Capistrano for a quick bite to eat. As we drove, I silently pondered the different examples of "powers" Marva had mentioned. I was struck by how normalized these have become, and how often they are viewed as necessary for success, even in ministry. How often are we bothered by someone wielding the force of his or her personality, but look the other way because it is for a cause we believe in? We may know of churches criticized for luxurious spending, but is this really an issue of spiritual warfare? Marva was arguing that we have accepted realities in our churches today that are deep and sinister problems. If she was right, then Kyle and I had to admit that unlike Paul and the early Christians, we were profoundly unaware of Satan's workings in the world (2 Cor. 2:11).

We sat down and ordered our meals, and the conversation continued. With a bit of trepidation, I pressed into the implications of what Marva had been talking about. "If we take the issues you raised—popularity, power of the show, and an entertainment orientation to church—it seems clear that this is not simply cultural accommodation, but a deeply troubling spiritual issue."

Marva's warmth remained, but her tone was serious. "People will say, 'We need to resist the temptation of cultural accommodation.' Well, yes, but it is more than that. We need to stand against these evil powers. Evil power will take all it can get; it will move stealthily and demonically to exert more and more power over the church. So, for example, I was at a pastoral conference once, and the pastors were trying to outdo each other as to who had the most important congregation. *That was demonic.*"

Marva had been hinting at this point throughout our entire conversation, yet the directness of these words hit like smelling salts. She got my attention, naming the problem directly, unafraid to call evil that which is evil. My temptation is to minimize the problem. It is easy to view things like competition in the church as minor missteps. I think, *Sure, we should avoid these things given our better judgment, but it's not that big of a deal.* Yet when we minimize the way from below in our own lives or within the church, we effectively embolden the powers. When we let down our guard and fail to take seriously the real powers at work in our world, we can easily get caught up in their path of destruction.

Our meals arrived, but we kept right on talking. One clear question remained in my mind, so I pushed into it: "Marva, when these powers infiltrate the church and become values, what position does that put the church in?"

Without hesitation Marva quipped, "When this happens we become a tool of the principalities and powers which are in direct opposition to God and his kingdom. Where churches should be the servants of the gospel, they are instead the proprietors of the powers."[4]

The scary truth is that we can become a tool of the powers, even in our zeal to do the right thing (maybe especially there). We can't assume that the church is abiding in the way from above simply because it is the church. Again, Kyle and I were brought back to James 3, where this way of evil is expressed through jealousy and selfish ambition. These traits are often treated as insignificant if not palatable flaws of effective and passionate leaders. But James tells us that where these fruits of the heart exist, "there will be disorder and every vile practice" (James 3:16). In other words, we can propagate the way from below in ways that are profoundly subtle, yet pervasively harmful.

After finishing our lunch, I (Jamin) left to pull the car around so that Marva wouldn't have to walk far. When I came out the front door of the restaurant, my eyes fixed on the half-dome of Mission San Juan Capistrano. I have seen it my entire life. It is a beautiful site, one of the few truly historical sites in south Orange County. There is something special about the Mission; its gardens are beautiful and its weathered adobe walls are captivating. Every year it attracts the migrating swallows and their fascinating mud nests. Today, however, I saw something different. For the first time I was able to see past its surface beauty, and I thought about the devious history that lay beneath. While the missionaries held good intentions of bringing the indigenous Native Americans to salvation, this noble cause was married to dynamics of domination and manipulation. The Native American neophytes who helped to erect the Mission were at times physically abused and held against their will.

I drove the car around and picked up Marva just outside the restaurant. As we turned past the Mission, I gave it one final glance. It occurred to me that the true history of the Mission could be instructive for the church today. We have grown adept at creating beautiful buildings and powerful-looking ministries. On the surface things look grand and magnificent, but the path to success and influence is often paved with dark powers. Like the progenitors of the Mission, we have allowed a beautiful end to justify our evil means.

RED TIGHTS AND HORROR MOVIES

Our culture has no time to take seriously "mythological categories" such as the devil and the powers. Sadly, the church often follows culture in this supernatural skepticism. We seem to accept that this language is only fit for fantasy novels, or at best belongs to an unenlightened time in history or more primitive cultures. In C. S. Lewis's *Screwtape Letters*, we find Screwtape, the demon, teaching his nephew Wormword: "The fact that 'devils' are predominantly *comic* figures in the modern imagination will help you. If any faint suspicion of your existence begins to arise in his mind, suggest to him a picture of something in red tights."[5] Many of us hold to this comic notion of the demonic, and according to Lewis that is precisely their strategy. However, for others of us, the topic evokes fear. Maybe we do believe in such things, but all we think of is ghoulish-looking demons and exorcism. The church has rarely explored the topic thoughtfully, so the horror movies and sensational tales of our culture have defined things for us.

Admittedly, until our encounter with Marva, Kyle and I had spent very little time considering these things ourselves. Somehow we can work our way through the stories of Jesus' life and ministry, exploring his teaching and miracles, and avoid discussing spiritual warfare. Yet this warfare is everywhere we look in Jesus' ministry. As we read the New Testament, we are consistently confronted with the powers and principalities. Our minds often roll over these passages, but they are there. If we ignore a clear theme of Scripture, a dangerous gap remains in our conception of God's work in the world. Notice the language in these passages (emphasis added):

¤ "For I am sure that neither death nor life, nor angels nor *rulers*, nor things present nor things to come, nor *powers*, nor height nor depth, nor anything else in all creation, will be able to separate us from the love of God in Christ Jesus our Lord" (Rom. 8:38–39).

¤ "He disarmed the *rulers and authorities* and put them to open shame, by triumphing over them in him" (Col. 2:15).

¤ "Through the church the manifold wisdom of God might now be made known to the *rulers and authorities* in the heavenly places" (Eph. 3:10).

¤ "For we do not wrestle against flesh and blood, but against the *rulers*, against the *authorities*, against the cosmic *powers* over this present darkness, against the spiritual *forces of evil* in the heavenly places" (Eph. 6:12).

¤ "[Jesus Christ] has gone into heaven and is at the right hand of God, with angels, *authorities*, and *powers* having been subjected to him" (1 Peter 3:22).

These representative passages speak of the "powers and principalities," highlighting some of the parallel terms used, such as *authorities*, *rulers*, *thrones*, and *dominions*. As we studied these sections of Scripture, we quickly realized the depth of this topic's complexity. What exactly are the powers and principalities? Are we talking about demons? Are we talking about sin or worldly systems of evil? We knew we had to find places in Scripture that could illuminate and help us understand how the powers functioned.

We returned to James 3 and found that the categories he offers us, "earthly, unspiritual, and demonic," provide a framework for understanding the powers and principalities. The church adopted these categories and crafted them into an axiom that we are perhaps more familiar with: the world, the flesh, and the devil. These three categories function as a triangular prism channeling the way

from below. Each side of the prism contains different things identified by Scripture as the powers and principalities. The devil and
the flesh, of course, have a certain chronological priority in their
participation in the way from below. The world is a category that
depends on these to exist—where functional and systemic features
of reality are commandeered by the way from below to further its
purpose. But operationally, all three work in concert to channel
evil to capture the attention of our hearts and minds.

Viewing the powers and principalities through this prism was
clarifying for us. The diversity of the powers and principalities
that Marva had spoken of began to find organization. There is the
power of sinfulness, or the human orientation toward evil, which
we call "the flesh." There is the work of the demonic, which we
can identify as "the devil." But maybe even more neglected than
the other two, hidden in plain sight, is "the world." We often reduce
"the world" to "worldliness," by which we are referring to bad values of the culture. However, there are real powers and principalities
at work in our world that function as systems of evil—such as racism, zealous nationalism, ageism, and materialism. This is why
the many terms Scripture provides can feel confusing. At times, it
seems clear that a power in Scripture is demonic. Elsewhere, this
is far from clear. For instance, governments can become fueled by
the demonic and become what is often called today "the Empire"
(or, in more biblical terms, Babylon).[6]

Fortunately, determining the exact nature of a power is not our
calling. Instead, we simply have to recognize the work of evil—in
and through the world, the flesh, and the demonic—and learn to
stand against it in all of its manifestations. To discern the way from
below, we have to take into account each side of this prism, since our
temptation will be to reduce the problem to one aspect and ignore
the others. Perhaps we believe the only problem we face is *worldly
systems*. In other words, we might believe the only real battles to

fight are systems of injustice or economic disparity. Consequently, we may not take into account the real spiritual battle we are in. Or perhaps we believe the only real problem we face is Satan. When we sin, we think, *The devil made me do it*, or when life doesn't go the way we want, we blame it on a "spiritual attack." As a result, we may not understand that sin is an issue of the heart, and we may ignore the depths of our own depravity and our own role in furthering the way from below.

We need to reject these reductionist approaches to the reality of evil in our world. All three elements are participating in the way from below, propagating the way of evil all around us. They all must be accounted for. At the same time, we should remember that these propagators of evil are not *fundamentally* evil themselves. This may sound counterintuitive, particularly with the demonic. But the devil was originally created good. He was a part of God's good creation, as were all the powers. Indeed, every aspect of this broken world was originally created good and was meant to be in the service of Christ. To grasp the comprehensive nature of the way from below, we must address the world, the flesh, and the devil, and recognize their interrelatedness.

ATTUNED TO DARKNESS

The interconnectedness of the world, the flesh, and the devil is on display even in the lives of Jesus' inner circle.[7] After Jesus reveals to his disciples that he must suffer and die, Peter rebukes him. Jesus responds to Peter's rebuke by exclaiming, "Get behind me, Satan! For you are not setting your mind on the things of God, but on the things of man" (Mark 8:33). Notice how the demonic is interconnected with what is worldly and fleshly. Jesus is not saying that Peter has somehow transformed into the person of Satan (and he is certainly not just name-calling). Jesus is claiming that

Peter's thinking is fueled by the demonic, and at the same time it is from the flesh and oriented around the worldly "things of man." Humanity is not neutral to the way of the demonic, but the flesh is particularly attuned to it. This is why Paul can say, "For while there is jealousy and strife among you, are you not of the flesh and behaving *only in a human way*?" (I Cor. 3:3, emphasis mine). To behave "only in a human way" is to sow to our flesh, to imbibe the ways of the world, and to utilize an approach to life that Scripture names as demonic.

When Jamin and I are seduced by the way from below, we tend to reduce the problem to the flesh. While the unhealthy desires of our hearts are certainly part of the problem, the devil and the world must be accounted for as well. When we see the way from below embraced or even heralded in the church, we tend to blame it on the vices of one individual leader or on bad theology. Once again, these are aspects of the problem, but they are not the only powers of evil at work. The problem of power in the church is a deeper and more complex issue than we had ever imagined. What does seem clear is that the critiques of the church, which are legion, appear to miss this fundamental insight. Like Peter, the church can be living out a way that is more attuned to the demonic than to Christ.

MONEY, SEX, AND POWER

Capitulation to the powers is seen in how we talk about money, sex, and power. These three are the currency our culture trades in. They represent another threefold prism of sorts, as three of the key inroads to seducing the flesh toward the way from below. Their insidious grip on our lives is easily ignored or excused. Living your life with the sole focus of accumulating more money is viewed as honorable as long as it doesn't result in stealing. Subtle forms of control and manipulation are fine as long as we don't explicitly abuse another person. Lust and pornography may be somewhat passé in certain quarters, but by and large they are excused as long as they don't result in outright adultery.

Practically speaking, only one of these three has been deemed a "real sin" in our churches. It (fortunately!) takes a lot for a pastor to get fired. But the one deal breaker seems to be sex. Outside of anything illegal, sex is really the only thing that matters to us concerning the pastor's personal life. Power? Not so much. Money? Very few care. Unless a pastor is caught stealing from the church's bank, a pastor can serve Mammon wholeheartedly and, generally speaking, find that few are really bothered. Power and money, of course, are tied tightly together. In these are the roots of all sorts of evil, bound up together in the way from below. It is curious that "power, sex, and money" are tied together in our consciousness, yet we only really view one of them as sin.

When a well-known pastor stepped down from ministry after a public outcry, his board made sure to note that although he had "been guilty of arrogance, responding to conflict with a quick temper and harsh speech, and leading the staff and elders in a domineering manner," he nonetheless was not guilty of any immorality.[8] Notice how "immorality" is not about living out of the way from below, a way to which the characteristics they listed clearly belong. Rather, they wanted it to be known that their pastor did not do anything that was against the common sensibility of North American leadership. He didn't cheat on his wife.[9]

It is easy to point fingers amid our own arrogance, or in our naivete to think that this is an isolated occurrence. It isn't. Before anything else, we must recognize these temptations in our own hearts, but we also must name it in our Christian culture. It is hard to admit, but we all have watered down the nature of immorality to make it more user-friendly. We remain content to decry the sins of the world. It is hard to hear John's words: "The one who practices sin is of the devil; for the devil has sinned from the beginning" (1 John 3:8 NASB). What this church board wrote is evidence that we have forgotten, as a people, how to distinguish the difference between the way from below and the way from above. According to Scripture, pride, uncontrolled anger, and domineering leadership are unquestionably "immoral." We read in Mark 7:21–22, "For from within, out of the heart of man, come evil thoughts, sexual immorality, theft, murder, adultery, coveting, wickedness, deceit, sensuality, envy, slander, pride, foolishness." Jesus places pride alongside murder and adultery. We read in Galatians 5:19–21, "Now the works of the flesh are evident: sexual immorality, impurity, sensuality, idolatry, sorcery, enmity, strife, jealousy, fits of anger, rivalries, dissensions, divisions, envy, drunkenness, orgies, and things like these." Paul views uncontrolled anger as a dynamic of the flesh alongside idolatry and orgies. When we ignore the sobering claims of these biblical passages and discount the impact of the powers, we miss the truth that our churches can become portals of evil in the world, baptizing death and selling it as life.

In the biblical view of the world that Marva had unpacked for us, there is an undercurrent of evil that seeks to seduce us to its way. But there is also a way to stand against the powers. The cross puts the rulers and authorities "to open shame, by triumphing over them in him" (Col. 2:15). Christ, the archetype of power in weakness, put to shame the powers at the high point of his embrace of power in weakness. When it appeared Christ was being put to shame, he was putting the powers to shame. When it appeared Christ was losing, he was triumphing. Where does this triumph occur? Paul is clear in this passage that the triumph is "in him." In the person of Jesus, these rulers and authorities are "disarmed." In 1 Corinthians we are told, "Then comes the end, when he [Jesus] delivers the kingdom to God the Father after destroying every rule and every authority and power. For he must reign until he has put all his enemies under his feet" (15:24–25). Christ defeated the powers in his person, but he has not yet destroyed them. Until he returns they still have power in the world. The church, therefore, as the body of Christ, has a special role as a witness to the way of Christ. Christ has defeated the rulers, and the church's calling is to bear witness to the world that still lives under these false authorities. Furthermore, Paul tells us that "through the church the manifold wisdom of God might now be made known to the rulers and authorities in the heavenly places" (Eph. 3:10).

The church, the place where kingdom values should reign, is the place where we come to know and participate in the way of God—where "we do not wrestle against flesh and blood, but against the rulers, against the authorities, against the cosmic powers over this present darkness, against the spiritual forces of evil in the heavenly places" (Eph. 6:12). The church is the place where the powers are to be exposed for what they are and are continually put to shame as they were upon the cross. Sunday morning worship in this sense is a spiritual battle, but the battle isn't limited to Sundays. This is why we need to discern the fruit of the church to see where it is rooted. Is the church walking in the way from below—a way that is unspiritual, earthly, and demonic, driven by selfishness and jealousy—or is it walking in the way from above, made manifest on the cross in love? This question should be at the heart of our small groups, conferences, seminars, and publishing; it should be woven into our parenting, friendships, and service. This question should drive us and deeply unsettle us.

DIGGING OUR OWN GRAVE

Often when we fail to stand firm against the powers, it is because we believe the powers can actually save us. We buy into the lie that we can employ evil powers for the kingdom. We may naively believe we would never be tempted in this way, but that is the subversive power of this evil. As when Jesus was offered bread after forty days of fasting, the temptation to grasp the way from below will feel natural and necessary. We will also be deceived in believing that we can destroy these means of evil on their own terms; but such a belief destroys us from within. Maybe we continually think that more money would solve all of our life problems, so we inadvertently begin worshiping the god of Mammon. Instead of being honest and caring toward others, maybe we subtly deceive by employing guilt, shame, or lying as tools to manipulate and control (Matt. 5:37). Maybe we try to align ourselves with famous people—in the church or outside the church—because we believe that their celebrity will fuel our success. Or maybe we use church resources to promote our own projects, books, or ancillary ministries, telling ourselves it is justified because they will bless the broader church community. Notice the goal is not necessarily nefarious. We often have good motivations. But if we try to employ the way from below for the gospel, what we find is that the gospel is undermined and the powers reign. We enlist the way from below in order to defeat it, but in doing so we join the ranks of its battalion ourselves.

In *The Gravedigger File*, Os Guinness argues that the church will become its own gravedigger as it continues to uncritically incorporate the values, principles, and techniques of the world. This is the strategy of the demonic, not to attack the church directly, but to trick her into attacking herself: to convince her that the ends justify the means and that she can wield the tools of darkness to make light. As one evil agent writes to another:

> The underlying strategy of Operation Gravedigger is as stark in its simplicity as it is devastating in its results. It may be stated like this: *Christianity contributed to the rise of the modern world; the*

modern world, in turn, has undermined Christianity; Christianity has become its own gravedigger. The strategy turns on this monumental irony, and the victory we are so close to realizing depends on two elementary insights. First, that Christianity is now becoming captive to the very "modern world" it helped to create. Second, that our interests are best served, not by working *against* the church, but by working *with* it. The more the church becomes one with the modern world, the more it becomes compromised, and the deeper the grave it digs for itself.[10]

The greatest battle strategy is always a defeat from within. Satan's way in the world is not outright devastation, but is a subversive sort of seduction. This way warps what is good into something that slowly and deceptively undermines its own existence. This is how powers created for Christ can be wielded against the way of Christ. The way of power for control that services the world, the flesh, and the demonic for ministry will always look powerful, but its power is superficial. Like a redwood that has rotted from the inside, it can boast in its size and grandeur, but it is not substantial. In her physical frailty and old age, Marva, on the other hand, seems nothing but weak in worldly terms. But Marva's power becomes evident when she hobbles up to her mic and proclaims the real power of God. Like the widow's mite, what Marva donates is actually more valuable to the kingdom than what worldly power can offer (Mark 12:42–44). Her way is the way of real power because her way follows along the pathway of Jesus.

THE LOCATION OF OUR CALLING

The way from below is a plague that has created, as Paul describes, this "present evil age" (Gal. 1:4). This evil age is a kingdom, and this kingdom has rulers, authorities, thrones, and dominions

(Eph. 6:12; Col. 1:16). This evil age even has a god, Satan himself (2 Cor. 4:4). The world and the flesh are servants of this evil age in which Satan reigns. Even as they seek to further its ends, implicitly or explicitly, they are servants of a master that is ultimately destroying them. Even death and sin are personified in Scripture as powers that war against us on the side of evil.[11] The flesh is the location where we live according to the rulers of this evil age, and it is a place from where we need deliverance. Sin and death are not simply idle notions, but are powers at work, even co-opting the law of God and waging war on God's people through it.[12] Like a cancer that turns good cells against the body, the way of evil has warped God's good creation and turned good powers into mechanisms of evil.

But in the place where Christ reigns over his people—the church—these authorities are judged. Although we knew this evil age as our original home, Jesus "has delivered us from the domain of darkness and transferred us to the kingdom of his beloved Son" (Col. 1:13). Paul tells us that we should be "strengthened with all power" (Col. 1:11), but this power is for service and love. Our King does not recognize people trading in power as the world conceives it (Matt. 7:21–23), because "God opposes the proud but gives grace to the humble" (1 Peter 5:5). The locus of God's dominion is in Christ, and therefore his body, the church, is the locus of his power and reign in this world. We clearly need to turn our attention more and more to the church as the place where these powers are undone. Following 1 Peter 5:5, the way from below is the way of pride and sinful autonomy, but the way from above is humility for love. As the people of God, the church is the location of those who trade in the economy of love.

Our call to stand against the powers and principalities must be seen as synonymous with our calling to be the people of God. These are not two calls, but one. We are called as his people to participate in Christ's triumph over these powers by submitting to the way of the cross. *We are called to be a cruciform people–to live according to the cross-shaped way of Jesus.*[13] We are called to receive power in weakness, not power in our strength or in ourselves. *We are the people known by their love.* We are called to proclaim, "Without you, Jesus, we can do nothing" (see John 15:5). *We are the meek who inherit the land of the kingdom.* Yet questions still linger for us in seeking to understand what a cross-shaped life really looks like. How does this impact the way we lead? How does this shape the way we relate to others? With these questions we continue our journey, attuned now to the deeper, more nefarious actors on the grand stage of redemption.

CHAPTER 5

THE POWER OF LOVE

OUR JOURNEY HAD TAKEN A DECIDEDLY UNEXPECTED turn. The words of Bilbo Baggins rolled around in my (Jamin's) mind: "It's a dangerous business, Frodo, going out of your door. . . . You step into the Road, and if you don't keep your feet, there is no knowing where you might be swept off to."[1] Marva invited us down a path we were unprepared for. The powers and principalities were not territory previously identified on our map. But now we could not ignore them. This idea that the church could be co-opted by the powers was deeply unsettling. Truthfully, it still felt extreme. But we couldn't question the church's role, historically, in systemic evil. All through our journey for this book, our nation was confronted with a string of race-related violence, exposing how deep-seated racism still is in the American conscious. Consequently, we reflected on the history of racism in America and the church's complicity in such an evil. As we thought about the history of racism in our country, we came face-to-face with a clear example of the church acting as a curator of the way from below.

SLAVERY, RACISM, AND THE SYSTEMS OF EVIL

Slavery was alive and well in nineteenth-century America. An evil system of power was on display in our culture, not hidden beneath layers of pretense but standing as a conscious apparatus of domination and dehumanization. Nor was it maintained in isolation. Numerous systems of racist power worked to create a culture of hate. The power of racism had seeped its way into many corridors of society, even taking captive the white church in the South.

One of the often ignored structures that fed into this culture was entertainment. The racist stereotyping of African-Americans found its way onto the stage in the early nineteenth century and proved to be America's favorite form of entertainment nationally for years. Minstrelsy was a dramatic, musical stage performance where white men covered in blackface makeup impersonated black men.

> The foremost characteristic of the African-American male in minstrelsy (as played by the white man) was that he was always clownish and foolish, in all important ways inferior to the white man. The audience was constantly bombarded with foppish, absurd costumes, corny, low-quality jokes and puns, and exaggerated comic behavior, all in the guise of exhibiting African-American culture.[2]

The demeaning, dehumanizing caricature of African-Americans served to cement in the minds of white America that slavery wasn't a problem. The justification of slavery was strengthened by other elements of this performative white appropriation of black people and culture. African-Americans were portrayed as morally and intellectually inferior. The minstrel performances also portrayed blacks as happy and content, enjoying a carefree life in between odd jobs. They were so happy, in fact, that they had no desire to leave the Southern world they were a part of.[3]

The minstrels traveled the country, codifying and reinforcing a denigrating view of African-American people and culture in the minds of white Americans everywhere. People saw the same shows in New York as they did in the South, and as a result a uniformity of perspective was established regarding people these audiences largely knew nothing about because of the segregation that slavery established. Sadly, these very performances and songs were permanently imprinted on the DNA of American culture, such that jokes and lyrics we know today find their origin in these racist performances.[4]

Minstrels were not the only means by which racist ideology and values were propagated in our culture. Unconscionable as it is, for many years a large number of churches in our country propagated the way from below through racist hate, deeply harming people made in the image of God. When people give themselves to this evil, they wield its power by utilizing physical, emotional, and economic oppression to lower others and raise themselves up.

Racism's infiltration of the church is not always obvious, because it is often mixed with other ingredients that dull its identification. Theologian Miroslav Volf argues, "Our coziness with the surrounding culture has made us so blind to many of its evils that, instead of calling them into question, we offer our own versions of them—in God's name and with a good conscience."[5] This is how the powers and principalities work in our world, covertly and beneath the radar. While overt racism is recognized as evil in our culture, we still make plenty of room for implicit, subconscious, and systemic forms of racism to flourish. These systems of power divide. Where God intended love, relationship, and community, the powers breed discord, distrust, and division. They are so subtle and ingrained in the fabric of our culture that we don't even recognize their presence. Racism is alive and well in our culture, but we often succumb to the lie that it died with institutional slavery and segregation.

Thankfully, our reflection on these systemic evils in the church led not only to recognition of the effects of the powers, but also to examples of individuals and movements standing against such powers. The problem we face is that most of us do not know how to attack a system. Racism is not simply the sum total of racists, but it is a system of evil that is greater than the sum of its parts. To stand firm against these evils, as Paul calls us to in Ephesians 6, we have to expose them to the light of the gospel. We must reject the division these evils sow and pursue reconciliation and unity in Christ. The church must be an alternate culture in which love reigns and division is rejected. If we are going to learn what it means to stand against the way from below and embrace the way from above, we have to continue to seek out those who can show us the way. We have to find sages of the power to love who have rejected the power to control, particularly in the face of systemic evils like racism. We must find exemplars of kingdom battle.

RESISTING EVIL WITH DR. KING

One of the church's greatest warriors against racism was Martin Luther King Jr. He utilized nonviolent resistance as a way to disarm the powers of evil. Unfortunately, we are so accustomed to violent resistance that when we hear "nonviolent resistance" we can easily interpret it to mean "nonresistance." But nonviolent resistance is *resistance*. King chose nonviolence because his movement was resisting evil itself, and not simply the evil person. Nonviolent resistance seeks to expose a system of evil to the evildoer so that he sees it for what it is.[6] Nonviolent action is still action, but it is the kind of action that unearths the truth of a person's heart. Nonviolent protests arouse "the dozing conscience,"[7] King proclaimed, and awaken shame and guilt in the oppressor.[8] King recognized that the powers at work in culture wreak havoc upon both the oppressed and the oppressor. This is why King was focused on standing against the system and not attacking a particular person. If he attempted to attack and undermine a person, he would lose the ability to befriend him. Befriending the oppressor, of course, is central to the way of love (Matt. 5:44).

King's ministry was formed by the way of love. In his words, "I would recommend to you a way of love. I still believe that love is the most durable power in all the world."[9] Love is a power, power at its purest, but as such, it is a power that runs contrary to the powers and principalities of the world. It is, as we have seen, power that is only known in our weakness. In the words of theologian Donald Bloesch, "We conquer not by the sword but by the power of the powerlessness of love."[10] It is in the power of love that we come to know life to the full, and, therefore, we lose our lives when we give them to hate. King explains what hate does to the one hating and how to resist it:

> Hate is a cancerous disease which distorts the personality and scars the soul. To return hate for hate only intensifies the existence of hate in the universe. Hate seeks to annihilate rather than convert. It destroys community and makes brother-hood impossible. We must learn that it is possible to stand up courageously and positively against an evil system and yet not resist it with physical weapons and inner feelings of hatred.[11]

The beginning point of nonviolent resistance, therefore, is not sit-ins, protests, or speeches. Provocatively, in the face of the kind of evil King confronted (threats, bombings, shootings), he claimed that the nonviolent resister must avoid "not only external physical violence but also internal violence of spirit. The nonviolent resister not only refuses to shoot his opponent but he also refuses to hate him. At the center of nonviolence stands the principle of love. . . . Along the way of life, someone must have sense enough and morality enough to cut off the chain of hate."[12] To resist evil one first must determine not to resist evil with evil—hate with hate—but to stand firmly on the foundation of love.

King's method of nonviolent resistance unveiled the nature of the powers and principalities by responding to them with love. He was following Paul's admonition, "Do not be overcome by evil, but overcome evil with good" (Rom. 12:21), recognizing that loving your enemy will "heap burning coals on his head" (Rom. 12:20). With these words, Scripture is not giving us a different method of domination—a surefire way to defeat and humiliate our enemies—but is showing us how to unmask the powers and principalities at work in the hearts of those rejecting the way of God. Unfortunately, when the powers are unmasked, they rarely submit to love but lash out against it. At the heart of King's method was the belief that if one chooses to love and resist nonviolently, the immediate response will be violence. This is exactly what happened. The powers and principalities thrive in darkness where they can subtly and deceptively undermine the way of love. When these are unmasked, violence is often unleashed (whether that violence is physical, emotional, or spiritual).

At the heart of our call to stand against the powers, for King, is the idea that the means of resistance must be as pure as the ends. If our goal is freedom and love, then the only way we can get there is through love itself. Hatred begets hatred, so another way is demanded. In his context, this meant that he suffered at the hands of the very people he chose to love, because suffering was the only way into their hearts.[13] King believed that this way was the only way to be faithful to Jesus, who also suffered at the hands of the very people he came to save. King called his people explicitly "to accept Christian Love in full knowledge of its power to defy evil,"[14] and proclaimed:

We must meet hate with love. We must meet physical force with soul force. There is still a voice crying out through the vista of time, saying: "Love your enemies, bless them that curse you, pray for them that despitefully use you." Then, and only then, can you matriculate into the university of eternal life. That same voice cries out in terms lifted to cosmic proportions: "He who lives by the sword will perish by the sword."[5]

To be faithful to the way of Jesus, who walked the way of the cross to defeat and expose the powers and principalities, King turned to the way of love. This way is an embrace of weakness, and as such, an embrace of our humanity; this way resists dehumanization, domination, and segregation. Nonviolent resistance takes the declarations of Jesus and puts them to work in a world that is still overrun with evil and still desperate to hear the message of Jesus, "who, though he was in the form of God, did not count equality with God a thing to be grasped, but emptied himself, by taking the form of a servant, being born in the likeness of men. And being found in human form, he humbled himself by becoming obedient to the point of death, even death on a cross" (Phil. 2:6–8).

DEHUMANIZED BY EVIL

Dr. King's vision provides a tangible example of how we might stand against the powers. His legacy of love is unrivaled in our country for good reason. However, we needed to find a living sage of the power of love. We had to find someone who was formed in the way of resistance that King embodied.

A little less than two years after King was shot, John Perkins was working on his own nonviolent resistance movement in Mississippi. He was not simply following King but was observing him while trailblazing his own path for freedom and equality. Perkins's movement overlapped with King's, but instead of becoming famous through his speeches, he became known for his community Bible studies. Unlike King, he was not in the national spotlight, but like King he stood firm against the systemic evil all around him.

On February 7, 1970, John led a nonviolent march in protest of the racial inequality in Mendenhall, Mississippi. A group of students who participated in the march left to return home and were followed by police. Once they crossed over the line separating Simpson County from Rankin County, a police car pulled one of the vans over. All of the students were ordered out of their van and were arrested, then taken to the county jail in the town of Brandon. Doug Huemmer, who had been driving the van of students, was taken in a police car by himself, and was beaten the entire way to the jail by Frank Thames, the officer who had pulled them over. The students were kicked, stomped, and beaten with blackjacks and billy clubs at the police station in Brandon. Their nonviolence was met with violence. After the students had been arrested, the driver of the other van contacted John to tell him what happened. He quickly connected with two other protesters and set out for Brandon, even though they were worried about another ambush from the police. When they arrived at the police station, a highway patrolman met them in the parking lot. He told them to wait outside for the sheriff. Instead, a dozen officers poured out of the station to arrest them. From this point on, five of the deputy sheriffs and seven to twelve highway patrolmen beat them within an inch of their lives. In and out of consciousness, Perkins recalls seeing a lot of blood, and remembers being forced to clean it up while they beat him some more.[16]

The anger I (Kyle) felt when I first read John's story churned my stomach and made my fists clench. I cannot imagine enduring this kind of indignity and pain. I found myself bubbling with rage against these men. And yet John's own reaction to this horrific story of dehumanization differs from mine. He recalls,

"They were like savages—like some horror out of the night. And I can't forget their faces, so twisted with hate. It was like looking at white-faced demons. Hate did that to them."[17] Like King before him, Perkins saw how evil defiled human beings. Evil power had destroyed them. While there is no question that John was being abused and dehumanized, he saw men who had been abused and dehumanized by evil. The very thing they turned to for power to control was warping them and making them less than human. John recalls, "I couldn't hate back. When I saw what hate had done to them, I couldn't hate back. I could only pity them. I didn't ever want hate to do to me what it had already done to those men."[18] That night, in and out of consciousness as the students cared for him, John prayed. "God, if You will let me get out of this jail alive . . . I really want to preach a gospel that will heal these people, too."[19]

THE ROAD TO RECONCILIATION

Fortunately, we didn't have to travel far to meet with John. In God's providence, when we tried to coordinate a time to connect, we discovered he was taking a trip out our way. We met John in his hotel lobby in Orange County, California. It was a hot Southern California day, but despite black jeans and a black long-sleeved shirt, John was unfazed by the heat and suggested we sit outside on the patio. He had a jovial but strong presence about him. For some reason the wrinkles in his face seemed less the result of old age and more the consequence of his consistent, beaming smile. With a cold glass of cola in his hand, John sat back in his chair. We were here to talk with him about what it meant to embrace the way of love as a means of standing against the principalities and powers. We began by talking with him about his painful ordeal in Brandon.

"John," I (Kyle) asked, "Can you talk a bit about your experience at Brandon and how it informed your own ministry? How did you turn to love rather than hate after all of that?"

John sat forward, his brow furrowed with thoughtfulness, and began. "After Brandon, I couldn't look at a white highway patrolman. But when I was in the hospital I was operated on by a white man, and a young doctor from Australia would come to my bed at night and read to me. I didn't care if he came or not. But as I healed, I began to feel the depths of his love for me. It took those white people to live out a faith that I could believe. It affected me. I felt that they loved me and had hope in me beyond myself. I think we are healed by that inner action of each other, by seeing love in that other person. Once a white man said to me, 'Tell me what you and your family need and add the cost of gas, and every two weeks I will send you a check for that so you can go on doing your ministry.'" As he recalled this exchange, John's eyes welled up with tears. He paused to collect himself and continued, "He was a Southern white man, and I was getting involved in all kinds of civil rights work to overthrow his system. Reconciliation can't take place until we believe we are all created in the image of God and have absolute value and worth. We have to become healed within the context of the people who have wounded us. We have to forgive each other."

Pausing for a moment, John sat back in his chair before continuing. "After Brandon, I came to know that my weakness came out of brokenness. I felt broken. I think I would have felt better if we had been gunned down, but handcuffing us and putting us in jail, and beating us? I was too weak. My wife came to jail and she had my oldest son, and when she looked at me, she saw fear in my eyes. My son thought I could do anything, and he had to see me look absolutely broken. My son talked about when I came home and he saw me, he wondered what could drive his father to walk through this. My child saw my weakness as absolute strength. But it isn't easy to embrace weakness. I know the call is, 'Your strength is made perfect in weakness.[20] Yeah, I can say all this stuff, but I can say it better than I can do it." John sat forward a bit, still looking intently at me. "So, I've got to embrace that too. Embracing our weakness, that is significant. Embracing our weakness and embracing our sense of calling will sound like an oxymoron. You have to embrace both at the same time."

John's story spoke of power to love. It spoke of reconciliation and forgiveness. But he also emphasized power in weakness, and how, in his son's eyes, the power of his father was only truly discovered in his father's weakness. John knew how difficult it was to embrace his weakness, and even though his life has been formed by this way, he still recognized its difficulty. But for John, this is simply the way of the gospel. There is no other way. In the face of evil in the world, the way of Jesus—the way of the cross—is power in and through our weakness. Up to this point Jamin had been listening quietly, but he quickly jumped on this idea with a question. "John, can you talk a bit about the gospel and reconciliation in light of your own ministry?"

Before he answered, John finally took a sip of the cold cola that had made a sizable water ring on the glass table. "The question we have to ask is, 'Does the gospel, as we currently preach it, have the power to deal with racism?' The evangelical church, whose basic theology is the same as mine, had not continued to preach the whole gospel. But I was convinced that we ought to preach the fullness of the truth and expect the power of the gospel. Reconciliation is an ongoing process, but it comes out of the gospel; it should not be taken out and dissected, but believed. That is the effect of the full truth of the gospel, that God was in Christ reconciling the world unto himself,[21] and has given us this ongoing proclamation of the gospel. That's the story. That's the longing. That God would come and live among us—Immanuel. Reconciliation is the display of that power that is really at work."

POWER FOR CONTROL

As Kyle and I drove home from our conversation with John, we spoke honestly about how foreign these realities felt to us. Growing up in Orange County, California, in a middle-class white suburb, wrapped me (Jamin) in a bubble of ignorance about the more profound realities of racism. John's stories brought to life what I only knew from history books. He made it personal. This man, whom I shook hands with, laughed with, and shared the joy of Christ with, had been radically impacted by racism throughout his life. He experienced violence, persecution, and disrespect by men like me, white Christian men. There were so many unsettling questions in it all. How could Christians justify such unchristian treatment of others? How could the way from below be so thoroughly accepted by the church, and establish such grave and oppressive division among God's people?

Incredibly, Christians even used Christ as a way to justify slavery. "What could be better for *these* people," they said to themselves, "than to be in a Christian household?" They allowed themselves to think that the possible *end* of evangelism could trump the *means* of slavery. Outright power to control was grotesquely distorted into something that seemed good. For many, no doubt, this was just a way to sleep at night—something they told themselves so they could still read the Bible without being overcome by guilt. But for many others, this was probably a genuine belief. Wendell Berry narrates the tension between holding faith in Christ and being a slaveholder, noting that the slaveholder:

> Placed his body, if not his mind, at the very crux of the deepest contradiction of his life. How could he presume to own the body of a man whose soul he considered as worthy of salvation as his own? To keep this question from articulating itself in

his thoughts and demanding an answer, he had to perfect an empty space in his mind, a silence, between heavenly concerns and earthly concerns, between body and spirit. If there had ever opened a conscious connection between the two claims, if the two sides of his mind had ever touched, it would have been like building a fire in a house full of gunpowder: somewhere deep down in his mind he always knew of the danger, and his nerves were always alert to it.[22]

It is, of course, easy to look back and judge our forefathers and mothers in the faith, just like the Pharisees who claimed they wouldn't have killed the prophets like their forefathers did (Matt. 23:29–31). What we must keep in mind is that we still see racial oppression, systemic evil, and a valuing of elitism in the church—which can lead people to employ dehumanization and evil under the guise of their own superiority, all in the name of Christ. When this happens, we come to think we are the answer to the church's problems, and while that might seem like a trite issue compared to racism, it is actually a manifestation of racism dressed in the preppy clothes of polite society.

Perhaps this elitism finds expression when the predominantly rich, white church decides it has a vision to reach the city, a vision it assumes nobody else has because "nothing is happening there." The assumption being made is that the churches that have been there for generations must not be making a kingdom impact because they are not doing things to the scale and "quality" of the rich suburban church. This attitude communicates that the inner-city churches don't really know what they are doing and assumes they might not have the same resources, education, or skill sets of their white counterparts; and this subtle idolatry can easily infiltrate our communities.[23]

The toxin of privilege has made its way into our ministry

mind-set. As Christena Cleveland notes, "*Privilege says* I'm called and equipped to minister to all people (but minorities are only called and equipped to minister to people who are just like them). *Privilege says* that the largest ministry with the most resources is the most effective ministry."[24] Cleveland's points forced us to grapple with some of our unhealthy ministry assumptions and caused us to ask some tough questions: Why don't we first turn to supporting and encouraging inner-city pastors, instead of assuming our presence is the solution? Why start a new "campus" with a video screen of a pastor preaching in a completely different context, foreign to this community and this neighborhood? The answer is that we want power for control, and we are convinced that if we are not controlling something, it will probably go wrong.

POWER FOR LOVE

Martin Luther King Jr. and John Perkins share something in common with the earliest Christians that I (Kyle) don't share. They lived in a culture that was antagonistic to their very existence. They lived amid a system of evil that sought to control them, literally *own* them. What we receive from these Christians is a unified witness calling us to peace and love in the face of dehumanizing powers. And yet, in the face of an evil much milder, I often turn to anger and my own self-assertion as a way to bolster myself against what I perceive as an injustice. I quickly assume that anything standing in my way is something to be destroyed. It is easy for me to look down upon those who are suffering because of evil, and instead of loving my enemies, I can harbor deep hatred against them. I find much anger within me about little things. I even find hatred welling up in my heart over bad traffic. In my heart I want to destroy bad drivers, whereas Perkins and King recognized Jesus' call to love even those who actually sought to kill them.

In Perkins specifically, Jamin and I discovered a focus on the gospel as the engine that drives this entire orientation—keeping us focused on love in the face of hate. He reminded us of what Paul says in Romans: "For if while we were enemies we were reconciled to God by the death of his Son, much more, now that we are reconciled, shall we be saved by his life. More than that, we also rejoice in God through our Lord Jesus Christ, through whom we have now received reconciliation" (Rom. 5:10–11). We can love our enemies because we first were enemies of God, and we can forgive because Christ forgave us. It is important that it was in our sin that we were forgiven (Rom. 5:8), and that Christ teaches us to pray, "Forgive us our sins, as we have forgiven those who sin against us" (Matt. 6:12 NLT). This, of course, is already anticipated by Jesus when he states, "You have heard that it was said, 'You shall love your neighbor and hate your enemy.' But I say to you, Love your enemies and pray for those who persecute you, so that you may be sons of your Father who is in heaven. For he makes his sun rise on the evil and on the good, and sends rain on the just and on the unjust" (Matt. 5:43–45).

John Perkins is a witness to the way of power in weakness for the sake of love. John did not choose his situation. At one point early in his life, he found a way out of the racist system of the South and into a good job in California. But he could not deny his calling, so he followed God in faithfulness back to the heart of the racist region he worked so hard to get out of. We too are called in unique ways to stand firm against systemic powers of evil. There are bigotries of all kinds in our world today, and there are systemic evils all around us. This is true both in our culture and in our churches. There are elements of the way from below at work within our churches seeking to steal, to kill, and to destroy (John 10:10). We are called to stand firm in the face of such evils, knowing that in so doing we stand against demonic powers.

As we seek to stand against these powers, we must heed the example of Perkins and King: People are not our enemies; our enemies are the powers of evil themselves. We are called in Christ to love all—to hope that God can save even those embracing evil—and we are called to believe that the gospel is good news for all. But we still resist. Our resistance, following both King and Perkins, should be the kind of resistance that exposes evil, so that the world and the person committing the evil can be confronted with their sin. Our resistance should expose attitudes, actions, and systems of oppression, no matter how small and insignificant we may believe they are. The way from below often hides in attitudes and actions that seem too small to matter, but with time and community, they blossom into deep hatred. Resistance in love is never easy, but perhaps is easier with those we already deem "other" or "different." It could be hardest with our own family. Nevertheless, such resistance is called for, not only as we observe injustice in the world around us, but also as we discover it within the walls of the church. We must stand against evil in the church first if we hope for the church to unify and discern what she is to stand against in the world around us. We must stand against the power to control in all forms, from racism to ageism, from issues like our idolatry of leaders (Christian celebrity) to the call to respond to violence by taking up the sword (guns), from issues of competition between churches to our systemic marginalization of people with disabilities.

To follow Christ we must accept the kind of power he offers and the kind of power he rested in. His power was funded by the God of love, and his life witnessed to the profound way God's love attacks the power structures of the world. The first temptation is that we seek to engineer a life of love in our own power. We get the *for* right (power for love), but not the *from*. Scripture is clear that "we love because he first loved us" (1 John 4:19). Power to love comes from God. If we wish to become the kind of people who love, we must first be the kind of people who abide in Christ's love for us in the truth of our weakness. The second temptation is that we come to believe power to love can be a fruit of power to control. We want love, but we want to achieve it through a method that is foreign and antithetical to it. But love is not the fruit of power to control. Love presses us into vulnerability. Love calls us to receive others different from ourselves, and it calls our stereotypes and bigotry into account. Love calls us to difficult things like forgiveness, reconciliation, and peace. The way of loving your enemies constructs a specific kind of resistance to evil. Love is a power that simultaneously calls us into our weakness and brings evil out of the darkness and into the light. Love demands courage and greatness, but it does so in the very places we are afraid of. Perkins offers us a picture of this greatness, and he highlights our calling to give ourselves to love in the face of evil.

SINS OF THE FAMILY

More than anything else we've wrestled with thus far, I (Kyle) feel the weight of the issues we explored in our conversation with John. I am overwhelmed that we face such fear and hate in the world today, and as MLK said, the more hate is lashed out, the more hate is intensified universally. It is as if there is an undercurrent of hate that has gained momentum, and people have failed to choose love as a way to undermine it. As Christians, this is something we should expect. But as Christians, we should never accept it in the church.

I am a systematic theologian who specializes in the theology of Jonathan Edwards. I spent four years reading and writing on Edwards for my dissertation, and since then I have continued to work on his theology. Edwards is widely considered to be the greatest philosopher *and* the greatest theologian America has ever produced. He had a once-in-a-generation mind, and he is considered by many to be the greatest thinker on beauty in the Christian tradition. And yet, despite his greatness, Edwards was a slave owner. While it is important that he raised his son to be fluent in Mohican, and that his son carried on his theology and utilized his father's insights to fight slavery, Edwards didn't fight it himself. Even though Edwards had a prophetic consciousness about him and attacked the evil and misguided ideology around him, this was an area he failed to see. Perhaps the greatest thinker in our nation's history was blinded to the most obvious system of oppression in our nation's history.

It may seem odd to reflect on Edwards here, but there is an important if not eerie connection. In Brandon, Mississippi, John Perkins was beaten with clubs, kicked, abused, and dehumanized, and all of it was done under the guidance of the sheriff of Brandon, who was named Jonathan Edwards. Sheriff Edwards's son, Jonathan Edwards III, was one of the policemen sent to watch the march. While there doesn't seem to be any direct relation between the sheriff and his son and the famous theologian I've devoted my time to studying, the name connection still sent chills up my spine. The reality, more often than not, is that things like racism flourish through family lines and systems. Like alcoholism and abuse, there are deep dimensions of hate that are fueled through our families and, in parallel, our churches. Edwards's theological failure to stand against slavery may have contributed to the American church's numbness to this particular evil. Two hundred years after his death, we still find deep hatred and racism flourishing in church-going men such as Sheriff Edwards and his son. The church, as the family of God, must seek to unravel these systemic forces in the world and in our own hearts, and confront this hate with love. "Love alone is credible," claimed one theologian, and its credibility is seen in its ability to undermine the forces of darkness.[25] While many of us think about the church in terms of years

("What is our focus this year?") and perhaps others think in terms of decades ("What season are we entering into?"), wisdom should help us think in terms of centuries. Small acts of love may not seem worthwhile or meaningful when we are shortsighted. But we have to think about what we are giving ourselves to, and how that may form the people of this place for decades and centuries. Edwards's failure to speak against the evil of slavery may haunt our nation even today, centuries later. Which of our failures will continue to wreak havoc and undermine our ability to be faithful to our call? Which of our failures will form our grandchildren's churches?

In our time with John, he focused his attention on the very heart of our journey, narrating his experience of finding strength in weakness by standing firm against the principalities and powers of his day. It was in John's weakness that he began to see the reality of his situation, and how tempted he was by power to control (even as he was oppressed by a system obsessed with control). It was in the face of an evil that can only be called demonic that John realized he needed a gospel that could save his oppressors. He understood that the greatest temptation in our stand against the powers is to respond in kind. Like the apostles, John had to lay down his hate and embrace love, recognizing that only love has the power to undermine hate.

The love John turned to was not romantic and directionless love, but the love that stems from reconciliation to Christ in our own rebellion. This love maintains a voice against the powers; it does not simply hold out open arms, but it continues the prophetic witness throughout Scripture against evil. John spoke directly to this, claiming, "What our system has done is put off the prophetic voice, so now we are only hearing what we want to hear. We are hearing what affirms our will. Take Elijah. He was telling truth to power, but we have lost that. The prophets surrounding Jezebel were telling her what she wanted to hear, and that's where the church is." Today, we try to numb ourselves to the work of the powers, rather than attending to how deeply they still infiltrate our culture. Andy Crouch claims:

> When evangelicals think about solving social problems like the legacy of slavery and racism in the United States, they think almost exclusively in terms of personal, one-on-one relationships—which is why so many white evangelicals can imagine the problem of racism is solved if they simply have a handful of friends of other races. To think of race this way is to miss the fact that race and racism are *institutional* realities built on a complex set of artifacts, arenas, rules and roles.[26]

When we are not members of the oppressed party, we seek to rid the world of the "artifacts" of racism and oppression. We think that if the artifacts no longer exist, then racism and oppression must not either. But this is to confuse what racism and oppression really are. These are powers at work, seeking to influence people and systems in the world, and these powers are not defeated by our domination but by our love. The other danger here is to assume that we stand in a position of modern maturity, such that we cannot possibly have deep-rooted evils like racism co-opting our churches. This is precisely what the enemy would wish, that historical snobbery and avoidance of prayerful self-reflection would lull us to sleep while the powers prowl around the household of God. Embracing the way from above means that we are ever watchful and honest.

Our time with John felt like a concrete step forward on our pilgrimage. Now armed with a clear picture of what it looks like to stand against the way from below by embracing power in weakness for the sake of love, we were ready to explore how else the way of Jesus might play out in other areas of our lives as Christians in a land that is not our own. There were certain features of life together that Jamin and I felt needed to be explored—community, ministry, and leadership. These three areas continued to surface as we reflected on the impact of our journey into true kingdom power. What sages might God lead us to next?

PART 2
EMBRACING THE WAY

CHAPTER 6

UNEXPECTED POWER

MY WIFE AND I (KYLE) HAD HOPED, PERHAPS FOOLISHLY, that our two-year-old would sleep during our overnight flight to France. Unfortunately, as we landed in Paris, Brighton was just as awake as when we left two flights earlier. We found my bags and headed over to the other side of the airport, past well-armed soldiers guarding a section of the terminal. My wife and toddler were continuing on to Aberdeen, Scotland, our old home. I was staying in Paris. As my wife checked in to their next flight and I attempted to entertain my very tired and disoriented daughter, I caught a familiar face out of the corner of my eye. Jamin, smiling as he approached, had arrived in Paris a day earlier. After touring the many terminals of Charles de Gaulle Airport for nearly an hour, he had finally tracked us down.

After I kissed my family good-bye, Jamin and I drove to the heart of Paris for lunch. We wandered around looking for a café where we could eat and rest for a bit. Remnants of the Tour de France, which had finished the day before, could be seen up and down the streets. Workers were tearing down seating along the Champs-Élysées, while T-shirt vendors tried to unload the last of their merchandise. We decided on a café just around the corner from the Arc de Triomphe. We sat down at a two-person table and gazed out the open window overlooking the bustling street. We were both tired. We could have easily made the café our afternoon home, embracing the unhurried leisure of mealtime in Paris. The warm sun and gentle breeze of this Parisian summer day were welcome companions, but we had important matters to attend to. We mapped out the drive, jumped in the car, and headed to the countryside. It was an hour-and-a-half-long car ride to our final destination.

Unlike most tourists, we had not come to Paris to take pictures of the Arc de Triomphe, visit the Louvre, climb the Eiffel Tower, or tour Notre Dame. As impressive as these feats of human construction and artistry are, in all their glory they paled in comparison to the man we had flown around the world to meet. The author of Hebrews tells us that Abraham went out of his own country in search of a "city that has foundations" (Heb. 11:10). Abraham sought something God had built, something that would stand the test of time, something that even the ancient monuments of Paris couldn't match. We were hunting for a monument God built, and we were both energized with excitement.

Unfortunately, a little over an hour into the drive, we were lost. Our journey had become a treasure hunt. We had driven to Trosly-Breuil, a quaint town northeast of Paris. At that point, our rental car's navigation system no longer seemed to know what to do. To add to our difficulties, finding someone who spoke English was not easy. We assumed a quick name-drop to a few of the locals would set us on the right path. We were wrong. To our amazement nobody seemed to know who this living monument was. Imagine it: Two young American men fly to France in search of deep wisdom from a man who lives in a town of twenty-five hundred people, and nobody in the town recognizes his name! The treasure we were hunting wasn't out in the open like the monuments of Paris, but was hidden, unknown by the neighbors around the corner. We continued down a main drive, thinking we hadn't gone far enough, when I saw the narrow street we had been looking for. We had arrived at the home of Jean Vanier.

We walked through the gate and up the driveway of his little stone cottage with blue shutters, pausing to take in the beauty of the flowers nestled against the home. Jean met us at his door and invited us in. Somehow, his six-foot-four-inch frame failed to exude even an inch of intimidation. He greeted us in meekness and tender hospitality, and it became clear that this was one of the gentlest and most kindhearted men we would ever meet. For most of his life, Jean has devoted himself to blessing people with disabilities. Many years ago Jean faced the disturbing and dehumanizing condition of government-run institutions for those with disabilities, leading him to invite two men with disabilities to live with him. Out of a desire to offer them a different life, Jean gave them what he had: himself, love, and community. This became the first L'Arche community, and is the model of the nearly 150 L'Arche communities that now exist around the world. Even though he has won numerous awards for his work, including being named the Templeton Prize Laureate for 2015, and even though he travels around the world to speak, he is still probably better known for whom he mentored than for anything else he has done. Vanier mentored Henri Nouwen, who became well-known for leaving the Ivy League to pastor one of the L'Arche communities (a move he made at Vanier's encouragement). Nouwen became one of the most beloved writers of Christian spirituality in the twentieth century, and in many ways, he became the face of Vanier's movement. It's fitting, really. Vanier has always been more interested in the people he ministers to than in how well-known his ministry is.

It was through Nouwen's book, *In the Name of Jesus*, that I was first introduced to L'Arche. I remember reading Nouwen's story and being floored. At the time I was in college and had fallen in love with reading and studying Scripture. I had come to believe that God was calling me to academic ministry. I had high aspirations, and I found Nouwen's story unnerving. Here was a man who had climbed every rung of the academic ladder and now sat atop it. He taught at Notre Dame, Yale, and Harvard, and he sold out lecture halls whenever he spoke. Then along came Vanier, who invited him to come off the ladder altogether. Nouwen had grown accustomed to impressing people with his Ivy League career, but he went to pastor a group of people who didn't even know what the Ivy League was. Nouwen's descent from the mountaintop had challenged me these many years as I saw the temptation for power and success in my own heart. It had piqued my interest in the L'Arche communities where Nouwen had spent his final years ministering.

What I discovered reading about L'Arche and reading Vanier's books was that the man behind the curtain, Jean, would serve as an ideal representative for the way from above. This is why we had traveled across the world to talk to him. He did not begin L'Arche with a vision for power, influence, or recognition. Jean had one thing in mind: love. He wanted to establish genuine Christian community so that others could discover a genuinely human existence. Jean doesn't only speak profoundly about community; he has lived it. He has lived it enough to be honest about what it looks like. This is one of the things that makes Jean so refreshing. He isn't interested in sugarcoating what it means to follow Jesus, nor is he interested in romanticizing his ministry. It is hard work. It is often painful work. In the words of Dostoyevsky, "Active love is a harsh and fearful thing compared with love in dreams."¹ To stand against the dehumanizing conditions these people endured, Jean turned to the weakness and vulnerability of community.

DEVELOPING COMMUNITY

Jamin and I sat down on the couch opposite Jean, who lowered himself into a chair framed by books. The room was simple yet homey. A few pictures hung on the walls, and there was a wall of shelves lined with books, pictures, and memories from his travels—all somewhat disheveled and in an order all their own. A red pot nurturing a fledgling plant grazed among the books, and a clock resting on a shelf reminded us that we were late. There was not a hint of pretension, and everything in the room felt personal and meaningful. Out the large sliding glass door we could see a trail running alongside another building before it disappeared into the trees. It was surreal being there. I was only a couple of hours removed from a sleepless overnight flight, but I had no trouble staying alert.

Years ago I read Jean's book *Community and Growth*, a profound treatise on living with others (and the difficulties of doing so). Jean's primary focus in the book regards living with people with disabilities, but what he says is true of family life, work life, dorm life, and other areas. Community life is difficult, so we often settle for something less. But community is essential. So I decided to start with a question about this specifically. "I find it interesting that community plays such an important role in recognizing and entering into our weakness. Can you speak to this a bit more?"

Shifting his weight slightly, and with his characteristic smile, Jean began. "When living with people with disabilities, whose cry is for friendship, community, and love, we discover it is difficult to love people. We have people here who can only scream, and our role is to reveal to them that they are more beautiful than they dare to believe. What I can say is that by living with people with disabilities I've discovered my own disabilities: the gradual discovery that there is anger within us, there is violence within us, and we have to work at that. It's the Holy Spirit helping me to discover who I am and how things are within me. We cannot really begin to know the truth of ourselves until we discover we have difficulties. Community is the place where we discover our own fragilities, wounds, and inability to love, where our limitations, our fears, and our egoism are revealed to us. We cannot get away from the negative in ourselves. We have to face it. So community life brings a painful revelation of our limitations, weaknesses, and darkness, and the unexpected discovery of the monsters within us.

"The immediate reaction is to try to destroy the monsters, or hide them away, pretending that they don't exist. Or we try to flee from community life and relationships with others, assuming that the monsters are theirs, not ours; they are guilty, not us. The heart of the message of Jesus is: Be compassionate as my Father is compassionate, do not judge so you won't be judged, do not condemn so you won't be condemned, forgive such as we have been forgiven. The heart of this is: Love your enemies, do good to those who hate you, speak well of those who speak badly of you, pray for those who persecute you. We think that you have to be strong, you have to win, you have to be the best. So we believe that we should all be winners, but we are not all winners. So our experience of being loved and accepted in community allows us to accept ourselves as we are. We are broken, but we are loved."

Jean's comments made me think about my (Jamin's) own experiences in community. As he spoke, I recalled my senior year of college when I moved into a house with a group of my closest friends. We were all so excited. Community with this kind of proximity and consistency is rare. It seemed like a dream come true to a group of idealistic Bible college students. Yet for me, the dream quickly faded. The reality of eight guys in their early twenties, living in a tiny house without air-conditioning, began to take its toll. I would get irritated at the littlest of things. I often felt excluded and isolated, but at the same time I chose to be aloof. It was a hard year for me. At the time, I blamed the others in the house, doling out responsibility to those I lived with for our failure to achieve the kind of community I had dreamed of. But in reality this intimate community had brought out my own fears, vices, insecurities, and selfishness. It exposed weaknesses I did not want to face. Ultimately, rather than facing what was in my heart, I retreated from the community.[2]

When our weakness is exposed, we can try to reject community, but we cannot escape it. We are inevitably intertwined with others. Healthy community will help us to walk in the way of Jesus, but rejecting it, or even trading it for something more superficial, puts us in a dangerous position. We turn to isolation because we are afraid of sharing our lives with others, or because our selfishness has become so calcified that we do not have space for others. In isolation we can become blind to our sins and our strategies to defeat our weakness rather than embrace it. In isolation we often think the worst of others, or, possibly, we see others as being everything we wish we were. We mistakenly dehumanize others in our isolation, by believing them to be either lesser or greater than they are. We can usually recognize the former, but the latter we rarely see. Vanier's words are poignant in this regard: "When you admire people, you put them on pedestals. When you love people, you want to be together."

VULNERABILITY AND WEAKNESS

If community is about being open to others in their weakness, and at the same time being open to our own weaknesses, then community necessitates a certain kind of vulnerability.[3] I (Kyle) asked, "Jean, can you talk about what embracing our vulnerability in community looks like practically?"

"I remember when I first met people with mental disabilities, I was anxious," Jean said. "But I came to see that their cry was simply, 'Will you become my friend?' Their weakness was a cry to be appreciated, understood, and loved in relationship. I have come to see that the vulnerability of people with disability, with deep mental handicaps, has been a cry for recognition—to be loved. And to love them is not to do things for them, but to reveal to them by the way we listen that they are important, and that they have value. To love, which is their cry, is a cry for recognition. Does somebody really love me? The heart of vulnerability is a cry for help. All weakness is a cry for recognition; not because we are the best, not because we have strength, not because we can do things on our own, or because we are independent. But weakness is the cry, 'I need your help.' Vulnerability is a cry for presence."

Jamin quickly responded, "Jean, I have found this to be incredibly difficult in my own life. Embracing our weakness in community and being vulnerable are wonderful ideas to talk about, but incredibly challenging in real life. Why is it so hard for us to live in the reality of who we are with others?"

Jean smiled and glanced out the window before responding. "We are born to live and we are born to die. We are born to grow and we are born to get weaker. We are necessarily vulnerable people. We are frightened. So, it is not a question of why is it like that. It is like that!" Jean chuckled and rocked a bit in his chair. It was as though he was amused at his own resistance to these truths. He continued, "Yet we are always trying to pretend it is not. We human beings, I think, are a little bit frightened of reality. Somewhere at the heart of our humanity we are frightened of our weakness. We believe we have to be strong and that we have to have power. Because of that we seek to be better and more power-ful than others. Jesus says the danger is that we try to take a speck out of someone's eye when we have a log in our own. Jesus tells us to take the log out." Jean laughed, leaned forward, and said, "But if I've got a log in my eye, how do I see it?!"

Jean helpfully highlighted how self-deceptive we can be. It is easy to assume we will readily recognize the way of Jesus, but if we attend to Jesus' ministry, the opposite seems to be true. Even his closest disciples seemed genuinely baffled at what Jesus was doing, and when he did explain his mission to them, he was often met with resistance. Jean recognized that this is still true for us. The way of Jesus pushes against our assumptions. It isn't easy to accept that the way of Jesus undermines our assumptions about life, and Jean wasn't pretending it is easy; but he highlighted that it takes real humility to follow in this way. Jean was acquainted with his own rebellion against Jesus' way because he was continually confronted with it. But because he had come to see the reality of himself, he could embrace Jesus all the more. He didn't need power; he had Jesus. He didn't need to impress us; he had Jesus. He didn't have to create a self in his own strength, because he had Jesus. He knew Jesus was with him in love, in the vulnerability of his weakness.

Jean continued, "So Jesus has come to help us accept reality. And in that reality Jesus is teaching us that weakness is not something terrible. Weakness can bring us together. This is community. Weakness is at the source of all that is beautiful. I often like to tell the story of a friend of mine who is a palliative care doctor. He was called into a prison in the US to treat one of the head people in the mafia who had cancer. This man had been abused as a child. For him weakness meant death, so he would hurt people. He had to be stronger than everyone because he was scared stiff of weakness, because when he was a child in weakness, he was hurt. And then my friend, because of the cancer, had to touch him and hold him, and he discovered that his weakness was not something horrible that you had to avoid. It became a source of togetherness.

"These two men, patient and doctor, became friends. As he became frail, the sick man could discover his own deep identity through becoming someone's friend. So weakness was no longer something to be rejected. It could become a path to living in the joy of friendship. So this is the question: How do we reveal to people that they are precious? We are in a society that says you are precious if you succeed. This is our reality. If we are in a group that is successful and powerful, then we feel secure. But then maybe we don't really walk in the Holy Spirit. What Paul understood was that when he lost all his security he was saved—he was looked after—and God was there. So as we go into that field of littleness and weakness, we don't succumb to our weakness, but we try to do what God wants us to. We need community, we need help, we need the personal, and we need the church, but even with all that, we need Jesus. It means I must cultivate my communion with Jesus. So this is what I hear with Paul. I hear it all the time: I need Jesus and I need communion. The Christian faith is not an ideal divorced from reality. It is an encounter with Jesus that invites us to live with others in reality and humility."

When the time came to leave, Jamin and I dragged our feet. We didn't want to go, but Jean had other people to attend to. So after wandering through Jean's neighborhood, enjoying the quaint village, we determined to get lost in the countryside of France. With our rental car's GPS in case of emergency, we meandered freely through the woods, open fields, and small towns. As lunchtime arrived we decided to look for a café in order to grab a light lunch and talk through our time with Jean. We navigated a tree-canopied road, winding through a forest before coming around a bend and finding civilization. As we came around a corner, we saw a massive castle overshadowing a small town. We had accidentally wandered into the village of Pierrefonds, with the Château de Pierrefonds (the imposing castle) towering over the little village. I'm not sure I had a precise idea of what the French countryside would look like, but this place matched every expectation. Pierrefonds is a quaint town with a beautiful lake, a town square lined with cafés, and Saint-Sulpice, the gothic church whose foundations are nearly one thousand years old. The town is surrounded by greenery, trees, hills, and the walled gardens of ancient homes. Before we toured the castle, we sat down to eat at an outdoor restaurant in the town square, surrounded by Parisians out for a summer drive to get away from the busyness (and tourists, no doubt) of their beloved city.

As we ate our lunch, we talked about Jean's comments regarding weakness, vulnerability, and relationships. It gave us pause to consider our own friendship. We had known the challenging yet beautiful reality of deep relationship that Jean spoke of. For more than a decade we have loved one another in our weaknesses. Our friendship has developed against the backdrop of tough life decisions, seasons of confusion and disappointment, the joy and difficulty of raising children, and our wrestling through the reality of faithfulness to Christ in our world today. The topic of weakness has been on our minds for years, and yet, even after years of practicing this in friendship, it remains a choice of courage and humility to continue to expose our areas of weakness to each other. This leg of the journey served as a helpful reminder that our deep friendship was forged through the kind of vulnerability and love that Jean spoke of.

EMBRACING OUR HUMANITY

The genuinely human existence is life in love. This is an ordered life, with the love of God as the primary facet of our existence, and love of our neighbor as its never-ceasing companion. We see this in the garden narrative in Genesis, where we hear the proclamation that "it is not good that the man should be alone" (2:18). We have always been called to be with others, not simply near them, but truly with them. This is even more true for the Christian seeking faithfulness. As one New Testament scholar has said, "Only in community . . . is it possible to follow in the path that Jesus walked alone."[4] Community is where we come to understand that vulnerability is how we are called to stand against evil. What Vanier and Nouwen seek to reveal is a way of following Jesus in our weakness and vulnerability. But, of course, in weakness and vulnerability we are trusting in Christ and his strength, so what we think of as weakness is only so from a worldly point of view. In actuality, it is real power. In the words of Bonhoeffer, "What may appear weak and trifling to us may be great and glorious to God."[5]

The problem, as we have seen, is how subtly deceptive the way from below is. Some have so embraced this way that they reject community altogether in the pursuit of something that feels safer. For some, this is a turn to domination and grandiosity, whereas for others it is fearful seclusion and busyness. For those of us who do lean into community, we can easily be tempted to do so through the way from below. We step into relationships seeking control, rather than pursuing love. What we often deem "community" is simply the people we use to become what we desire; this is when others become resources amid our quest for self-actualization. In sin, others become objects to use for our own benefit, and it is all too easy to baptize this practice in the name of spiritual growth, love, or whatever else we hide our sin under. In our quest to feel whole, we can end up consuming others rather than embracing them in love.[6]

Surprisingly, it is often those who appear the most relationally engaging and vulnerable who are using others to gain power and control; there are some who reject community by seemingly embracing it wholeheartedly. They assume that they can throw themselves into community by generating a false vulnerability—a kind of exposure of themselves that appears revealing but costs them nothing to share. This person seems like the most honest and vulnerable person you have ever met, and yet he floats from one person or group to another, luring others into sharing their own pains and fears as if he were a spy. This is not community; it is a kind of emotional exhibitionism that mimics community and leaves a wake of emotional wreckage behind.

It is only in Christ that we find a foundation that can support the weight of our selves. In Christ we learn that we do not have to generate a self in our power, but we can find ourselves in him: "Your life is hidden with Christ in God" (Col. 3:3). A life of faith is trusting that in Christ you are redeemed and in Christ you are secure; that he is your redemption and even your sanctification (1 Cor. 1:30). Likewise, it is only in weakness and vulnerability that we can find ourselves in Christ, because we are so broken that we will always seek out idolatrous ways of creating a self. These ways will be driven by the power to control and will be fueled by structures of the powers and principalities. Power to control may mean domination, or it may mean using people to feel whole or find self-fulfillment. Our fallen hearts are skilled at finding idolatrous paths to self-growth. As those who are in Christ, however, we are called to give ourselves for the good of others, to genuinely move toward them in the truth of their weakness in love, cherishing them as God's beloved. In the words of Bonhoeffer:

> God did not make others as I would have made them. God did not give them to me so that I could dominate and control them, but so that I might find the Creator by means of them. Now other people, in the freedom with which they were created, become an occasion for me to rejoice, whereas before they were only a nuisance and trouble for me. God does not want me to mold others into the image that seems good to me, that is, into my own image.[7]

What Vanier shows us, in light of this, is that the community has a fundamental role in living according to the way of Jesus.

We are often blind to our weakness and vulnerability because our hearts turn God into an idol, into something we can use to generate the life we desire. But when we are confronted with others and must take them into our lives (and allow them to take us in), we are confronted with the truth about ourselves. This is one reason why those who embrace worldly power are almost always unable to be known by others. Worldly power cannot thrive when honesty and vulnerability reign. They are thorns in the flesh of those seeking power to control, but they are the nourishment of those seeking power for the sake of love.

A COMMUNITY OR A GROUP?

Becoming a Christian means that we are a part of a new people—where I am theirs and they are mine. The biblical category for this is family. Immediately after Jesus rose from the dead and ascended back to the Father, the earliest Christians started referring to each other as *brother* or *sister*. This became more profoundly difficult when they came to realize that Gentiles and Samaritans were now brother and sister as well. Foreigners were now their closest relations.

The temptation here is twofold. Either we will allow the terms *brother* and *sister* to become meaningless, or we will cease to be a family at all and become something else. These temptations have come to pass for many of us. When we lose the deep meaning of brother and sister, and when we give up on the church as a family, then we simply become a group. When this happens, we cease to be a family of God with Christ at its center and instead become a group with issues at its heart. Jean notes:

> The difference between a community and a group that is only
> issue-oriented, is that the latter see the enemy outside the group.
> The struggle is an external one; and there will be a winner

and a loser. The group knows it is right and has the truth, and wants to impose it. The members of a community know that the struggle is inside of each person and inside the community; it is against all the powers of pride, elitism, hate and depression that are there and which hurt and crush others, and which cause division and war of all sorts. The enemy is inside, not outside.[8]

Groups are loosely held together by a common vision, but real Christian community is bound together in love. Sadly, our churches are often more groups than communities. In the body of Christ it is clear who is the "head" of the community—it is Christ. It is easy to assert this, but it would be foolish to assume that this is true of all our churches. This is the reality that continually confronts Jamin and me. Churches do not have a magic force field around them protecting them from falling victim to a way of life apart from Christ.

To become a true community, we have to embrace the way of Jesus in the truth of our weakness and neediness. Like the men and women Vanier ministers to, we have to accept that we all cry out to be loved and accepted. We must first recognize that the problem is not only out in the world, but is already defiling us from within. The answer is not persuasive vision-casting, but Jesus. In Jesus we see that others are not "things" to protect ourselves against, but people to give ourselves to in love. Jesus' mission entails self-giving to undeserving people, and we are those undeserving people. As we receive his gift of himself, we find that we are not simply called to follow him, but to live within his life. This is why Paul's letters are riddled with the phrase "in Christ." He is our life, and in him we come to know the love of God and the love of neighbor. In him we find our true selves, and the genuine human existence that James Houston talked about. This genuine humanity is never in isolation, but is always with others.[9]

To be with God, who is always with us, is to be in community. To receive Christ entails that we partake in the life of his people. This is not somehow separate from Christ's mission in the world but is essential to it. The breakdown of genuine community is the fruit of the way from below. Worldly power is allergic to vulnerability—really sharing life with one another and receiving others as intrinsically valuable. Worldly power always wants to identify people in worldly ways (like status), so that we can decide if we find them valuable. In contrast, Christ calls us into the very place where we can know his power—community. It is in genuine community, offering ourselves and receiving others as our brothers and sisters in Christ, that we come to know God's power in weakness. Community teaches us how much we need others and how beautiful and good that need itself is. Christian community is the incubator for God's power in weakness for the sake of love.

STANDING AGAINST THE POWERS IN COMMUNITY

Jean's life has become a compelling witness to the way of Jesus against the systemic work of evil. Evil denies that community is actually true power in Christ, but Jean's stand against institutionalizing people with disabilities is a helpful image of kingdom power in weakness against the powers of the world. The dehumanizing structures of evil had all the advantages, it would seem. People with disabilities had no real voice of their own against the prevailing power systems that did not give them the considerations human beings deserve. There were cultural assumptions that "This is just what we do with *these kinds* of people." There were government programs, systems, buildings, and employees who "knew what to do" and were funded to do so. Furthermore, there was no real precedent to do anything different. Jean, of course, would disagree, and simply point to Jesus.

Amid these grim realities, there was Jean. He was only able to take in two men. It seemed like a generous but insignificant act in the face of the deluge of systemic evil being fostered by the world around him. But like Jesus, Jean wasn't interested in how powerful his ministry seemed (Jesus, after all, particularly at the end, was left with only a small cadre of followers who ended up abandoning him). His interest gravitated to how profoundly loving an act was, more than how powerful it seemed. Jean wasn't aiming to achieve "world domination for Jesus," but to bear witness. Jean was a witness to the kingdom by loving people who were not being loved; he was doing Jesus-things in Jesus-ways. But, also like Jesus, by giving himself to power in weakness, he is now heralded around the world; and his communities thrive in thirty-five countries. Jean is an ambassador of the way of Jesus. The two ways we've been looking at, the way of power in weakness for love, and the way of power in strength for control, are rarely set in contrast as clearly as in Jean's ministry. His attack on the dehumanizing institutions in mid-twentieth-century Europe reveals exactly what we have found in Scripture about living in our weakness and rejecting the power offered by the world, the flesh, and the devil.

Jean's approach to humanize the dehumanized was to give himself in love to them. There was a clear imitation of God's own act of grace, where he gave himself in love and entered into the broken reality of the world. Jean did the same. He gave himself by fostering a life of community, generosity, and love. Life together is an underappreciated reality in a hyperindividualistic culture like ours. But the reason we ignore deep community is the very reason we need it—because we believe we can find power on our own. Community is hard because community pushes against our flesh, magnifies our insecurities, and reveals our strategies to manipulate and control. Like Jean asking two men to live with him, community often feels as though it isn't accomplishing much.

Nothing about genuine community feels *powerful*. Part of the reason for this is because true community takes time, and there is no possible substitute for that. Like a tree that "yields its fruit in its season" (Ps. 1:3), it takes real patience for the fruit of community to come into season. It takes wisdom and love.

Against the temptation to exert power for control, Jean has accepted a power for love. Against the structure of the powers in the world and their dehumanizing force, he did not turn to domination, but to love and self-giving as the prevailing way of Jesus. While Jean has focused his life on one specific group that has been neglected, this way is available to all. This is the way of Jesus. And like Jesus' ministry, Jean's ministry has been imitated around the world, but most famously, as noted earlier, by Henri Nouwen.

DOWNWARD MOBILITY

Henri Nouwen has had a lasting impact on how Jamin and I think about all of these things. Nouwen has become famous for *downward mobility*, the term he used to describe leaving the heights of the academy to pastor people with disabilities. Nouwen writes, "The story of our salvation stands radically over and against the philosophy of upward mobility. The great paradox which Scripture reveals to us is that real and total freedom is only found through downward mobility. The Word of God came down to us and lived among us as a slave. The divine way is indeed the downward way."[10] He continues, expanding upon this vision of Jesus:

> Indeed, the one who was from the beginning with God and who
> was God revealed himself as a small, helpless child; as a refugee
> in Egypt; as an obedient adolescent and inconspicuous adult; as
> a penitent disciple of the Baptizer; as a preacher from Galilee,
> followed by some simple fishermen; as a man who ate with

sinners and talked with strangers; as an outcast, a criminal, a threat to his people. He moved from power to powerlessness, from greatness to smallness, from success to failure, from strength to weakness, from glory to ignominy. The whole life of Jesus of Nazareth was a life in which all upward mobility was resisted."

Nouwen has become a witness to the way from above—that is, the way of weakness—but in so doing he has inevitably become a symbol of something *extra*ordinary, in its literal sense (as in, not normal). In other words, it is easy to hear his story and find it incredible, but also find it impossible. We simply cannot follow that way. Over the years Jamin and I had wrestled with this tension. Because of this we had decided to ask Jean about Nouwen during our time with him. We wanted to hear a bit more about the real man, Henri Nouwen, and not merely the idealized version of him.

"Jean, could you tell us a bit about Henri and his acceptance of the way of downward mobility? What was that like for him? Every page of his writing seems to be marked by loneliness. Was that always what it was like for him?"

Jean sat back and glanced over our heads for a moment. He was clearly having a warm memory of his friend, and as a smile came over his face, he began. "I remember going to hear him when he was giving talks at Harvard to hundreds of people. He was right at the top, but he lived alone and he was a mess. He was a mess and he knew he was a mess. He would come away from giving the talks that everybody praised, and would experience terrible loneliness at night. He saw it, and he was going crazy from loneliness. That's when he came to see me and he came to live here at Daybreak. But it was never too easy for him because he would always want to flip off and write another book. We would say, 'Henri, you have to stay. You are the priest of the community.' He didn't like that too much,

123

but he knew that was the path, and there was something in him that wanted to be faithful to this role of being a pastor. But somewhere on the other side he also wanted to write new books, and he would be a pain in the neck with editors. So he had left but he hadn't found a real peace within him, but he was working toward it, and he had chosen to take the Road of Daybreak."

Jamin and I glanced at each other. Neither of us knew what we were expecting when we asked the question, but it wasn't that. When we talked later, we discovered that we were both encouraged by Vanier's words about his friend. Henri was humanized. He did not have to be the picture-perfect representative of the way of Jesus. His struggle gave us hope that we, too, could accept this struggle. When Jean paused, Jamin took a chance to jump in, asking, "Jean, what about his peers in the academy? How were those relationships when he left?"

Jean continued, with the same honesty and fondness. "His peers weren't interested. They either adulated him or rejected him. He didn't really find the peace he had hoped for in the community, because the community put brakes on him. He couldn't keep running off to see this friend and another friend and write a book. But he knew what the journey was and he had accepted the pain. He was a beautiful man on that journey, but an anguished man; as you say, every page was marked with loneliness. He just couldn't stand being alone. But he was an excellent pastor in the community. Excellent. If somebody fell sick, he would go to the hospital every day. He was compassionate—very compassionate—and a wonderful man. But he was a man struggling through his own wounds. He knew what it was to feel lonely, and he could see what it meant for people with disabilities. So his path was a good path but a painful path."

Jean paused for a moment and smiled again, and with a quiet chuckle he continued, "Even his death was a funny thing because he had a heart attack in Amsterdam, and he had about four hours waiting for a plane change. He went to a hotel and in the hotel he saw it coming, so he rang up, but they couldn't take him down in a lift because the lift was too small. So they had to get the firemen." Vanier began laughing hard now. "Henri said he couldn't do it like everybody else!" Jean, still laughing, added, "All the streets were blocked, the firemen coming, the ladder going up—he was theatrical to a degree which was fantastic. I loved that." Jean paused, still smiling from the memory of his friend, before turning a bit more somber. "I had him on the phone the night before his second attack, which killed him. He was such a beautiful man. He was a man that God used in the most amazing way. The fact that he had taken the downward path even though it still hurt was a beautiful thing."

There is something beautiful about the downward path, but its beauty has nothing to do with how easy it is. Jesus, Paul tells us, "emptied himself, by taking the form of a servant. . . . He humbled himself" (Phil. 2:7–8). Jesus' gracious entrance into the world was not met with welcome and celebration (John 1:10–11). He was rejected. This is the harsh reality we must come to grips with as we consider this downward path. Jesus makes it known that the same world that hated and rejected him will hate and reject us as well (John 15:18–19). Often, we hear God's call to embrace our weakness or move in sacrificial love and we imagine that ultimately this will result in our heroism—overcoming all odds and becoming powerful. In other words, we imagine that Jesus has just given us a more surprising and challenging way to achieve power and success. We still believe we will get what others want, but the difference is that we will go about it "in the right way." This is simply not what Jesus tells us. Embracing the way from above is often a hard and lonely road, but it is the true path of life.

The way of community is the way of vulnerability and love. These are two central features of living a genuinely human

existence, and yet they are often the very things we are afraid of.
We want love, but we want love without vulnerability. We want
love in our strength, but not in our weakness. But that is not love.
We think we want community, but deep down we want to be in
a group that makes us feel special. Jesus offers something else,
something distinctively more profound. Jesus calls us to himself,
that we may partake in *his* life. But Jesus' life was marked, not by
success, domination, and victory, but by love. In this world, love
is marked by suffering, crying out, and a deep and abiding longing for the day when God "will wipe away every tear" (Rev. 21:4).
While being a witness to the invisible way of Christ won't often
feel like the path of life, it is the calling of faith to embrace this way
regardless. This is the way against evil, and as such, it is the way
of Christ.

CHAPTER 7

THE POWER OF THE LAMB

"I AM PRETTY SURE A SMART, PRODUCTIVE ATHEIST COULD do my job well," said a successful pastor. By *successful*, I (Jamin) mean what we tend to mean when we use this term in the church: He was at the helm of a church that was growing significantly. His words shifted the tone of the conversation, and I paused, trying to process what he had just admitted.

He had come to realize that much of his success was built on his own talents and abilities. The power driving the success of his ministry was his own. It scared him. He was disturbed by the notion that he could succeed in ministry without depending on God; it troubled him that he could do ministry in the flesh and be praised for it. Even more disconcerting was the fact that he could lead confidently, think strategically, and cast an exciting vision for his church—and none of this required he even be a Christian. It wasn't that he was doing ministry in the flesh that unnerved him, although that was certainly enough. More disturbing was that his view of ministry didn't depend on God even existing for things to work well.

This conversation was a sobering moment for me. As I reflected on my life in ministry, it occurred to me that I also devoted much of my time as a pastor to relying upon my own strength. I relied on my communication skills, my academic training, and my own thoughtfulness and creativity rather than God. I also used these strengths for the wrong reasons. My strengths are not negative—I could have used them as opportunities to sow in the Spirit—but instead I used them to sow to the flesh (Gal. 6:8). Rather than using them as gifts given by God for his glory, I used them to gain more power. I employed rhetoric instead of pointing to the cross. I tried to self-will growth in my life and in the lives of others rather than abiding in the way of Christ. I was pursuing significance, influence, and position. In short, I was pastoring in the way from below.

The way from below forces pastoral ministry into professional categories where the focus is on what *I* can get done and make happen. A profession is something *I* choose, *I* develop, and *I* earn. To succeed in a profession, I build a strong résumé, develop core competencies, and emphasize my strengths (while hiding my weaknesses). When someone offers me advice on career development, the guiding assumption is that change and improvement are within my control. *Control* becomes the obsession. Success in a profession largely comes down to my work ethic, talent, and confidence, because success is defined by my productivity and power. Leaving aside the factors that are outside of my control, it is assumed that as long as I work hard enough, things will go the way I want. In the church, this might mean: "I am an effective communicator and powerful preacher, therefore my church will grow"; "I am passionate about evangelism, therefore people will come to Christ"; or even "I know how to initiate and think strategically, therefore our church will make a difference in this city."

After a decade of ministry, I have grown weary of this professional orientation. I believe God is inviting me to pastor in the way from above. This changes everything. Now, ministry is not primarily a profession, but a vocation. A vocation is a calling—a gift, a grace, and an invitation. My calling is not based on *my* résumé, *my* abilities, or *my* power. It is based solely upon the résumé, ability, and power of the One who calls me. This is not something I control, but something I receive. Success is not determined by what I accomplish, but rather by my faithfulness—faithfulness to the One who called me and to his gracious invitation. This still requires work, because faithfulness is not sitting around and waiting for God to do something. But the work is sowing to the Spirit in the way of Christ. It is not our effort that is the problem, but the source of our action.

This shift in mind-set has changed my understanding of ministry from the building of a career to the continual embrace of my calling. This has made a major difference in my posture as a pastor. There are, of course, moments when I digress into grasping for control. There are moments when I want "real power," and I begin plotting how I can get it. (It's amazing how easy it is to equate worldly power with "real power" in my heart.) The way from below is always wooing us, and our hearts are never fully immune to its seduction. When I am tempted by the way from below, the only solution is to abide in the One who called me and open my heart to his way.

One of the unexpected challenges of accepting the invitation to minister in the way of Jesus is how lonely it has been. I remember wading through a season of loneliness a few years ago. I was weary and in need of a companion. That's when I met Eugene Peterson. Not in person, mind you, but through his books. At the time I only knew Eugene because of his translation of the Bible: *The Message*. I had no idea he had a series of books on the pastoral vocation.[1] I remember sitting down with *Working the Angles*; it was like hearing someone else sing a tune I had long been humming, but didn't quite know the words to. I was just one page in, and Eugene was already narrating my experience back to me.

American pastors are abandoning their posts, left and right, and at an alarming rate. They are not leaving their churches and getting other jobs. Congregations still pay their salaries. Their names remain on the church stationery and they continue to appear in pulpits on Sundays. But they are abandoning their posts, their *calling*. They have gone whoring after other gods. What they do with their time under the guise of pastoral ministry hasn't the remotest connection with what the church's pastors have done for most of twenty centuries.[2]

I think I underlined that entire first page. This was precisely what I had witnessed in my own life. I was tempted to reject the very heart of my calling. This is what I felt so acutely as I navigated the world of pastoral ministry, often feeling so alone. I began to read more and more of Eugene's books because he spoke right to my heart. His words were like a beacon of light amid the dark, cloudy realities of pastoral life. I wasn't alone! I had found a companion.

It was around this time that Kyle was finishing his PhD in Scotland. Kyle and I didn't get to talk all that often, but when we did I told him about Eugene, about what I was learning about my calling as a pastor. You can imagine both Kyle's and my surprise when he was invited to an event where Eugene was speaking to a small gathering of pastors, at a church in northern Scotland. Kyle, as I had been, was fairly unfamiliar with Eugene's writings, but after months of listening to me talk about Eugene's pastoral influence on me, Kyle had to go. After listening to him read a story from *The Tales of Winnie-the-Pooh* and muse on ministry and the church, Kyle was captivated by his vision for the pastoral life. At the end of the event, Eugene gave Kyle his address and encouraged him to write. We both took Eugene up on the invitation. Over the next several years, we both wrote letters back and forth with him. With each letter we were encouraged and given much insight into the temptations in ministry, and how the powers have infiltrated the life of the church.

Here we were, years later, on a journey to learn what it meant to embrace the way from above. As we wrestled with the competing ways of power, we kept coming back to how our view of power has impacted pastoral ministry. We needed to find someone who could guide us as we explored these realities. It was obvious who we needed to see. We wrote Eugene a letter, asking if he would connect with us to explore the issues of power and pastoral ministry, and he invited us to Montana. Before we knew it, Kyle and I were flying into Glacier Park International Airport in Kalispell, Montana. The tiny airport signaled the slow-paced, small-town world we were about to discover. We rented a car and headed into town, finding a nice little diner for burgers and shakes before heading to our B&B to get some sleep. In the morning we would head over to the Peterson residence.

THE PASTOR

When we drove past the mailbox at the base of his driveway, I caught my first glimpse of the place Eugene encountered letters from Kyle and me. As we slowly drove down the long driveway, we saw a couple of deer grazing nearby at the neighbors' house. We climbed out of the car and stretched in the cold air, our Southern California lungs breathing deep the crisp Montana air. We were both tired from our multileg flight the day before, and incredibly full from the massive breakfast at the local B&B. As we walked down the stone steps toward the wood cabin Eugene calls home, we paused to look out over the lake behind it. It was a beautiful day in Montana, and we were going to spend it with "the Pastor."[3]

Eugene and Jan greeted us at the door as though we were familiar neighbors. Jan vibrates with hospitality, and Eugene beams with joy as he watches her entertain. We made our way to Eugene's study and settled in as Jan brought glasses of water. I slowly took in my surroundings. The room bore the signs of a writer—a wall full of books, and scribbles written on notepads on the desk. On the wall adjacent to the desk hung a series of tiles depicting the stations of the cross. Next to Eugene's reading chair was a Greek New Testament, and on his desk were letters from folks like Kyle and me. The glass windows lining the room gave us a majestic view of the lake. It felt as though we were in a sacred space. In many ways, I suppose we were.

"Must be a hard place to write," I joked. Eugene laughed. Even though we had never met before, I felt as if I already knew him. Years of corresponding and reading his books had created a familiarity, a relationship that already felt established.

Kyle began our discussion. "Eugene, as you know from our letters, we are on a bit of a journey. We are trying to learn the way of power in weakness. In particular, we want to explore with you what this might look like for the pastor. But first, we want to explore how pastoral ministry is particularly impacted by power. When you think about power and the life of a pastor, what comes up for you?"

"Jamin and Kyle," Eugene began, in a more serious tone, "being a pastor is a precarious position, because you usually don't know this beforehand, but you are in a position of power. Being a pastor automatically puts you in a position of power; you don't have to do anything to get it. We don't realize how people treat us. And gradually it kind of seeps into our bloodstream, and without even making decisions, it feels good. It feels good to be in a place of power. It becomes addictive. I think power is a very addictive thing, and we're just sitting ducks for it."

"Eugene," I said, "what I hear you saying is that pastors can easily become tempted by power and status and find their identity in that. This really taps into my own struggles in ministry. I see this in myself when I worry about how I am perceived outside of the church. Truthfully, being a pastor isn't always viewed as a powerful position."

"Oh yes, that's right." As Eugene often would, he elaborated with a story. "I was sitting on an airplane once, going someplace—I had a couple of books published at this point—and the guy next to me asked what I did. I said, 'I'm a writer.' The minute I said that I thought, *Eugene, you're not a writer, you're a pastor.* Why does *writer* sound better than *pastor*? But it does. I wanted to identify myself with something that was special. Pastor is not special. Pastors are a dime a dozen, but if you are a writer, you're in the elite. That was part of those early years, and I was a competitor my whole life, and to rid myself of that competitive stuff was really hard. So I embrace being a pastor because there is nothing pretentious about it. It is a label that carries no distinction in our culture. In fact, it is a negative, if anything."

As Eugene talked more about what drove this competitive spirit, I was brought back to a story from his memoir, *The Pastor.* In it he talks about a pastor friend of his who had chosen to leave his congregation for a bigger church. Eugene was concerned. He believed his friend's decision was fueled by "adrenaline and ego and size."[4] In his memoir Eugene includes a letter he had written to the pastor at the time. He writes, "Classically, there are three ways in which humans try to find transcendence . . . through the ecstasy of alcohol and drugs, through the ecstasy of recreational sex, through the ecstasy of crowds. Church leaders frequently warn against the drugs and the sex, but, at least in America, almost never against the crowds. Probably because they get so much ego benefit from the crowds."[5] Eugene made a point of stating in his memoir that moving on to another church wasn't in itself bad, nor were big churches; but his concern was that his friend's driving motivations for making the move were unhealthy. I asked Eugene to reflect a bit more on this story, and he said something that gripped me.

"It is easy to draw a crowd if you know how to do it. And religion and athletics are the two easiest ways to do it. But there is something addictive about that. It just really is."

I was raised in the church and had been in ministry for many years, and never once had I heard a pastor talk about the addiction of crowds. That fact, if nothing else, was incredibly telling.

A LONG WALK TO THE CROSS

With that we briefly parted ways. It was time for Eugene's "liturgical nap." We made plans to pick up the conversation in an hour. While Eugene rested, we walked the edge of the lake. After a few minutes we came to the shoreline of a Christian camp. Right at the edge of the shoreline, buried deep in the ground and wedged between water-smoothed rocks, was a cross. As we looked at this reminder of true kingdom power, I shared with Kyle my struggle to resist the way of power to control. I could see myself in Eugene's friend. I knew the competitive spirit, the desire for a crowd, and the hunger for power. As I confessed to Kyle my own temptations in ministry, I reflected on my journey in the church.

I grew up at Saddleback Church. Large crowds, influential pastors, and radical growth were norms for me growing up. I didn't know it at the time, but my heart was crafting a vision of pastoral ministry during these years that would come to haunt me. It was not a vision anyone at Saddleback encouraged directly, but rather what my flesh began to form amid my experience. What I viewed as "normal" for the pastoral vocation was anything but. By the time I felt called into ministry, the expectations formed in those earlier years had developed into a vision of success. I expected one day I would lead a church with thousands of people. I would write books, be famous, and teach others how to do it. *This is just what happens when you succeed.* I was somewhat aware of the less "successful" pastors in the world, but they were just that—"less," and probably wishing they could be more.

When I became one of those less successful pastors, I remember how jarring it was. To be in a church of a few hundred people, and still not even be "the guy." It was difficult for me to process. Was I doing something wrong? Why wasn't this "working"? I could relate to Eugene's friend, his itch to get somewhere bigger, somewhere more significant.

I can distinctly remember being at a crossroads in ministry. I felt God was calling me to move into a new role, and at the time I had two different jobs open to me. One was at a big, influential church, and the other was at a small, unknown church. God's calling at this moment in my vocational journey could not have been clearer. He had called me to the small church. I remember wrestling with him. Yet, he made it known he was calling me into a season of hiddenness. Just when I felt it was my time to make a name for myself, God invited me to hide. As frustrating as this season was, it was during this time that I learned all the ways I had sought out power and rejected weakness, and it was there that the Lord taught me what it truly means to be a pastor.

As we walked back down the shoreline toward Eugene's house, our hearts were heavy. We could still feel the tug of grandiosity at work in our own hearts. We thought of friends in ministry who had completely given themselves to the quest for power. I knew many pastors who were busy building careers, seeking to get to the top, all the while dreaming of bigger crowds of adoring fans. They had no idea they were headed down a path that led to death and destruction, not life and fulfillment. We wanted to hear more from Eugene. What made a pastor successful in God's eyes? How might a pastor learn to embrace the way of power in weakness? How might a pastor pursue the way of love rather than the way of fame and success?

THE RELATIONAL PASTOR

Jan greeted us warmly at the door once again. The Peterson home exudes a sense of warmth, and Jan and Eugene's hospitality made it feel as though we were in our own pastor's home. Even for a day we were with a shepherd, and we were treated like members of his flock. We headed back upstairs to Eugene's study to continue our conversation.

"Eugene, we can see how much the pastoral vocation has been co-opted by the way of power to control. It is not unusual to see pastors longing to win, dominate, and seek fame. What does this mind-set produce? What do you believe is the heart of the problem?"

He spoke to us as friends. "Jamin and Kyle, the great temptation of power is control, and the great consequence of control is lack of relationship. The reason that intimacy is so difficult in ministry is you're not in control—you're in relationship. You have to enter a person's life and they have to enter yours. The minute you start becoming obsessed with control, you lose the relationship. Sadly, pastors can get really good at seeming relational, but they are just being manipulative. They know how to play the emotional angles. I think that probably the leading characteristic of successful pastors today is their control. Is that part of your experience?"

Kyle quickly responded to Eugene's question. "That does speak into my own experience. I see this running rampant in the church today. In my experience, this seems to come up most obviously in our obsession with systems and programs as a way to achieve and quantify."

"That seems right," said Eugene. "The minute you develop a programmatic mentality, you depersonalize it because you don't have to know this person, like them, or pray for them; you just do your job and make sure they do their job. The one thing we can do, we can learn people's names, we can be in their homes, and they can be in our homes. We can assiduously cultivate a sense of relationship. There is no hierarchy in friendship. We can cultivate relationships with the outsider, with the person who doesn't think I'm important. So I think somehow we have to find ways to cultivate a sense of nobodyness. Paul certainly did that. Weakness was his strength."

I had spent years striving to be "somebody," and now Eugene was encouraging me to be "nobody"! The emphasis on being personal, on leaning into relationships with people inside and outside the church, was refreshing and convicting. I think many pastors, and I include myself in this, operate within our own "class" as it were—separate not only from nonbelievers but also from the very people we are called to shepherd. Eugene offers us a different vision. While the reality of church ministry today still weighed heavily on us, Eugene's vision was a hopeful one. This isn't rocket science. It is being with people.

After a delightful conversation over the dinner table with Jan and Eugene, talking about our families and ministry, we went out on the back deck and looked over the water. It was cold, but it was beautiful. "I love how peaceful it is here," I said out loud, to no one in particular.

Eugene responded with a smirk. "Yes, but did you see the abomination of desolation?" Eugene glared at a new vacation home on the lakefront. Its elaborate architecture and size made for an eyesore against the backdrop of humble homes built by local residents. It was an interesting image. Eugene grew up in this place and helped his father build the original cabin he now lives in. But something else came in from the outside, something he believed tainted this place. Throughout his ministry he was a "hometown" pastor, knowing the names of his congregants, having people in his home, and ministering in the midst of everyday life. But around him the world was creeping in—not as residents, but as vacationers, offering whatever was new, big, and exciting.

THE WAY OF THE DRAGON OR THE WAY OF THE LAMB

A few months after our time in Montana, Kyle and I were reading through several of Eugene's books. We were both a bit shocked by the number of books he had written that we knew nothing about. In one of his books, *Reversed Thunder*, we came across a quote that connected with our journey. *Reversed Thunder* is Eugene's exposition of the book of Revelation. In it he offers a summary of the two ways depicted by John the Apostle in his visions:

> We choose: we follow the dragon and his beasts along their parade route, conspicuous with the worship of splendid images, elaborated in mysterious symbols, fond of statistics, taking on whatever role is necessary to make a good show and get the applause of the crowd in order to get access to power and become self-important. Or we follow the Lamb along a farmyard route, worshiping the invisible, listening to the foolishness of preaching, practicing a holy life that involves heroically difficult acts that no one will ever notice, in order to become, simply, our eternal selves in an eternal city. It is the difference, politically, between wanting to use the people around us to become powerful (or, if unskilled, getting used by them), and entering into covenants with the people around us so that the power of salvation extends into every part of the neighborhood, the society, and the world that God loves.[6]

Eugene was narrating the way from below versus the way from above. Grabbing rich imagery from the book of Revelation, he described these two ways of power as the way of the dragon versus the way of the Lamb.[7] The dragon represents the devil and his way of power against Christ, the Lamb of God. I could not let this passage go. I kept returning to it. In using this imagery Eugene painted in bright colors the nature of the spiritual battle of power. Which way will we put our faith in: the way of the dragon or the way of the Lamb of God? We march in the procession of one kingdom or the other (Col. 1:13). The way of the dragon is fixated on the spectacular, obsessed with recognition and validation, intoxicated by fame and power. The way of the Lamb is committed to worship, pursues God in the ordinary, and is faithful in hiddenness. The dragon devours and dominates, while the Lamb humbly and sacrificially serves.

As I thought about these two ways, I noticed that they play out practically in a pastor's posture. These two ways show up on the everyday landscape of ministry. I began to make a list. I wanted to discern my own posture as a pastor.

First, the way of the dragon . . .

¤ The pastor uses the church as a platform for personal fame, fortune, and influence.[8]

¤ The pastor views ministry as an arena of performance, where some win and some lose.

¤ The pastor uses the people of the church as tools to accomplish their big dreams.

¤ The pastor relegates prayer and care, the heart of pastoral work, to "lower-level" staff because they don't have time to waste.

¤ The pastor views other pastors primarily as competition.

Second, the way of the Lamb . . .

¤ The pastor gives their life for the sake of the church, regardless of what they gain.

- ¤ The pastor views ministry as an arena of love and service, not winning and losing.
- ¤ The pastor embraces their congregation as people to know and love, not tools to use for other ends.
- ¤ The pastor views prayer and care as the centerpiece of their work, rather than an interruption.
- ¤ The pastor views other pastors not as competition, but as fellow shepherds on the journey whom they need for encouragement and wisdom, and who they are called to encourage and love.

EXPECTATIONS FROM BELOW

The pastoral vocation is in crisis. We may not be aware of it, but the calling is being threatened. Eugene reveals what he has seen over decades of pastoral ministry:

In the process of realizing my vocational identity as pastor, I couldn't help observing that there was a great deal of confusion and dissatisfaction all around me with pastoral identity. Many pastors, disappointed or disillusioned with their congregations, defect after a few years and find more congenial work. And many congregations, disappointed or disillusioned with their pastors, dismiss them and look for pastors more to their liking. In the fifty years that I have lived the vocation of pastor, these defections and dismissals have reached epidemic proportions in every branch and form of church.[9]

The problem Eugene identifies is the result not only of pastors embracing the way from below, but also of congregations embracing it. Eugene noted that those in ministry "can impersonate a pastor without being a pastor," and they can do so simply by meeting the

criteria for success and power placed before them by their congregation.[10] Too often what congregations look for in a pastor has nothing
to do with being a pastor. We want someone who can wow us. We
want someone who exudes confidence. We want someone who can
"get things done" and "make things happen."[11] We are looking more
for a proven professional than someone humbly called. We are looking more for a polished businessman than a seasoned shepherd. We
are looking for someone who is powerful and in control. We are
looking more for a dragon than a lamb. Yet these kinds of pastors
are much like the shepherds in Ezekiel 34, who were fixated on
feeding themselves and disinterested in actually feeding the flock.

As a result of expectation, many who feel called to ministry
don't even consider pastoring as a part of their calling. I (Jamin)
had a conversation with a pastor friend of mine a few years ago. I
was encouraging him in his vocation, affirming what I believed
to be a passion and desire to shepherd (which is what *pastor* means
in Scripture). I was surprised by his response to my affirmation.
"Well, I wouldn't really consider myself a shepherd, but more of
a leader or a teacher. That's not really my gifting." But shepherding isn't one option among many for the pastor. It is the heart of
the vocation. The primary tasks of the pastor are not determined
by personal interests or affinities. We can't reduce the vocation to
what excites us most or what we feel we excel in. The pastoral vocation is a call to embrace our weakness, not to actualize our abilities.

Instead of seeing the pastorate as an office some of us are called
into, we often view pastoring (and by extension, the church) as
something the pastor gets to define based upon gifts, desires, and
perceived calling. When pastoral ministry is something the pastor gets to define, the task of shepherding quickly digresses into
a ministry of power. But pastoring was never this kind of a thing.
It always carried with it images of care, provision, and protection.
The shepherd was always one who sought the safety, well-being,

and good of the sheep first and foremost. The sheep need to know their shepherd, and they need to be known by their shepherd. The pastor attends to them personally, cares for them, and sacrifices for their good. If the pastor's primary task is to care for the sheep, then this cannot be done from a distance; it is an up-close-and-personal endeavor. Peter gives us this kind of vision for pastoral ministry.

> So I exhort the elders among you, as a fellow elder and a witness of the sufferings of Christ, as well as a partaker in the glory that is going to be revealed: shepherd the flock of God that is among you, exercising oversight, not under compulsion, but willingly, as God would have you; not for shameful gain, but eagerly; not domineering over those in your charge, but being examples to the flock. And when the chief Shepherd appears, you will receive the unfading crown of glory. (1 Peter 5:1–4)

This passage includes a charge not only to shepherd, but also to shepherd in a certain kind of way. Again, we have a contrast of two ways. The pastor can lead out of either compulsion or willing love. The pastor can approach ministry either for selfish gain or with eager care. The pastor can lead either in a domineering manner or by example. The contrast could not be clearer. The pastor can embrace the way from above or the way from below. What is interesting to note in the passage is that Peter grounds this idea of shepherding God's people in the person and work of Jesus. Jesus is the "Shepherd and Overseer" of the soul, Peter says earlier (1 Peter 2:25). He is the chief shepherd, the good shepherd (John 10), and this reminds those of us who are pastors that the sheep are not ours. We are under-shepherds of the chief shepherd. We serve a role of stewardship, not ownership. This also means that we must look to the chief shepherd to know how to shepherd, and we must learn his way of shepherding. Jesus did not lead out of compulsion, but in willing love. His pace and rhythm in ministry reveal this. He did not approach ministry for selfish gain, but we are told he had no place to rest his head (Luke 9:58). The one who washed the disciples' feet did not lead by domineering, but by an example of service. When Jesus explicitly cast a vision for ministry, it followed the same contours as his own, even grounding the work of ministry in his own mission as the Son of Man:

> "You know that those who are considered rulers of the Gentiles lord it over them, and their great ones exercise authority over them. But it shall not be so among you. But whoever would be great among you must be your servant, and whoever would be first among you must be slave of all. For even the Son of Man came not to be served but to serve, and to give his life as a ransom for many." (Mark 10:42–45)

Jesus invites pastors into his way of shepherding. In his way, power is found in weakness, and power is expressed in love. We don't shepherd faithfully by simply observing his behavior in the Gospels and trying our best to copy his act, but by participating in this way by the Holy Spirit. The word Peter uses is *partaker*. We are invited to partake in his way. We become shepherds who serve in hiddenness, and are surprised when recognition comes. We become shepherds who are committed to being personal and present. Like Jesus we believe that the localization of our calling is not a curse to be overcome, but a blessing to receive. We are called to shepherd a certain people in a certain place. Such is the way from above.

In light of this, we might ask the simple question: What makes for a "good" pastor? As members of Christ's body, we need to know what we should be looking for in our pastors. We need to look for those who have embraced the way from above. We need to look for shepherds who seek to guide, care for, and protect the flock. We need to look for those who have embraced their weakness and depend upon God's power. We need to look for those who sacrificially love. We need to look for those who have humbled themselves "under the mighty hand of God" (1 Peter 5:6).[12] But we also need to recognize that we are all called to be faithful in ministry, and that the way of Jesus is something we all need to embrace. We are not all called to pastor, but we are all called into faithfulness in the way of Jesus.

CHAPTER 8

THE POWER OF FAITHFULNESS

AS WE FOUND OUR WAY BACK INTO DAILY LIFE, FROM TIME to time Jamin and I caught ourselves daydreaming about Montana. We would remember the quaint, small-town diner where we had milkshakes, the mountains colored green from dense forest, and more than anything else, our conversations with Eugene. What a joy it had been to sit with him—to talk, listen, and open our hearts to the way of the kingdom together. I (Kyle) found myself reread-ing some of the old letters Eugene had sent me over the years. As I read, I could hear his soft yet determined voice. I was encouraged by his vision for pastoral ministry that was at once profound and profoundly simple.

As my family moved around for several years—finishing up degrees, moving back to the States, trying to find a job, finding a job, and then finally landing where we had hoped to be—we changed churches a lot. Eugene's insights altered how I looked for churches. I hesitated now when I went to judge a church service. I was more gracious. I looked at the nature of the community, the way the church worshipped together, and whether there was a shepherd (or shepherds) helping to lead the people.

I may not be a pastor, but wherever my family lands, I end up in some kind of leadership position in the church, and I end up serving in a variety of ways. The same is true for many of us. We may not be in full-time pastoral ministry, but we are all called to minister. We may not be pastors, but we will find ourselves in positions of leadership within the church. So we cannot just stop with pastoral ministry when we think about power and weakness, and the powers and principalities. We have to talk about leadership itself.

There is no shortage of talk about leadership today. It is something of a cultural obsession, and it is perhaps even more alive in the confines of the church. With the decreasing emphasis on the "pastor-shepherd," we have seen the rise of "the leader." When we talk about leaders we often assume they should have strong personalities, be able to make difficult decisions, and gather people aroud them and wield influence over them.

A few years ago I (Jamin) was talking to a friend about some coaching he had received regarding his "career path" in ministry. He wanted to know what qualities and training he needed to "advance" his pastoral career. He was told that the key thing he was missing was the "it factor," which would hurt him in advancing as a leader in the church. This is the kind of thing we look for in leaders: the "it factor."[1] Leadership, on this understanding, is easily discerned: You know it when you see it. If pastors have a lot of followers, if they magnetically draw people toward them, or if they have charisma and gravitas that stand out in a social setting, they must be leaders. This worldly approach to leadership has nothing to do with the way of the kingdom. Quite often, having the "it factor" is simply a sign of a dangerous, unhealthy, and toxic leader.

THE RISE OF TOXIC LEADERS

"Toxic leaders" are easy to find, and their influence has become increasingly pervasive in our culture, perhaps most evident in politics. Toxic leadership has become something of a presumption in the political sphere, but that is certainly not the only realm in which it resides. Leadership of any kind will always be alluring to unhealthy, domineering, and narcissistic individuals. The church is not immune to this, because the church can provide a context for power. A toxic leader is someone who maintains power and significance by manipulating followers through their own fundamental drive to be powerful and significant. Toxic leaders dominate and control.[2] Toxic leaders wield their personalities to cement their power, relegating their followers to a position of dependence upon them rather than on Christ. Toxic leaders subvert the systems designed to hold them accountable and quickly establish scapegoats when they fail. Toxic leaders do not develop other leaders, because they pose a threat to their own power. Toxic leaders create an unhealthy symbiosis between themselves and the organizations they lead, such that their absence would equal the collapse of the organization.[3] In other words, a leader is toxic if he ceases to live according to the way of Jesus—the way of love, humanization, and truth, giving himself instead to the way of manipulation, dehumanization, and deception.

Many of us have experienced toxic leaders. For some of us they have been coaches. For others they have been bosses. Sadly, for some of us they have been our pastors. Oddly, as damaging as these leaders may be, we often desire them. These are precisely the people we believe possess the "it factor." *This is what we are looking for.* As counterintuitive as it sounds, because of our fears, our wounds, or our desire for grandiosity (and inability to become great in ourselves), we seek these kinds of leaders and buy what they are selling wholesale. This is precisely how cults are formed. Jean Vanier claims that "a cult is a community that is closed in around the figure of a guru and built on fear. People join because they are afraid—of loneliness, of feeling lost, of going to hell—and they stay there for the same reasons, for fear of the consequences if they leave."[4] We can easily become cultlike when we surround a Christian guru and end up following that person rather than following Christ. The reason we desire toxic leaders, according to Jean Lipman-Blumen, is because toxic leaders promise to "keep us safe, anoint us as special, and offer us a seat at the community table."⁵ We want a sense of safety, significance, and belonging, and they are offering it in exchange for loyalty.

We must stand against domineering, manipulative, and power-hungry leadership. It is tempting to believe simply over-throwing such leaders would solve the problem. However, this approach is naive. Toxic leaders are the products of toxic cultures. So we don't seek out shepherds, but gurus. We don't desire serv-ants, but kings. We don't long for pastors, but celebrities. Such a leader is not known by his or her congregation, not personally, but serves more as the logo of an organization. But this is what we ask for, and, unsurprisingly, this is what it takes to be considered "suc-cessful" in much of evangelicalism today.

Unfortunately, the things that make leaders dangerous are the very things that earn them affirmation. This is where we see the subtle temptation of grandiosity seeping into ministry. The ways of the world have been so thoroughly internalized in our church culture that we don't even see them anymore. I recall one pastor who used to remind his congregation, on almost a weekly basis, that if people went to a different church, it meant they really didn't want to hear God's Word preached. He presented himself as the sole authoritative interpreter of the Bible.

Where pride and arrogance reign, so do other vices. It came out that he had seduced a woman in a pastoral care session and had an affair with her for fifteen years. People were surprised that such a great teacher could be such a great sinner. But why? Wisdom and talent are not synonyms. Arrogance and pride never reside alone, but are woven within a faithfulness to the way from below that pro-duces death. When leadership is governed by the principles of the way from below, then we are "anointing" priests not of the kingdom of Jesus but of the kingdom of darkness. This is a scary reality, but it is the truth. Satan would like nothing more than to wrap his claws around the hearts of leaders, to use their influence as a means of propagating evil. The church and its leadership are strategic points of attack in Satan's work. Power, ambition, jealousy, and pride are all bait for those who seek to influence the people of God.[6]

Fortunately, there is another vision for leadership not married to the ways of worldly power. Leadership in the kingdom has always been servant leadership. It is always a different sort of leadership from that promoted by the world. As Jesus told his disciples, "You know that the rulers of the Gentiles lord it over them, and their great ones exercise authority over them. It shall not be so among you. But whoever would be great among you must be your servant, and whoever would be first among you must be your slave, even as the Son of Man came not to be served but to serve, and to give his life as a ransom for many" (Matt. 20:25–28). *Whoever would be great* among you must become a servant. Jesus takes grandiosity by the horns and wrestles it to the ground. He reorients it according to the way from above, against worldly motivations like jealousy and selfish ambition. What would it look like to embrace Jesus' vision for leadership? What would it look like to put off the obsession with worldly values of power and prestige? What would it look like to have healthy leaders as opposed to toxic ones?

RURAL LOS ANGELES?

We went looking for answers in Los Angeles. Perhaps LA seems like an odd place to find someone to speak into Jesus' way of leadership. After all, isn't LA the very bastion of worldly power? Isn't this the factory of celebrity culture and branded identity? Perhaps. But we knew of someone there who could offer us a radically different vision of life in the kingdom. He was a leader of unusual wisdom who had embraced the way from above. So for two and a half hours we sat in LA traffic. That was expected. What wasn't expected is what we saw just moments after we exited the parking lot Southern Californians call a freeway.

As we wove our way through quiet surface streets toward our destination, it felt as if we had left LA and been transported to a country town. We drove past a small general store and wound our way through rolling hills filled with open land and unassuming homes. It seemed fitting that this boy from Missouri would manage to find a rural part of LA. As we drove, Jamin and I shared our enthusiasm in having this next conversation on our journey. We both had been influenced by this man's writings early in our lives. I had a deep sense of connection to him, having been mentored by people he mentored. He was somewhat of a grandfather to me in my faith.

We rounded the corner in a sleepy neighborhood and drove up the small hill and parked in front of Dallas Willard's home. We walked past the white picket fence and rang the doorbell. Jane, Dallas's wife, answered and welcomed us in. Jane had been gardening. She set her gloves on the kitchen counter and grabbed us a couple glasses of water before returning to her work. Dallas met us in his living room.

The house was warm and inviting, just like a grandparent's home should be. An old baby grand piano sat grazing in a jungle of book piles. There was an old typewriter on a cabinet and a corded telephone that looked as if it had been lifted from a hotel in the sixties. The mid-century modern style was of an age that is currently in vogue. However, the wear and tear were not contrived but were the effects of real living. The home felt welcoming and unassuming, draped in simplicity and adorned with the ordinary. Dallas lumbered over to a chair and sat down. I pulled up a chair next to him as Jamin took a seat on the couch. Out of the corner of my eye I noticed the Ten Commandments hung above the fireplace, and a framed quote from John Wesley sat next to the couch. It was a distinctively Christian home, not in a cliché sense, but in a natural and meaningful way.

Dallas is a quiet and unassuming man with huge hands. As you shake his hand, you almost check to make sure he isn't wearing a catcher's mitt! There is no question when you interact with him that he is a weighty and powerful man. Not the kind of power academics are usually known for, but a humble power. Dallas exudes a calm, unhurried, and grounded sincerity that is equally as strong as it is inviting. What is most unusual, perhaps, is that Dallas spent forty-eight years as a professor of philosophy at USC, but he is more known for his writing on spiritual formation. Through his books and lectures, he has become one of the most influential evangelicals of his generation.

There is no question that Dallas was a successful person, but it is hard to pinpoint that reality in our current cultural assumptions. He was a bestselling author, but he didn't flaunt or exploit it. He had a wide-reaching platform into the Christian world, but he didn't seek to create it (or, for that matter, sustain it). He was told, early on, that he wasn't a good speaker, but conferences kept begging him to come. He once told me that he only wrote books on the Christian life because people asked him to! In an age when people are desperate for success, a platform, or a way to seem meaningful, Dallas sought out faithfulness and trusted the rest would work itself out. The success of his life can't be quantified in books sold or audience numbers, but in the hearts he personally touched. After his death, a deluge of comments poured out articulating how Dallas had been the one who woke people to the reality of God's reign, and what Dallas called the "with-God-life." His impact proved to be incredibly wide.

While we could have talked to Dallas about nearly anything and found his answers profound, we were particularly interested in hearing his understanding of success in ministry and the nature of Christian leadership. These weren't the sorts of questions he was normally asked, but it was clear that he was the kind of person who understood success. He was near the end of his time and therefore could look back and assess our current cultural realities with clarity.

SUCCESS OR FAITHFULNESS?

After some small talk and discussion of mutual friends, we turned to the questions at hand. "Dallas," I (Kyle) began, "can you address our current ministry culture and highlight the ways we might not trust in the way of Christ? What concerns do you have, and what guidance would you offer?"

"The real issue for the evangelical church today," he said, "is what counts as success in ministry? If you go back several decades, you will see that people didn't think about ministers in the same way. They didn't really think in terms of success. The whole idea of being a success was more in terms of being faithful to a calling. For example, you could be a minister who wasn't a very good speaker and be regarded as someone who was faithful to their calling, someone of character. So the problem is how you think about success, and today it is very difficult to think about success except in terms of a great deal of money and a lot of accoutrements—like buildings and programs. And the model of success that is largely projected by our seminaries is tied to these outward symbols, and a very low percentage of people who are in the ministry can succeed in those terms. I'm sorry to say this, but much of what we call

Christian is not a manifestation of the supernatural life of God in our souls; much of what we call Christian is really just human.

"So now the positive side. What is ministry? Ministry is bringing the life of God, as it would be understood in terms of Jesus and his kingdom, into the lives of other people. That's ministry. We minister the kingdom of God. That gives you a new way of thinking about ministry because now you are a carrier of the kingdom of God, which is how Jesus trained his first disciples. You are a carrier of the power of God, the kingdom of God, and the grace of God; and so you watch that work with people and try not to get in its way. But that is the secret of ministry. You bring the power of God, the truth of God, and the presence of Jesus into the lives of other people and you watch it work."

"Dallas," Jamin interjected, "what has this done to leadership in the church? I have a lot of friends who are pastors who feel like they have to keep up to be considered relevant. They have congregants who can download better sermons, listen to better worship music, and who can jump in their cars and go anonymously to dozens of churches in a short driving distance. What are the key temptations here?"

Dallas paused to consider Jamin's question. "The underlying assumption of this way of doing our church services is that you are putting on a performance, and if you are going to put on a performance, then you want people who are stellar. This is in terms that are understood by the consumers of the performance, and a humble man or woman who has simply been faithful in serving the Lord is not stellar. It is a great temptation to put on a performance. By the way, this is one of the things that crushes pastors, the idea that every Sunday they have to put on a performance. God's provision for us and for his work through us is adequate. We do not have to make it happen. We must stop shouldering the burdens of outcomes. These are safely in his hands."

THE LITTLE THINGS

As Dallas talked, it was evident that this was a person who had lived through decades upon decades of fads in the church. He had seen one technique after another come and go, and had walked alongside pastors who had run themselves into the ground trying to "succeed" in ministry only to find misery. But the temptations are more acute than ever. Pastors, more than most, are bombarded with blogs, magazines, conferences, books, and degrees to help them "get it right," win, and succeed. It is not surprising that many who began ministry desiring to serve God end up burned out or jaded. This discussion of success, faithfulness, and ministry brought me back to a moment in Dallas's book *Divine Conspiracy*. It had been a decade since I had read it, but it stuck with me.

"Dallas, in *Divine Conspiracy* you argue that we are always tempted by trying to do big things for God and neglecting the small things. This seems relevant here. Can you spell this out a bit more?"

"Well," Dallas said, "the main thing is, such a person leaves the big things to God. The word that came to Jeremiah's secretary was, 'Seekest thou great things for thyself? Seek them not.'[7] And then he goes on to promise that God will take care of him. We should just get out of the business of seeking great things. Now, if we do that, then we will be more observant of the small things; we will, for example, have time and energy because we are resting in God to really do justice to the small things. And that will be to approach them as one who lives in the kingdom of God who actually cares about the people who are closest to them. Those people are the 'neighbors' in Scripture, they are the ones who are close to us, and we care about them. But you know, you can't do that if you are in a hurry."

As Dallas paused, Jamin prodded him a bit. "Dallas, as you talk, I think of Peter and his expectations. Peter wanted a messiah who offered big things like power and success, and he wanted to pick up a sword and dominate. Jesus offers him the cross. We find Peter and the disciples arguing about who is greatest, and Jesus tells them to become like little children.[8] What do we take away from this for embracing the little things?"

Dallas quickly replied, "Well, what is revealed, not only by Peter, since he was expressing what every one of the followers thought, is that the Messiah has come to serve us, that we're going to hitch our wagon to his star and we're going to be sitting pretty from here on. The only issue is how we're going to divide up the goodies. That's what they are arguing about. Over and over while he was talking about 'I'm going to go up and they're going to kill me,' they are talking about who is going to be the chancellor and the exchequer or whatever, because they were thinking in terms of human power. And he is saying, 'No, I have something much greater to give to you, which comes through death and the abandonment of control.'

"When the pastor leads and speaks, that's where he needs to be standing: no power except what comes through the presence of God with him. And again, you see, you're going to have to break a lot of habits, because your whole life has been devoted to something else. Probably how you've experienced church and then perhaps how you've experienced your theological education, is not in that direction. That is why, for example, it is so extremely hard to get meaningful programs on spiritual formation integrated into the course of studies in seminaries. It is always regarded as something like, 'Oh well, if you are interested in that . . . but you don't have to be. What you really need to be up on are your languages and your history and your knowledge of the Bible and so on, and then perhaps you learn something about preparing sermons and counseling. That's what you really need to know.' No no no. That's not what you need to know. You need to know how to abandon yourself to God. Methods are often temporary, but what God is looking for is a life."

LEARNING TO LEAD

Jamin and I left Dallas's home not knowing that this was the last time we would see him. Within a year of our conversation he had died. What Dallas articulated so helpfully in our discussion was that people's perception of the purpose of Christian life and ministry had changed from faithfulness to success. Dallas talked about the emphasis on getting things done, rather than being faithful. He talked about ministry that flows out of a person who has abandoned oneself to God, rather than one who strives to keep up with what is relevant. Dallas talked about a weighty person, and how the person of depth witnessed to God's invisible kingdom in a world desperate for it. In this sense, the call of every Christian is to mediate God's kingdom to the world by living according to the invisible reign of God. This sounds nice, but in reality our hearts reject Christ's way. We want power. Christ claims that without him we can do nothing. We want to win. Christ offers the cross. We want to do big things. Christ waits for us to be faithful with little things. The whole enterprise runs contrary to our sensibilities. So what does it mean to lead and "succeed" in ministry? It means to serve. Dallas writes:

> "Whoever wishes to become great among you must be your servant" (Mark 10:44). By the way, it is dreadful to see this recommended as only another *technique* for succeeding in leadership. Jesus wasn't giving techniques for successful leadership. He was telling us *who the great person is*. He or she is the one who is servant of all. Being a servant shifts one's relationship to everyone. What do you think it would do to sexual temptation

if you thought of yourself as a servant? What do you think it would do to covetousness? What do you think it would do to the feeling of resentment because you didn't get what you thought you deserved? I'll tell you. It will lift the burden.[9]

Dallas's life and ministry provide a vision for our own lives and ministries that is ultimately about clinging to Jesus and his way in the world. The goal is not generating a great and powerful ministry, but becoming weighty people who serve like Jesus. For Dallas this means doing Jesus-things in Jesus-ways; it is embracing a way of life that is invisible and runs contrary to our modern sensibilities. Ultimately, this is a call to the way of wisdom, which is precisely why there is no secret formula for success in God's kingdom other than love, and love is often messier than we want to deal with. But as we trust in the way of Jesus, we must not look around and ask if others are watching, if we are seen as important, or if we are doing something "meaningful." Rather, we need to ask: If we are pierced, what do we bleed? Do we bleed forgiveness, love, and grace, or anger, hatred, and domination? If our church is confronted with the chaotic wind and waves of the world, what is its foundation? What reveals itself when struggles come? If the clothing I put on to project an image to the world is stripped away, what lies beneath?

WALKING IN THE WAY OF WISDOM

As we are confronted with these questions, we have to turn to wisdom. Wisdom helps us discern what we do to partake in the body of Christ fruitfully, and it also helps us discern whether the fruit of an individual or an organization is good or bad. But we don't need worldly wisdom; we need *Christian* wisdom. Christian wisdom is living along the contours of Christ's life and living in harmony with his reign. Christian wisdom, therefore, is not living according to how the world *is*, but how it should be. When Job inquires about wisdom, he realizes it is not discovered through a careful pondering of reality, at least not in its deepest sense. "It is hidden from the eyes of all living and concealed from the birds of the air," we are told, and "God understands the way to it" (Job 28:21, 23). Whereas Christian wisdom is a long process of growth into maturity, counterfeit wisdom is always easier to come by. Counterfeit wisdom is fast food for the soul. It is easy to find, cheap to get, and never fulfills its promise to satisfy you. We are all tempted by counterfeit wisdom.

I (Kyle) once worked for a Christian organization that was run by fear and domination. A colleague of mine called it dehumanizing, and that is exactly what it was. On the one hand it proclaimed Christian values and had an evangelical doctrinal statement, and on the other it baptized a leadership structure that constantly reminded us that we were replaceable, unimportant, and unvaluable. The values were always connected to marketing, big enterprises that looked impressive, and the latest technology and style. When my boss, a man who had been championed as the future of our department, was fired out of the blue, we were left wondering if we were all going to lose our jobs. For the next week, we all did our work in a fog, many of us frantically looking for jobs in case we too were fired. At the end of the week we had an emergency meeting off campus so no one saw us (always a bit dubious, but in keeping with a culture of fear). We were told that people had noticed we looked shell-shocked, and that if we didn't put smiles on our faces, there would be a price to pay. Needless to say, that piece of pastoral care didn't quite help.

Because of the dehumanizing nature of the organization, there was constant turnover of employees. But no matter how many stories like this surfaced, they were always drowned out by the praise of all the "big" things going on. When people were neglected, someone reminded them how lucky they were to be a part of the *bigness* of the place. I was there long enough to see its fruit and really taste it. It was bitter and rotten. The system was driven by power structures of fear and manipulation. No doubt the leadership believed the organization was built upon the rock, but at the end of the day, sand was beneath (Matt. 7:24–27). Everything about the place exuded worldly forms of power, success, and strength, and the way it got there was by employing the way from below (and hiding its methods beneath its doctrinal statement). The structures of this institution tapped into worldliness in an attempt to baptize it for Christian gain. But this will always be the way of death, and its fruit will always be dehumanization.

Of course, it is easy simply to point fingers at such infractions and angrily decry the demise of contemporary Christianity. In reality, I have a log in my eye as well. I can preach with theological accuracy and biblical dedication while at the same time be estranged to the ways of Jesus. When things don't go my way, I can turn to strategies and techniques to win before I turn to abiding and trusting. Deep in my own heart is the desire to have faith in God, but this doesn't always include trusting in his ways. In my self-deception I separate Jesus from the example of his life, and think I can have one without the other. I still focus on the way I can see, the way that *makes sense* to me, rather than submitting to the way of the kingdom. We must be able to name these realities. It is not arrogance to know what the way of evil looks like in the world and to name it. It is deceptive, however, to name it everywhere other than in your own heart. Dallas helps to focus our attention: "The issue, so far as the gospel in the Gospels is concerned, is whether we are alive to God or dead to him. Do we walk in an interactive relationship with him that constitutes a new kind of life, life 'from above'?"[10] He goes on:

What must be emphasized in all of this is the difference between trusting Christ, the real person Jesus, with all that that naturally involves, versus trusting some arrangement for sin-remission set up through him—trusting only his role as guilt remover. To trust the real person Jesus is to have confidence in him in every dimension of our real life, to believe that he is right about and adequate to everything.[11]

Many of us seem ready for Jesus to save us, as long as this saving has little to do with how we engage everyday life. We are tempted to tack Jesus onto things we are doing, while at the same time we are desperately afraid that he will undermine them. We can try to use Jesus to obtain power, but we are often less interested in the cross he bears.

So what might it look like to be faithful to Christ in our churches and various ministering opportunities? What might this look like for leadership? The first reality we need to swallow is that the discussion does not start with leadership. Are there Christian leaders? Yes. Is this the focus of Scripture? No. The focus of Scripture is wisdom, holiness, and love as we abide in Christ. We can still talk about leadership (and should), but when we do we need to recognize that we are talking about becoming someone wise. This fits well with where this journey has taken us thus far. What does it mean to seek wisdom and really lead in our weakness rather than our power? What does it mean to be faithful where the Lord calls us in the midst of this present evil age?

LEADING WITH WISDOM

Leading in the way of wisdom constructs a house on a certain kind of foundation, one that will not be destroyed when the chaotic winds of life smack against its walls. But what does this way entail? Dallas claims, "According to the wisdom of Jesus, then, every event takes on a different reality and meaning, depending on whether it is seen only in the context of the visible or also in the context of God's full world, where we all as a matter of fact live."[12] There is a hidden way of life that we must trust in, and that way is God's wisdom. It is the way of the cross. This is the way of faith, or, as the author of Hebrews puts it, "Faith is the assurance of things hoped for, the conviction of things not seen" (Heb. 11:1). Faith is the conviction of an unseen reality that we know to be true in Christ. Right after this declaration in Hebrews, the author goes on to narrate several Old Testament figures who lived according to the unseen way of God: "By faith Abel offered to God a more acceptable sacrifice than Cain . . . . By faith Noah, being warned by God concerning events as yet unseen, in reverent fear constructed an ark for the saving of his household . . . . By faith Abraham obeyed when he was called to go out to a place that he was to receive as an inheritance. And he went out, not knowing where he was going" (Heb. 11:4, 7, 8). It is easy to read about these heroes of the faith and miss where their power was found. We are told that they "conquered kingdoms, enforced justice, obtained promises, stopped the mouths of lions, quenched the power of fire, escaped the edge of the sword," and "*were made strong out of weakness*" (Heb. 11:33–34, emphasis mine). It was in their weakness that they were able to live according to the power of God.

To lead is to do exactly what these biblical figures did, to set our eyes on the invisible country, the New Jerusalem, which is driven by an economy of love. Wisdom is learning how to live in this way. Wisdom is trusting in the unseen ways of God and his reign in the world. This is why Paul tells us to "look not to the things that are seen but to the things that are unseen. For the things that are seen are transient, but the things that are unseen are eternal" (2 Cor. 4:18). It is also why James warns, "Whoever wishes to be a friend of the world makes himself an enemy of God" (James 4:4). To be a friend to the world is to trust in its ways. But God's reign is antithetical to worldliness. God's reign defines its own understanding of wisdom that is seen as folly by the world. Therefore, there is no silver-bullet leadership strategy in the kingdom of God. There is only wisdom in love through abiding in Christ. This wisdom in love is by faith, and as such, it is an embrace of our weakness and Christ's strength.

DISCERNING THE POWERS IN LEADERSHIP

Jamin and I have both worked in environments that claimed to be Christian but had developed a toxic leadership structure that embodied the way from below. In these places, somehow, the ways of below are marketed as virtues, and power is given to those who grasp for it. In these environments, choosing the way from above is incredibly challenging. It is easy to get caught up in the excitement and the vision for success. It is easy to see such a place as a vehicle to succeed. It is in these places that setting our eyes on the invisible country is so difficult. Leading here will mean that we will always be seen as suspicious. Leading here will entail pushing so hard against the stream that we're seen as a nuisance at best, and incompetent or insubordinate at worst. Your own desire for wisdom, holiness, and love will be seen as destructive to the quest for power, and therefore, it will be recast as laziness, elitism, or aloofness. Or, with Jesus, you may be rebuked and called demonic by those who have set themselves up as the experts of the Bible. When Jesus tells his followers that the world will hate them because of him, we have to remember that he had no context of a "secular world." The "world" that Jesus was talking about included the people of God. We too must realize that the most ardent opposition to the way from above—the way of Jesus—may come from within the church.

The call to wisdom for leadership will necessarily require the church to change her view of what it means to succeed. Toxic leaders thrive in toxic cultures. If our desperation for meaning and significance drives us toward worldly leaders, we will overlook their toxicity in lieu of the payoff they provide. As the evangelical church has thrived in its technique, technology, skill, rhetoric, platforms, publishing, and building, it has also lost its true power. The power of Christianity is found not in these things but in Christ, who walked the way of the cross. We have focused on the visible when we are called to set our minds on the invisible. Power is choosing the way of love, which is the way of wisdom and faith, against the way of the world, the flesh, and the demonic seeking to seduce us. Leaders in the church are to be the watchmen steering us away from the evil that so easily entangles us, pointing instead to the life God has for us.

DISCERNING THE WAY

Christian leadership must always embody a different form than leadership in the world. Those who are considered leaders in God's kingdom are those defined by wisdom, love, and service. While the evangelical church culture promotes young leaders, Dallas reminds us that youth and wisdom don't usually go hand in hand. Our focus on youth reveals how little concern we have for wisdom, which comes from decades of faithfulness. It is not surprising, therefore, that we've been inundated in recent years with stories about famous pastors having waves crash into their houses, revealing the foundation of sand beneath. We've tasted fruit that looked good and found that it was rotten. But as we reflected on our time with Jim, Marva, James, Jean, John, Eugene, and Dallas, it was clear that these people bore fruit of the kingdom. In their final seasons, all of them were living lives of profound of love and wisdom: They were gracious, kind, gentle, loving, and encouraging. They didn't hesitate to name the way from below when they saw it, but they didn't gloat over this either. They had seen too much, and knew their hearts too completely, to allow arrogance to overtake them.

I (Jamin) heard Dallas speak at his final conference. Others were billing this as his legacy moment. I wondered how he would approach his final chance to proclaim his message. Would he cling desperately to legacy? Would he erect a statue of himself on the stage, demanding that we never forget who he was or what he had done? I sat down with a friend for the final session of the conference, and we were shocked by how counterintuitive Dallas's approach was. He chose to spend his final speaking opportunity blessing others—literally. His final talk was on what it means to bless others and how to do it. He even took the time to bless us personally and directly. This is how a kingdom leader exits the stage. This is how he goes to the grave. He was not seeking to cement his legacy or write a gravestone header for everyone to see. It reminded me of John Calvin's request for an unmarked grave. He wasn't interested in his legacy, but wished for others to shift the attention off of himself to God. Calvin knew something focused on himself was doomed to fail. But God's kingdom has no end. The evil penetrating reality through the world, the flesh, and the demonic shall not defeat it. In Dallas's final moments onstage, he followed Calvin's lead. He left an unmarked grave.

CHAPTER 9

WALKING IN THE WILDERNESS

KYLE AND I QUIT CHURCH AT THE SAME TIME. WE GREW UP in Christian homes, then did what we thought "really serious" Christian kids did and went off to Bible college. We soaked up our theology classes, led on-campus ministries, and regularly attended chapel. Our lives were inundated by things of the faith. In this context, church felt superfluous. We were still committed to following Jesus, but it seemed that everything we needed for life and godliness could be found outside the church. We had come to believe the church was impotent, unnecessary in our quest to follow Jesus. Our personal devotion and the resources provided by our colleges seemed better and more substantial. On campus we had deep community, wise and faithful professors who mentored us, regular chapel to exhort and encourage us, and classes to sharpen our theological convictions. We had all that we needed to live a powerful Christian life without ever having to step foot in the assembly of God's people. What else could the church add?

People give up on church for many reasons. Some are devastated by an abuse of power in leadership, and in a state of disillusionment and hurt, they flee. This kind of departure from the church can entail an exodus from the faith altogether. Others leave for similar reasons as Kyle and I did; their divorce from the church isn't the result of direct conflict or pain, but it's a slow and undefined drift. These people remain committed to growing in Christ, and many, in fact, leave in order to do "big things for the kingdom." The church just doesn't seem necessary to accomplish their spiritual goals. As a pastor, I am aware that there are many people still attending church on Sunday mornings who believe this internally but have yet to leave. Church attendance has been reduced to another ineffectual part of "normal life." Ultimately, many have come to believe that the church really doesn't matter, just as Kyle and I did in college.

One might suspect that the journey Kyle and I embarked on in this book would drive us into another season of suspicion about the church, perhaps this time for more concrete reasons. A sustained observation of the failures of the church might leave us so disenchanted that we couldn't possibly find our way back again. But the sages along our path would never have permitted such foolishness. Their commitment to the church was unwavering, even in the face of faithlessness, because the church rests on Christ's power and faithfulness. In every conversation, no matter how sobering, a tone of hope remained.

FAMILY OF THE WAY

A rejection of the church is a rejection of Jesus' way.[1] Christ made this known: His way of power continues to pour forth in this world by the Spirit through the church. When we come to think that the Christian life is about our own development rather than about our calling in Christ as a family of God, we inevitably confuse the church for a secular entity. The church simply becomes the sum of its parts, which need to be slick, skilled, and led by a guru with a strong vision. Too often people give up on the church because, as a secular entity, it is impotent! But the church is a different sort of venture, on a different sort of mission, with a different power system up and running. People reject the church because they have failed to grasp what it is.

In the Upper Room discourse, Jesus tells his disciples about his upcoming departure. After his resurrection, he will ascend to the right hand of the Father. He will continue to be with his disciples through the ongoing presence of the Holy Spirit, but he will not be present physically. When we turn to the Great Commission, we find ourselves on the precipice of this departure. Jesus, who is the way from above, is ascending above. How will God's power to love continue to go forth in the world? This is precisely what the Great Commission seeks to answer. We read in Matthew 28:18–20: "All authority in heaven and on earth has been given to me. Go therefore and make disciples of all nations, baptizing them in the name of the Father and of the Son and of the Holy Spirit, teaching them to observe all that I have commanded you. And behold, I am with you always, to the end of the age." Incredibly, the disciples are invited to share in the cosmic power of Christ. Jesus says elsewhere, "I saw Satan fall like lightning from heaven. Behold, I have given you authority . . . over all the power of the enemy" (Luke 10:18–19).

Jesus' ascension does not snuff out the candle of God's power, but the eternal flame of God's kingdom burns within a new lantern: The way from above will continue to pour forth in this dark world through the church. The radical nature of this plan is emphasized even further as Jesus states, "Truly, truly, I say to you, whoever believes in me will also do the works that I do; and greater works than these will he do, because I am going to the Father" (John 14:12). Christ guides people in his way through his body—not his physical body (which has now ascended), but his spiritual body, the church. The church was first known as *the people of the Way* (Acts 9:2). The "Way" these people embraced was the way of Jesus—the way of power in weakness for the sake of love. This was not a loosely connected group of individuals, a social club of sorts, but a family united in Christ (Eph. 2:19). It is this ancient family that we now are a part of in Christ by the Spirit. We are bound together as those who live in, through, and for the way. We are the family of the way, called to walk not according to the flesh, but according to the Spirit (Rom. 8:1–8), called to walk the path of Jesus to the cross (Matt. 16:24), and called into his death and resurrection.

We are still prone to walk an old path, one of self-reliance and self-glorification, so we are called to "put off" the old and "put on" the new (Eph. 4:22–24). Putting off the old means dying to the way of the world, the flesh, and the devil. Putting on the new means living into the way of Christ Jesus. Paul sums this up nicely in 2 Corinthians 4:11: "For we who live are always being given over to death for Jesus' sake, so that the life of Jesus also may be manifested in our mortal flesh." The church, therefore, makes manifest the way from above by embracing life in death—power in weakness for love. Remarkably, God makes his way known through his church, not only to a watching world but to spiritual forces as well. We read in Ephesians 3:10: "Through the church the manifold wisdom of God might now be made known to the rulers and authorities in the heavenly places." The church militant is shining the light of the gospel into the dark encampment of the forces of evil.

FAMILY RITUALS

Every family has its rituals. At times they are merely traditional, but often they are chosen. The values and beliefs of a family find their expression in their daily, weekly, and yearly rituals. Some families decide that personal communication and intimacy must be supported through a daily evening meal together uninterrupted by work, friends, or media. Yearly vacations are often a ritual of family life, one that supports the values of relationship, adventure, and rest. Much of the time these daily or yearly rituals are assumed; they are "what our family does." When we get married, we unite with another person who has his or her own history of family rituals, and the clash of these rituals can make for interesting family holidays: "You're not supposed to open presents on Christmas Eve," or maybe "We should never watch television at the dinner table." Our generation may not think we believe in antiquated things like rituals and traditions, but rituals function as the subconscious programming of our expectations and understanding of the world.

The family of God is no different. Every congregation has its own rituals and traditions (not just "liturgical" churches). The same kind of conflict that arises when we experience our in-laws' version of Thanksgiving happens in the life of congregations. "This isn't how we have always done it"; "But we've always gone to this camp"; or even "That's not when or how we do Communion." As I (Jamin) write this, I am a few months into a new pastoral position. I am mindful of the ways in which making even the slightest change can create dissonance in a church body that has an established sense of tradition. Just changing where the piano is onstage can be cause for concern. The truth is, despite our disagreements, there remain several rituals (habits or practices) of the church that are biblically commissioned and historically rooted, and they help shape us into the way from above. In this chapter we seek to explore four of these rituals of the church—baptism, Communion, corporate singing, and reading or preaching the Word—and show how they are means of putting off the ways from below that still reside in our hearts. Before we examine specific rituals, however, we must first show how they are a means by which the people of God are formed in Christ's way.

PRESENTATION, PARTICIPATION, AND PROCLAMATION

I (Kyle) recall a friend venturing into church planting with great enthusiasm. He had a vision to reach his city and make a pronounced kingdom impact. He oriented the church service with a focus on recovering distinctively Christian rituals, believing that these would spark a renewal in the church. It was quickly evident that things weren't having the powerful effect he imagined, so he left his church in search of another way to accomplish his grand vision. In other words, the church had become a vehicle to achieve his vision (one of the greatest idolatries among pastors), and these rituals had failed to give him the edge he needed to leverage his ministry. This exemplifies the subtle temptation to turn the traditions of Christian practice into devices at our disposal—tools to make things happen. Yet it isn't only a temptation for pastors. We all can succumb to a functional rejection of things like Communion or the reading of Scripture because we view them as antiquated and incapable of meeting our "felt needs."

The rituals of the church are an essential means by which the church *presents* herself to the way, *participates* in the way, and ultimately *proclaims* the way. As a means of presenting ourselves to the way, the rituals of the church invite us to offer ourselves as living sacrifices (Rom. 12:1). Every ritual to which Christ calls us invites us to die to the way from below—to put to death our autonomous power to control—and invites us to live and embrace self-giving, sacrificial love. The entire movement of the church service is a way of opening to God's presence and power. These rituals invite us into the rhythm of dying and rising, and are means of participating in, or abiding in, the way from above.[2] As such, these are necessarily cross-shaped means of God's power, and our sharing in them catches us up in this heavenly movement here on earth.

As a means of presenting and participating in the way, these practices are also a means of proclamation. As we have seen, the church is called to make manifest the way from above, and the practices of the church are a means of doing so. Paul's words in Romans 6:13 are instructive for us here: "Do not present your members to sin as instruments of unrighteousness, but present yourselves to God as those who have been brought from death to life, and your members to God as instruments for righteousness." What is made clear by Paul's language in the very next verse is that "sin" here is a personification of the powers.[3] The word for "instruments" can be translated as "weapons." We have weapons to present, either to Christ, as we present ourselves as living sacrifices, or to sin, as we present ourselves as weapons of unrighteousness in the way of death. The language of "weapons" is significant in light of our calling: "For we do not wrestle against flesh and blood, but against the rulers, against the authorities, against the cosmic powers over this present darkness, against the spiritual forces of evil in the heavenly places" (Eph. 6:12). As we present ourselves to God and participate in his way of power through the habits of the church, we are practicing a life against the world, the flesh, and the devil. This is spiritual warfare, and the way we live determines to whom we offer our "weapons" in service. Through the rituals of the church, the Holy Spirit invites us to participate in Christ's triumph over the powers in his death and resurrection. This means that through our ongoing participation in the way of the cross, Christ is continuing to put to shame the powers and principalities of darkness. His work on the cross continues forward by the work of his Spirit through the cruciform church.

RITUALS FORMED IN THE WILDERNESS

Unlike some of our family rituals, the rituals of the church are not arbitrary but were birthed through Israel's journey out of slavery and into freedom. As such, the practices link us to the entirety of God's story. As we look at the story of the exodus, we find a narrative that colorfully informs our understanding of baptism, Communion, singing, and the proclamation of the Word. We can easily forget that the exodus was for proper worship of God. God was calling his people out of Egypt so that they could worship and serve him in the wilderness. When we go to church, therefore, we are reenacting the exodus—the deliverance from the land of slavery into the kingdom of the Son—and are receiving habits of mind and heart to abide in God as we journey through a land that is not our home. Every church service, in this sense, enacts the grand drama of redemption that we might become the kind of people who can thrive in God's kingdom. To be faithful actors in this drama, we must present ourselves to God, open ourselves to participation in God's deliverance, and proclaim the truth of our God who delivers.

The Israelites had endured four hundred years of slavery at the hands of the Egyptians when God heard the groaning of his people and redeemed them through his servant Moses. God not only delivered them out of a land of slavery, but also made good on his promise to lead them to a land where they would live in shalom with him. But before they found refuge in this promised land, they traveled through a very unpromising land in the wilderness.

In one sense, Israel was redeemed when God led them out of Egypt and through the sea, just as we are redeemed when God leads us out of this present evil age: "He has delivered us from the domain of darkness and transferred us to the kingdom of his beloved Son, in whom we have redemption, the forgiveness of sins" (Col. 1:13–14). However, just as the flood cleansed the world but left the roots of sin untouched (planted deeply in the hearts of Noah's family), so too did Israel's journey through the sea and our own journey through the waters of baptism cleanse, without eradicating, sin from our hearts.[4] This became evident in the exodus when Israel continually longed to return to enslavement in Egypt. Egypt still resided in their hearts, even after they were led out of the land (Acts 7:39). Amid freedom, they longed for the comfort of being bound. The wilderness brought out the truth of their hearts—they wanted the familiar, even in the face of God's miraculous deliverance. Similarly, in the face of rituals that seem weak, such as baptism, singing, Communion, and preaching, we often long for something more powerful—something more akin to Pharaoh's power. Israel's own impatience with God's way led them to create and worship a golden calf, and our own impatience tends to bear similar kinds of fruit. As we are being delivered from our flesh and desire for worldly power, we grow impatient and grumble with God, longing for practices of power rather than weakness.

FOLLOWING THE EXODUS OF JESUS

When Jesus is transfigured alongside Moses and Elijah in front of Peter, James, and John, we are told by Luke that he speaks with Moses and Elijah about his upcoming *exodus*. Unhelpfully, this is often translated as his "departure" (Luke 9:28–36). Jesus looked forward to his upcoming death as a retelling of the exodus story of freedom from slavery into life with God. At the cross, freedom from the age of sin, death, and the flesh, and safe passage into the promised land of life with God in Christ by the Spirit, would be realized. In short, Jesus re-narrates the story of the exodus in his own life and work. Consequently, as those found within this exodus of Christ, we are called to reprise the Israelite story in our lives. Romans 6:17–18 tells us, "But thanks be to God, that you who were once slaves of sin have become obedient from the heart to the standard of teaching to which you were committed, and, having been set free from sin, have become slaves of righteousness." We, the family of the way, have been rescued from a land of slavery and are now embarking on a journey to the heavenly promised land. Just like the Israelites, we find ourselves in a wilderness (Heb. 3–4). Just like the Israelites, we are prone to return to our former manner of life, to long for old rituals, and to cling to the strange comfort of tyranny once known in our hearts. The hearts of the Israelites repeatedly turned back toward Egypt in the face of danger, opposition, and need. They reminisced about the days when their stomachs were full (Ex. 16:3); then they made a golden calf like the idols of Egypt (Ex. 32). The wilderness was supposed to be a time of "putting off" the way from below and "putting on" the way from above. The wilderness was supposed to be an education in faithfulness. God led his people in specific ways to shape their hearts and minds to present themselves to God, to participate in his way, and ultimately to proclaim his name to the world (Isa. 49:6). These now serve as types for our own exodus from worldliness to life in the kingdom. As we travel through the wilderness of the world, longing for the heavenly city (Heb. 11:16), God has given us particular rituals designed to guide our feet toward the promised land set before us, not to follow the example of Israel but to follow God in faithfulness:

> I do not want you to be unaware, brothers, that our fathers were all under the cloud, and all passed through the sea, and all were baptized into Moses in the cloud and in the sea, and all ate the same spiritual food, and all drank the same spiritual drink. For they drank from the spiritual Rock that followed them, and the Rock was Christ. Nevertheless, with most of them God was not pleased, for they were overthrown in the wilderness. Now these things took place as examples for us, that we might not desire evil as they did. (1 Cor. 10:1–6)

We are now in a different sort of wilderness—led out of the world and into the kingdom of Christ—awaiting the promised land that will come when Christ returns. We journey in this wilderness daily, knowing God's presence is with us but also longing for the day when he will be present in full. But there is also a time we set aside for togetherness that serves to calibrate the tune of our hearts to the kingdom of Christ. When the people traveled through the wilderness, rescued from the harsh work of slavery, they were given the command to set aside a day of rest. It is hard to grasp how counterintuitive this was, particularly after the overbearing command to work from Pharaoh. Christians have historically located our day of Sabbath in the resurrection of Christ. As churches gather on Sunday, they engage in certain rituals, specific to this day of Sabbath, which are not known the other six days of the week. On our day of rest we remember our own leaving behind the land of slavery (the world, the flesh, and the devil), and we fix our hearts on the journey toward the promised land. While Sabbath might have seemed odd, lazy, and utterly counterintuitive, it was God's way of realigning the hearts of his people to his way. Our actions on the Sabbath day will seem odd and worthless to others as well, but when they are grounded in God's work to bring us through the wilderness and into his kingdom, they reveal God's deep recalibration of our hearts to his way.

BAPTISM: DYING TO FLESH AND RISING IN CHRIST

Soon after the Israelites found themselves released from the clutches of Egypt, they faced a familiar foe in the wilderness. Trapped between the Red Sea and Pharaoh's army bearing down on them, things seemed hopeless. It appeared to anyone with worldly wisdom that God had made a tactical error in his plan by leading the Israelites into a defenseless, perilous position (Ex. 14). This was Israel's first challenge in the wilderness. God rescued the Israelites not by creating an alternate route, but by calling them through the same body of water that would ultimately kill Pharaoh and his army. The Israelites had to journey through the water of death in order to journey toward the promised land. Picking up this theme, Paul exhorts, "Do you not know that all of us who have been baptized into Christ Jesus were baptized into his death? We were buried therefore with him by baptism into death, in order that, just as Christ was raised from the dead by the glory of the Father, we too might walk in newness of life. For if we have been united with him in a death like his, we shall certainly be united with him in a resurrection like his" (Rom. 6:3–5).

Just as the Israelites passed through the water of death on their way toward the promised land, Christians enter the water of death in baptism that we "might walk in newness of life." In baptism we present ourselves to the pattern of Christ's death and resurrection that we may die to our old selves and rise to embrace lives that are "hidden with Christ in God" (Col. 3:3). In this watery death we put off our self-empowered and controlling manner of life to participate in Christ's way of power in weakness for the sake of love. But also in baptism we leave Egypt behind us—the age of sin and death no longer defines and controls us—"For the law of the Spirit of life has set you free in Christ Jesus from the law of sin and death" (Rom. 8:2). Just as Egypt was put to shame by God's defeat of their gods, so too in our baptism is Satan put to shame. Baptism connects us to Christ's victory over the powers of sin and death at the cross because we are baptized into Christ. This act is a proclamation of the "powerful working of God" who raised us from the dead with Christ (Col. 2:12). Each and every baptism serves as a manifestation of God's way and, as we witness baptisms, we can celebrate the power of God in his deliverance.

SINGING: LONGING FOR THE GOD OF POWER

When God's people saw how the Lord had rescued them from death, they worshipped him. In Exodus 14:31 we are told, "Israel saw the great power that the LORD used against the Egyptians, so the people feared the LORD, and they believed in the LORD and in his servant Moses." This people, who had once improperly feared Pharaoh, now properly feared the Lord. In awe of God's power, their hearts turned to faith in him. We read in Exodus 15 that the response of their hearts was to corporately give God praise. Similarly, we gaze upon the exodus of Jesus, the defeat of the powers of evil and death at the cross, and the only fitting response is praise. We have seen God's mighty power on the move in our lives, so we present ourselves to him in worship. And yet, presenting ourselves in worship entails honesty about where we are. We are in the wilderness before Christ's return, and thus worship will entail not only praise, but also lament. The Lord calls us to worship "in spirit and truth" (John 4:24); therefore we must never neglect the truth of our hearts and its connection to what our lips proclaim. Even in our praise we are called to participate in the way of the cross. We may find ourselves crying out to God much as Jesus did in the Garden of Gethsemane: "My God, my God, why have you forsaken me?" (Mark 15:34).

If we are to share in the exodus of Christ, surely our singing will include songs of desperation like the ones we see in Christ's prayer in Gethsemane and the songs of the Psalter. Whether in praise or lament, our worship of God in the wilderness is a proclamation of his power. We are the people who cry out to God in lament, praise, petition, joy, and fear from our hearts, that we might journey in truth with the God who has rescued us from death and leads us in life. In the book of Revelation we read that a new song is sung in heaven that only the redeemed can learn (14:3). Likewise, there is a sense in which we are all learning the song we will sing for eternity, but we are still out of tune in the flesh and still tone-deaf because of the world. In this proclamation of our hearts, we are trusting that our God is the God who hears, and that our singing is not desperate futility, but the longing of love. Through such singing we participate in Christ's ongoing defeat of the powers and principalities. It may seem foolish and inconsequential, perhaps as effective as blowing trumpets while marching around the walls of an enemy city (Josh. 6), but the battle cry is the outpouring of a people of love who live and thrive in the kingdom of love. Our song is a hopeful longing to the day when every tear will be wiped away, and when we will be participants in the wedding feast of the Lamb.

COMMUNION: EATING THE MEAL OF POWER

As the Israelites journeyed through the wilderness, they were in a land bereft of basic human necessities: water and food. When the people "came to the wilderness of Sin" (Ex. 16:1), they grumbled against Moses because they were hungry. They longed for sustenance. God had rescued them from a land of slavery, but now they found themselves in a cruel, dry land, very hungry, and no doubt very weak. God provided for their need and rained down manna from heaven. Jesus again pulls this part of the exodus story into his own life and work, proclaiming, "Truly, truly, I say to you, it was not Moses who gave you the bread from heaven, but my Father gives you the true bread from heaven. For the bread of God is he who comes down from heaven and gives life to the world. . . . I am the bread of life; whoever comes to me shall not hunger, and whoever believes in me shall never thirst" (John 6:32–33, 35). In the wilderness of faith there is only one source of nourishment: Jesus.

So we come to the Communion Table desperately in need of food and drink. We present ourselves to God as those who are weak. At the Communion Table we acknowledge that it is in Jesus' death that we have life, and it is in weakness that we find power. We read in John 6:53–56: "Jesus said to them, 'Truly, truly, I say to you, unless you eat the flesh of the Son of Man and drink his blood, you have no life in you. Whoever feeds on my flesh and drinks my blood has eternal life, and I will raise him up on the last day. For my flesh is true food, and my blood is true drink. Whoever feeds on my flesh and drinks my blood abides in me, and I in him.'" We need his provision, lest we die.

To come to the table of the Lord, therefore, is to come to a place where our hearts and bodies are shown a new kind of longing. In our flesh, we do not call out for these things. In our flesh, we avoid even talking about death. But at the Lord's Table, we come to partake in the meal of Christ's death so that we might "proclaim the Lord's death until he comes" (1 Cor. 11:26). As we share in the death of Christ at the table, we make manifest the power of his way. As Jesus shared the wine and the bread with his disciples, he made it clear that this meal was for the sake of remembering his work on the cross (Luke 22:14–20). This practice invites us to seek life in an unusual place, Jesus' death, and it quenches our thirst precisely where Jesus called out, "I thirst" (John 19:28). Partaking in this kind of meal unveils the peculiarity of the kingdom we are called into.

From the perspective of worldly power, this practice is meaningless and feeble. Perhaps this is the reason so many evangelical churches have dismissed Communion from regular practice in corporate worship. In the Lord's Supper we proclaim a power in weakness for the sake of love that is foolishness to the world. Such a proclamation is the result of not merely the facets of the ritual, but the way in which the ritual is practiced. When Jesus established this meal as the centerpiece of community life for the people of the way, he did so in the context of washing his disciples' feet. Jesus was demonstrating the way of power and leadership he was calling his followers into (John 13:15). Power in the kingdom gives birth to service, rather than power forcing servitude as the world continually presumes. But the table flattens out the hierarchies we like to create. At the table, we all come equally; and at the table, the power structures of the world collapse. As much as we tend to reject this idea, we do not come to this table only as individuals, but as members of a family, as brothers and sisters in Christ.

The Communion Table is a place of partaking in the love of Christ at the cross, and therefore receiving the kind of love that Christ offers. Similarly, to partake in this meal is to receive and accept the call to love Christ's body, and to give ourselves to one another in life and in death (John 15:13). The Communion Table, therefore, provides us with a pattern of reconciliation for the church. It is here that we walk the way of power to love, humbly receiving what we cannot create in our own power, but manifesting the way from above alongside those with whom we would not normally share a meal. Furthermore, with John Perkins, we see that reconciliation is not simply an act of love, but an act of love against the powers and principalities of the world. Communion is the meal of those who are enemies of the way from below; believers who trust in the bread from heaven rather than the bread of Egypt.

PREACHING AND PUBLIC READING: HEARING THE WORD OF POWER

The people of God traveled through the wilderness and headed to the promised land, saved through the waters of death and nurtured by the manna of heaven, and found themselves encamped at the foot of Mount Sinai (Ex. 19:2). These weak and needy pilgrims had been provided for in many ways, but here they were given a unique gift, the Word of God. In Exodus 20 God speaks a Word we are most familiar with, the Ten Commandments, and the response of the people is interesting: "They stood far off and said to Moses, 'You speak to us, and we will listen; but do not let God speak to us, lest we die'" (Ex. 20:18–19). They were in need of a Word that would clarify the nature of their relationship with God and their unique vocation as his people. They had journeyed out of Egypt, and now this Word was going to call the way of Egypt out of them. They were given tablets of stone with the Word of God written by the finger of God (Ex. 31:18) so that they could have the Word with them; and they were given Moses, who could proclaim the Word to them. Without this Word, they were helpless, lacking in wisdom and understanding of God's ways. But the people of God did not listen with soft hearts. They hardened their hearts against him. We too are now given the warning against a hardened heart: "Today, if you hear his voice, do not harden your hearts as in the rebellion, on the day of testing in the wilderness, where your fathers put me to the test" (Heb. 3:7–9).

Our journey through the wilderness of faith is much the same as the Israelites'. Having been saved from a land of sin and death, and now headed to the promised land, we too are in need of a Word from God. We need to hear from him. The two rituals of the church that fulfill this aspect of Israel's narrative are preaching and the public reading of Scripture. In both, the Word of God is proclaimed. Paul encourages Timothy, "Until I come, devote yourself to the public reading of Scripture, to exhortation, to teaching" (1 Tim. 4:13). In both rituals, the people of God are called to stand under the Word and be listeners. The centrality of the public reading of Scripture, and possibly the reason for its absence in so many churches, is that the Scriptures read aloud cannot be controlled or filtered to our liking. In the public reading of Scripture, we hear the raw proclamation of God through his Word and must receive it, in the Spirit, as a Word for us. A public proclamation of Scripture helps to keep the preacher accountable to the Word that was read. But while the public reading of Scripture is straightforward, preaching is less so.

The proclamation of the Word of God in preaching is a Christ-centered and cruciform reality. As Paul says about his own preaching, I "preach Christ crucified" (1 Cor. 1:23). This kind of preaching calls for listeners with ears to hear, who have become attuned to the wisdom from above (1 Cor. 1:21). As such, this kind of preaching is a "stumbling block to Jews and folly to Gentiles.... For the foolishness of God is wiser than men, and the weakness of God is stronger than men" (1 Cor. 1:23, 25). The word preached should always point to Christ, trusting that where Christ is illumined his way will shine forth.

Whereas the Israelites waited for Moses to bring the word from the Lord down the mountain, we are those who have received the Word of God descended in the flesh to live among us (John 1). Whereas the Israelites cowered under the descending fire from God, we are empowered by the fire of the Spirit that descended on Pentecost. As the author of Hebrews says, "Long ago, at many times and in many ways, God spoke to our fathers by the prophets, but in these last days he has spoken to us by his Son" (Heb. 1:1–2). Now, to hear in spirit and in truth, we must be those who are attending in our hearts to the Word that commands our lives. When we listen to a sermon, we surrender our own word as the authority, bowing a knee to the Word of God that leaves us "naked and exposed" before him (Heb. 4:13). It is in listening to the Word in the Spirit, opening our hearts to that Word, that we can become those who know his voice (John 10:27).

When Paul articulates the power of his own preaching he says, "My speech and my message were not in plausible words of wisdom, but in demonstration of the Spirit and of power, so that your faith might not rest in the wisdom of men but in the power of God" (1 Cor. 2:4–5). The power of preaching is that it points to Christ.

Preaching Christ crucified is a continual invitation to the body of Christ to participate in Jesus' way of death and resurrection. When this happens the church proclaims the way from above. Whereas the world's wisdom and proclamation came in sophisticated rhetoric and attractive style, Paul's own preaching rejected "lofty speech," what the world would call "wisdom," and came in "weakness and in fear and much trembling" (1 Cor. 2:1–3). Importantly, and somewhat provocatively, Paul proclaims that Christ sent him "to preach the gospel, and not with words of eloquent wisdom, lest the cross of Christ be emptied of its power" (1 Cor. 1:17). It is not only that the mode of Paul's message *should* match its substance, but they *must* align for God's power to be known. The way from above is proclaimed through Christ-centered, cross-focused preaching, both in its heralding and in its reception.

Everything for the Christian begins with "God said."[5] We are those called to stand under the Word, to hear the Word, and to become the kinds of people who can actually receive the Word God proclaims (Heb. 5:11–14). Like Israel in the wilderness, we are those who have the Word proclaimed over us as the Word is read aloud, and we are those who have received the written Word of God. The Word we hear is always the Word of the cross, and we are those who either harden our hearts or soften them to the way of God. This means that the corollary practice of reading Scripture and preaching is listening. The people of God are hearers primarily, because our God is the God who has spoken, and who claims, "For as the rain and the snow come down from heaven and do not return there but water the earth . . . so shall my word be that goes out from my mouth; it shall not return to me empty, but it shall accomplish that which I purpose" (Isa. 55:10–11). The purpose of this Word is to lead God's people in deliverance to the way of the kingdom. Likewise, the author of Hebrews admonishes, "Therefore we must pay much closer attention to what we have heard, lest we drift away from it";

and "Today, if you hear his voice, do not harden your hearts as in the rebellion" (Heb. 2:1; 3:15). The Word comes to us "today" because, in the Spirit, God's Word still speaks. The Word of God is not dead and lifeless, but alive and active; and it exposes the depth of the human heart before God (Heb. 4:12–13).

CO-OPTED RITUALS

Unfortunately, the very rituals that are intended to be ongoing means of walking the way from above can become devices of power to control. Just practicing baptism, Communion, singing, and the reading or preaching of the Word is not a guarantee of our participating in the power of God. We must be watchful and on guard, even in the practices of the church (1 Peter 5:8). The practices can quickly become co-opted by the powers and principalities. Paul admonishes those who walk in Christ to be on guard against the "elemental spirits of the world" (Col. 2:8), something he claims he and his audience were enslaved to as children (Gal. 4:3). Paul claims that these elemental spirits (or elemental principles) undermine the rituals and practices of the faith, causing them to be used in the flesh and not the Spirit. (Such practices included dietary restrictions, festivals, Sabbath, and even the Law; see Gal. 3:23–4:5; Col. 2:16.) Paul's language here is quite provocative. The things of the faith, even the Law, can be co-opted by the way from below. The powers and principalities can manipulate any of the rituals of the church while we still practice them in the wilderness. With the most devious of deceptions, the very practices given to us to align our hearts to the way from above can become co-opted. This deception lulls the modern church to sleep amid a battle for her soul.

The rituals of the church can be used to propagate the way from below, and this can happen in leadership as easily as it can happen in the hearts of everyone else present. The sermon can be used to prop up the idol of personality, where the crucified Christ is not preached, but instead the pastor is glorified. Baptism can be used as a means of control and self-congratulatory growth for the church, where baptisms are tallied because they look nice on our ministry scorecard, and individual members bask in the feeling that big things are happening. We can sing songs, take Communion, and sit under beautiful preaching while harboring the world in our hearts. These aren't just minor missteps in our style or approach, but debilitating distortions of the rituals of Christ's family. Cross-shaped endeavors are not merely to be done, but to be done Jesus' way.

When the rituals of the church are infused with the way from below, the church voids the cross of its power. When this happens we manifest the wrong kingdom. We become weapons of unrighteousness. We see this in Corinth, as Paul critiques the Corinthian church for their practice of Communion, admonishing, "But in the following instructions I do not commend you, because when you come together it is not for the better but for the worse" (1 Cor. 11:17). They were rejecting the way of Jesus even as they partook in the meal of Jesus, and this meant that they weren't eating the meal of Jesus at all (1 Cor. 11:20). They voided Communion of its meaning entirely by embracing a way contrary to the cross. It had become a meal done in power and status instead of weakness and love.

What does it take to be watchful over the rituals of the church, so that we might not become like the Corinthians? First, we must be watchful over our own hearts. We are all duplicitous in our walk. While we walk in the way from above, we continue to flirt with the path of the world, the flesh, and the devil. As such, when we come to church and participate in the family rituals, we carry unhealthy beliefs and desires with us. When we approach the practices of the church, we must be honest and repentant in our self-reflection before the Lord. We may stand before the Communion Table and realize our hearts scoff at the notion that this is the source of life, in the same way the religious leaders scoffed at Jesus upon the cross. In this sense, the practices of the church are always a mirror to our hearts. The rituals of the church are a means of exposing our commitment to the way from below. The cross-shaped nature of the rituals unveils our continued desires for control and domination. In short, the rituals reveal where we truly believe power is found.

Second, we must remain watchful over our particular community. The rituals serve as an excellent mirror here as well. If we want to know the degree to which our church continues to embrace power to control, we need look no further than the way we actually engage the rituals of the family. If we find that preaching is the centerpiece of everything we do—not because of our hunger for the Word, but because of our affinity for a particular speaker's personality, wit, or stage presence—we can discern that our community is in need of repentance. If we find that Communion no longer has a spot in our corporate worship because it doesn't fit the kind of atmosphere we seek to develop, or because it is too logistically difficult to do in our service, we know we have something to repent of. As we allow the Lord to use the rituals of his body as a means of mirroring the truth of our hearts, so too must we bring our entire congregation before the Lord as we practice them, asking that he search our hearts as a community and see if there be any wicked way in us (Ps. 139).

In the book of Revelation, Jesus refers to the church as a lampstand (Rev. 1:20). With this image we are drawn back to the idea with which we started this chapter, namely that Christ's light is to shine forth through the church. What we discover in Revelation is that there are seven lampstands (churches) to whom Christ speaks a specific word. We are told that Jesus walks among these churches (Rev. 1:13; 2:1) and that he knows they have submitted to the way from below. He has searched them and known them, and he calls them to repentance (Rev. 2:16, 23). For example, he says to the church in Laodicea, "For you say, I am rich, I have prospered, and I need nothing, not realizing that you are wretched, pitiable, poor, blind, and naked. I counsel you to buy from me gold refined by fire, so that you may be rich. . . . So be zealous and repent" (Rev. 3:17–19). The spiritual battle these churches face, in succumbing to the way from below, is repeatedly brought to the forefront (Rev. 2:9–10, 13). The churches are to guard themselves against "the deep things of Satan" (Rev. 2:24), lest they become like a "synagogue of Satan" (Rev. 2:9; 3:9). Jesus warns them that if repentance does not take place, he will come and "remove [their] lampstand from its place" (Rev. 2:5). The cosmic context of our churches, standing in the spiritual realm with Christ walking among us, is a reality we rarely submit to. We continue to stand with the seven churches of Revelation as those found faithful in some things and unfaithful in others. The call to repent, therefore, is ours to hear. Christ walks among us, searching and knowing the truth of his body, calling for us to have ears to hear and eyes to see. The warning that echoes forth ominously through the ages is that if we fail to repent, he may remove our lampstand. The question we have to wrestle with is: If he does, would we even notice?

THE WAY OF TRIUMPH

The church that does have eyes to see and ears to hear is the church that walks in the triumph of God. We read in 2 Corinthians 2:14–16: "Thanks be to God, who in Christ always leads us in triumphal procession, and through us spreads the fragrance of the knowledge of him everywhere. For we are the aroma of Christ to God among those who are being saved and among those who are perishing, to one a fragrance from death to death, to the other a fragrance from life to life." If we are not careful, we can begin to think that our triumphing means that we do, in fact, have the power we are so desperate for. We are a powerful agent of God "triumphing" in the world.

This is often how this passage is understood, but it is actually saying something quite different. The image we get in this passage is not of the church triumphing, but of one who has been triumphed over. The image of triumph had a cultural correspondence for the Corinthians of Paul's day. Triumphing was an allusion to the Roman processionals following a victory in war.[6] As New Testament scholar Paul Barnett states, "The verb was not used to describe victorious troops but defeated prisoners who had been brought to Rome to be paraded as the spoils of war."[7] What the apostle Paul is telling us here is that in Christ God has triumphed over us, and in him we are now paraded before a watching world. We are caught in the victory parade of Christ, celebrating his defeat of the world, the flesh, and the devil. The image is not of our power, but God's. We are viewed in a position of weakness. And yet, as the church embraces the role of Christ's captive, we make Christ's way known in the world.

As we walk the way from above, continually embracing our own dying and rising through the rituals of the church, we emit a fragrant aroma. The language of aroma evokes an image of sacrifice, and our "spiritual worship" requires that we "present [our] bodies as a living sacrifice" (Rom. 12:1). Paul goes on to add, "And do not be conformed to this world, but be transformed by the renewing of your mind, so that you may prove what the will of God is, that which is good and acceptable and perfect" (Rom. 12:2 NASB). At Sinai, the Israelites learned that leaving Egypt was not simply a location change. They had moved out of one way of life into another. Like the Israelites, we too are confronted with the unusual way of power that God presents to us, as he calls us out of the world and into the way of his kingdom more and more. We too feel like a fragile people wandering in the wilderness, and we too receive commands that seem odd—to organize our week around rest (Sabbath), to care for our neighbor, and to place God above all else.[8] These ways may not seem like the path of power, but they are the ways of the kingdom.

The formative education of the church is to renew our minds and hearts around the way from above as we participate in the family rituals of Christ. Each Sunday we participate in an exodus of the soul: repenting of the worldliness within and walking through the wilderness into the ways of the kingdom. The rituals are not magic, nor are they mechanistic ways of formation; they are means of abiding. Walter Brueggemann narrates the exodus helpfully: "Without knowing what would happen at the mountain with YHWH or what it would be like to meet the emancipator God of the exodus, Israel came to the mountain to enact and acknowledge 'regime change,' an embrace of the rule of God of the covenant as an alternative to the rule of Pharaoh, who was still so well remembered."[9] Each week we bear witness to this regime change, but only if we come to hear the Word anew, relive our journey through the sea of baptism, praise him for who he is and what he has done, and partake in the meal that sustains us on this particular journey. As we give ourselves to these practices of the wilderness, we learn the way of eternity; and the orientation of loving God and neighbor becomes the recognized tune of God's kingdom.

CHAPTER 10

THE WAY OF RESISTANCE

I (JAMIN) WISH I COULD SAY OUR JOURNEY THESE PAST few years completely overhauled my view of power. By the grace of God there has been significant transformation of my heart. I am more and more willing to embrace my weakness and pursue the way of love in the face of evil. And yet, there are times when I fully commit myself to the way from below. When faced with challenges in ministry, I turn inward looking for the strength I need, rather than going out to a God who has promised to be my strength. As my writing "career" grows, I am tempted to grasp for control when I sense an opportunity for greater influence. When I come face-to-face with problems at work, my first thought can be, *How can I just fix this?* rather than *What does it mean to abide in Christ here?*

I am learning what it means to embrace power to love. Perhaps nowhere more consistently than in parenting. Fatherhood is a vocation vested with power. Discipline, instruction, and protection are all facets of fatherly power. Children (shockingly enough!) don't always respond to fatherly power with humility, openness, and appreciation. They misbehave. They reject wise instruction and grasp foolishness. In these moments I am presented with two options of power: I can seek to control my kids and force them to bend to my will so that I feel powerful, instructing them and disciplining them for the sake of keeping them "under control." Or

I can choose the way of power to love. I can embrace my rightful position of authority in my instruction and discipline, but do so in love and for the sake of love. Sometimes I succeed and sometimes I fail. I am growing in the way from above. I am on a journey.

I (Kyle) have had a similar experience these past several years. I have struggled against the power structures of the academy with its built-in system of value and status. I am still allured by these things. But even in my weakness, as I long to follow in the way of Christ, the power of God is at work. I often consider Jean, who resisted systemic evil and dehumanization by giving himself in love. I think of James and Rita, and the love they shared until the end of their life together. Their love was like a flower that had broken through cement to bask in the sun, as they fought through sickness to be faithful unto death. I think about Marva, who struggles with continual pain to stand firm against evil, using whatever God has given her to resist the powers and principalities. I think of John and the dehumanization, oppression, and racism he looked in the face, and how he turned to love so that he could save his enemies. I think of Eugene and Dallas and how they modeled the way from above in vocations that ceased to value it. I found hope in these brothers and sisters because I saw their imitation of Christ enfleshed before my eyes.

The sages we met showed us a close connection between how they gave themselves to the body of Christ and how they lived the entirety of their lives. The rituals of our church family should correspond with our identity, value system, and approach to life as a whole. There should be a harmony between the church, our household, and our individual life. But like Israel in the wilderness, we can easily be led through these rituals without the desired effect. Our ability to walk faithfully through the practices is directly connected with our life lived in the world, and our ability to walk with Christ in the world is connected to how we give ourselves to the family rituals of the body of Christ. The interwoven tunes are either harmonious or discordant—leading to unity in purpose or hypocritical disenchantment.

In ancient churches, and some modern ones, stained-glass windows catch your attention quickly when you enter the building. Unlike paintings, the windows were always to be understood as windows—things you look through, not things you simply look at. You look "through" a stained-glass window by seeing the outside world as defined by the true depiction of reality in the window. The windows are supposed to be portals into reality. Similarly, the movement of our church services as a re-narration of Israel's deliverance from Egypt should tune our hearts to the way of God in the world—so that when we leave, our hearts are still tuned that way. The whole of our lives should be formed by the harmony of God's order, and should therefore become more and more obviously out of tune with the world.

It may feel more like we are bringing the harmony of the world to church. We struggle to pay attention, let alone have our hearts tuned to the way of God. Confronted with the aspects of our hearts that the wilderness raises within us, we may fight against the Spirit, grit our teeth, dig in our heels, and just do it our own way. Or we can try to hide, hoping that if we don't think about how much our flesh still governs us, God won't notice. These responses are driven by fear. We are so overwhelmed that we don't want to face the truth of our hearts. However, we need not fear, "for whenever our heart condemns us, God is greater than our heart, and he knows everything" (1 John 3:20). The way from above exposes our hearts, but the exposure is an opportunity to abide in Christ and not desperately seek to create a self in our own power. The practices of the wilderness are practices of exposure that lead us into abiding trust.

This abiding trust, what we can call prayerful abiding, is the tune of the Christian's heart whose cadence is love. The practices of the wilderness, alongside all Christian practice, must be grounded in habits of mind and heart that conform to the same movements of God's own holiness. As Christians, we are not simply trying to be good, or even trying to achieve holiness; as Christians, we are those who live in Christ, who is holy, and we are those indwelt by the *Holy* Spirit himself (God's own Spirit of Holiness). Then to learn and grow in the Christian life, we need to have a certain rhythm of heart that is tuned by the grace of God; and the only way to have one's heart tuned to God's grace is to have access to the Father, in the Son, by the Spirit (Eph. 2:18). We become tuned to God's life as we live in his presence. Even though God's presence will expose our idolatries, fears, and anxieties, we must come to walk with him. The world we journey in now is the wilderness of the Christian. The challenge of living in this particular wilderness is not merely external, in which we fight opposing forces from without. There is an internal reality to this wilderness, in which we must navigate the depths of our souls, souls that still long for the things of this world. As we are delivered from our enslavement, we must not only engage in practices with the body, but also open in the freedom of the Spirit to have our hearts move in harmony with the kingdom.

INNER POSTURES OF POWER

We often suppose that our inner lives are irrelevant to our service. This is simply naive. As Kyle and I have become aware, we show up at work every day with our hearts in our hands. If our lives are chaotic and our hearts are anxious, we cannot simply pause for an hour to craft a sermon or prepare a lecture in a way that is meaningful and thoughtful. It just doesn't work that way. Our lives are integrated. My ability to thoughtfully counsel a couple in my office

and Kyle's ability to think deeply while studying a difficult theological text are informed by who we are.

To live out the way from above, to actively walk the way of
Jesus, we have to move with both our bodies and our hearts. We
read in James 1:22–25:

> But be doers of the word, and not hearers only, deceiving your-
> selves. For if anyone is a hearer of the word and not a doer, he
> is like a man who looks intently at his natural face in a mirror.
> For he looks at himself and goes away and at once forgets what
> he was like. But the one who looks into the perfect law, the law
> of liberty, and perseveres, being no hearer who forgets but a
> doer who acts, he will be blessed in his doing.

Hearing and doing the Word is not a mechanistic act, as if our
calling in sanctification is just doing the right thing. Our inner
lives need ordering. We need habits, as we've seen, not simply of
body, but of heart. Family rituals fail when the bodies move but the
hearts are left behind; they become hollow acts of tradition without
the values, narrative, or purpose that fueled their original creation.
For the rituals of the church family, our hearts and bodies need to
be in harmony as we present ourselves as living sacrifices to God
(Rom. 12:1). This is a call to put on the armor of God, to embrace
Jesus *and* his way, so that we can enter our battle against evil with
a Christian kind of strategy. We read in Ephesians 6:10–18:

> Finally, be strong in the Lord and in the strength of his might.
> Put on the whole armor of God, that you may be able to stand
> against the schemes of the devil. For we do not wrestle against
> flesh and blood, but against the rulers, against the authorities,
> against the cosmic powers over this present darkness, against
> the spiritual forces of evil in the heavenly places. Therefore

take up the whole armor of God, that you may be able to withstand in the evil day, and having done all, to stand firm. Stand therefore, having fastened on the belt of truth, and having put on the breastplate of righteousness, and, as shoes for your feet, having put on the readiness given by the gospel of peace. In all circumstances take up the shield of faith, with which you can extinguish all the flaming darts of the evil one; and take the helmet of salvation, and the sword of the Spirit, which is the word of God, *praying at all times in the Spirit*, with all prayer and supplication (emphasis added).

In this passage Paul reorients our understanding of standing against evil and engaging in battle. At every turn, the armor of God is an issue of the deepest parts of our souls, entailing an embrace of truth, a cultivation of righteousness, a readiness of heart, and a strength of faith. Unlike real armor, these things are not external to us like clothing and the tools of war. The armor of God requires that we internalize these realities so that our hearts become tuned to truth, righteousness, readiness, faith, and the Word. How are we to put on such armor? How are we to become faithful soldiers in the spiritual battle God has called us to participate in? Paul's answer points us to the work of God and the posture of our hearts. Our weapons are hewn by the Word and Spirit, and our fighting stance is prayer.

THE POSTURE OF PRAYER

Beginning with prayer is not merely a tip of the hat to God. It's not a cliché: "Don't forget to pray first." Rather, we begin with a posture of abiding in, and depending upon, God in the deep places of our hearts, because God is the source and goal of our power. When we open our hearts in prayerful abiding, what we first discover is that we have false beliefs residing there. Therefore, we don't begin with prayer as a device for getting things done, but as a means of communing with God who transforms the heart and leads us in the way. Prayer is being with God who is always with us, and "being with" necessitates honesty. We are with God in the truth of our hearts. In prayer we open our hearts to his loving presence, exposing areas where unbelief reigns. Only his presence can purge these places of darkness and form them in love. In prayer we enter into the reality of our power in weakness, particularly when we "cease to set the agenda" in prayer and when we "'make space' for God to be God."¹ In prayer we can know the silence and lament of the psalmist, ceasing to strive in the power of ourselves and, in our silence, knowing that *he* is God.

In prayer we embrace our weakness and depend upon God's power to transform the heart. The heart is the first, but not the only, battlefield where God's power in weakness must conquer in love. We can call this conquering of the heart "recollection," and prayer is where we find recollection for the heart. The word *recollected* or *recollection* is not often used these days, even though the term was one of the more important words to describe the Christian life in early Protestant spirituality. John Fletcher, an eighteenth-century evangelical writer, describes recollection this way:

> Recollection is a dwelling within ourselves; a being abstracted from the creature, and turned towards God. Recollection is both outward and inward. Outward recollection consists in silence from all idle and superfluous words: and in solitude, or a wise disentanglement from the world, keeping to our own business, observing and following the order of God for ourselves, and shutting the ear against all curious and unprofitable matters. Inward recollection consists in shutting the door of the senses, in a deep attention to the presence of God,

and in a continual care of entertaining holy thoughts for fear of spiritual idleness.[2]

Recollection is not merely remembering, but re-collecting the truth of oneself in Christ. We need recollection because we are prone to lose ourselves; we attach ourselves to things other than God in search of power and value. We attach ourselves to work, to people, and to accomplishments. We lose ourselves in the world, and *the world* is not neutral in the cosmic battle. In prayer we recollect ourselves in the truth that power and value are found in Christ alone and that our life is hidden with Christ in God (Col. 3:3). In this sense, prayer is where we embrace our finitude, our frailty, our neediness, and the truth of our identity as beloved children of the Father in Christ by the Spirit. Recollection is not something we generate, but something we are invited into. We come to know the truth of our identity as we abide in honest relationship with God in prayer.

The posture of prayerful abiding is a way of life, but it also entails intentionality. For many of us, our lives are dominated by noise, busyness, and a melodic chaos that never ceases. More so today than ever before, we are inundated with distraction. As a result, silence and solitude are incredibly helpful practices to intentionally open ourselves to the kind of prayer needed to live the way of the kingdom. Even in the first-century world, which did not have anywhere near the kinds of distractions our world has, Jesus retreated alone, away from the crowds and his disciples (Matt. 14:23; Mark 1:35; Luke 4:42). Jesus recognized, as have Christians throughout the centuries, that silence and solitude are helpful practices in being attuned to Jesus' way of living in the world.

Giving ourselves to times of silence and solitude helps to expose the ways in which our lives are truly oriented by distraction, achievement, and escapism. Silence and solitude reveal the ways in which we are swimming in the stream of worldly power and we aren't even aware of it. We do not practice silence and solitude as a means of self-help, or to feel better about ourselves, but to be with God in the truth of ourselves and open to his movement of love. The formation of a person who is prayerfully abiding in Christ leads to maturity, and Christian maturity is defined by discernment and wisdom. Prayerfulness, silence, recollection, and peace allow us to stand under the Word in truth, not dulling our hearing but becoming "those who have their powers of discernment trained by constant practice to distinguish good from evil" (Heb. 5:14).

The posture of prayerful abiding is what allows us to grasp the rituals of the family deeply. As we richly embrace these rituals we can, in turn, carry that tune into our lives, relationships, and households. Abiding in the love of God becomes the oil that greases the interlocking gears of our homes, churches, and individual lives. By the presence of the Spirit we can find the harmony of love interconnecting every aspect of our lives. This is not something we achieve alone. We must give ourselves to God such that he tunes our hearts to himself.

RESISTING FROM WITHIN

Hearts tuned to the grace of God in prayerful abiding and love will instinctively harmonize with three broad expressions of the way: generosity, reconciliation, and nondivisive resistance. While there are many more expressions, these three are central inclinations that account well for the kind of resistance Christians are called to *within* the church. But this means we have to become the kinds of people who can live this way in community, in our worship together, in our listening, and in our openness to the Word proclaimed. These things do not happen by magic, as much as we might desire that. We are called to individual acts of generosity, reconciliation, and nondivisive resistance so that we can partake in a community that embodies these things and is known by its love. While more could be said, we highlight these three expressions because they exemplify areas in the church today where we tend to capitulate to the way from below. We too easily turn away from generosity, away from reconciliation, and toward divisive acts of resistance that leave the church fractured. The way of prayerful abiding in love should always be pressed into this three-fold mold, because a prayerful life witnesses to the way from above by exposing evil wherever it resides.

THE POWER OF GENEROSITY

As Jamin and I initially reached out to the individuals interviewed in this book, we held out little hope that they would be open to meeting with us. With a few exceptions, these figures had no knowledge of who we were and had no prior relationship with us. What struck us about every person we spoke with was his or her generosity. Each person gave not only time, but also hospitality, grace, vulnerability, and wisdom. They opened their hearts and their lives to us and welcomed us in. We heard of personal struggles, learned about their ministry goals late in life, and were personally invested in beyond our expectations. One person we interviewed even gave us financial support toward our trip to France to meet with Jean, telling us that Jean's witness was too important to leave out of the book. These people embodied, in every aspect of their lives, the biblical call to generosity.

The problem with our conception of generosity is that we tend to think only in terms of money. But a generous person is more than someone who gives money. A generous person gives himself or herself to another. Self-giving entails a habit of the heart to value others, and a certain elasticity of the heart to move in love. While the financial aspect of generosity can be a barometer of one's generosity as a whole, it is not the only form of meaningful giving. Jim Packer, James Houston, Marva Dawn, John Perkins, Jean Vanier, Eugene Peterson, and Dallas Willard all had generous hearts, and for the short time we spent with them, they gave of themselves extravagantly.

But generosity isn't simply a better way to live (in contrast to, say, stinginess). Generosity is a form of resistance. A heart that is formed by greed, pride, self-centeredness, and anger will very quickly adopt forms of living that affirm the power structures of the world, the flesh, and the devil (even within the church). But people formed for the kingdom, formed by generosity of spirit, are those who unmask demonic initiatives and bear witness to a different way.

When Paul calls Christians to love one another and outdo one another in showing honor (Rom. 12:10), or when he tells us that we should count others as more significant than ourselves (Phil. 2:3), he is narrating the call to generosity. The generous person considers the interests of others (Phil. 2:4) and is called to submit "to one another out of reverence for Christ" (Eph. 5:21). Furthermore, this person receives the call to "be kind to one another, tenderhearted, forgiving one another, as God in Christ forgave you" (Eph. 4:32).

We need look no further than God's movement of redemption in Christ to see what generosity looks like. "For God so loved the world, that he gave . . ." (John 3:16). Here is the heart of God's generosity toward us. He loved so he gave. He gave himself. God's grace is "lavished" upon us in Christ (Eph. 1:7–8). His lavishing, gracious generosity is the ground of our own generosity. Generosity begins in the heart as a movement of the soul in love. Generosity is having a heart that can open wide to receive others in love, taking them within your heart and giving yourself to them in return.

Generosity of heart is having the same kind of heart as God, lavishing grace and mercy upon others in the same way God has done for us in Christ.

Christians have at times believed that the idols of money (Mammon), time, and security are enemies to destroy. Money, time, and security in and of themselves are not bad, but they can be fashioned into idols of the way from below. They can be mechanisms of power to control. Success often equals a kind of self-sustained and protected life that is void of self-giving and the vulnerability of generosity. When we give of our money, time, and security, the very things that prop up our own power, we reject the quest for control and instead choose the way of love. As we do, we may discover how deeply we cling to power and control, providing an opportunity to prayerfully present our hearts to the Lord. Ultimately, the heart given to the way from above will be inclined toward generosity and away from vices such as lying, greed, and selfishness. In the face of such brokenness and sin in the human heart, this person will move to bless instead of curse, give abundantly, and seek the kingdom before all else. This is why hospitality has always been one of the major virtues of God's people (e.g., Rom. 12:13; Heb. 13:2; 1 Peter 4:9). The family of the way has an open-door policy. As we give to the poor, spend time with the elderly, and set aside our comforts to be with those with disabilities, we begin to accept the contours of kingdom power and resist evil within and without.

THE POWER OF RECONCILIATION

The early Christians were immediately confronted with the reconciling dynamic of the gospel. From the outset of the church, Christians were immersed in racial tensions and animosity that forced them to grapple with the nature of the way. Jewish Christians were told that their former enemies—Romans, Samaritans, and Gentiles—were now their brothers and sisters, and so the scourge of racism was revealed. The good news of the gospel, that God had reconciled them to himself in love through Jesus, was married to horrifying news, that those "other people" were given the same good news. Perhaps we moderns imagine ourselves to be much more enlightened. Yet churches today are often broken down into factions based on ethnic, social, generational, and economic markers. Whereas the world recognizes that segregation is a kind of moral failure, in the evangelical church it is basically the go-to strategy. Instead of seeking to be unified in our diversity, we segregate into communities that look alike, make similar amounts of money, appreciate the same kind of music, and share the same social status.[3]

The early church had to face the realities of racism, exceptionalism, and segregation right from the start. Reconciliation was the foundation of their resistance against these evils. What we learn in the New Testament is that these issues can only be overcome by unmasking them and the power structures that fuel them. For instance, Paul confronted Peter because of his refusal to stand by his Greek brothers and sisters in the face of pressure from other Jews:

> But when Cephas [Peter] came to Antioch, I opposed him to his face, because he stood condemned. For before certain men came from James, he was eating with the Gentiles; but when they came he drew back and separated himself, fearing the circumcision party. And the rest of the Jews acted hypocritically along with him, so that even Barnabas was led astray by their hypocrisy. (Gal. 2:11–13)

Paul goes on to say that their "conduct was not in step with the truth of the gospel" (Gal. 2:14). The truth of the gospel is, as Paul says in Ephesians 2:18, that "through him [Christ] we *both* have access in one Spirit to the Father" (emphasis added). The "we both" in this passage is the Jew and the Gentile. Jew and non-Jew alike have access to the Father in the same way—through the Son and in the Spirit. It is in Christ that reconciliation is known for them both, not only reconciliation with God, but with one another. The gospel presses us to accept the difficult reality that we do not become reconciled to God in isolation, but as members of a covenant community in Christ. This community is not a homogeneous group of look-alikes, but it exists in palpable and beautiful diversity.

Reconciliation, as the foundation and fruit of the gospel, is the embodiment of power in weakness for the sake of love. Reconciliation and control are rivals, so reconciliation resists, and will stand against, forms of communal control and homogeneity. Whereas control leads to unity by demolishing diversity, reconciliation leads to unity *within* diversity—which requires us to lay down our own control. To accept the call of reconciliation is to reject power for control. It entails standing against the powers and principalities that seek division and segregation. When we are told that "there is neither Jew nor Greek . . . slave nor free . . . male nor female . . . you are all one in Christ Jesus" (Gal. 3:28 NASB), the idea isn't to collapse difference into an un-individuated humanity, as if gender and ethnicity no longer exist. Rather, the bedrock of all our collective identities is in Christ, and his body should reflect that unity. The call of the church is reconciliation *in* diversity and not reconciliation that collapses it. As people of the way, we are charged to seek reconciliation:

All this is from God, who through Christ reconciled us to himself and gave us the ministry of reconciliation; that is, in Christ God was reconciling the world to himself, not counting their trespasses against them, and entrusting to us the message of reconciliation. Therefore, we are ambassadors for Christ,

God making his appeal through us. We implore you on behalf of Christ, be reconciled to God. For our sake he made him to be sin who knew no sin, so that in him we might become the righteousness of God. (2 Cor. 5:18–21)

As ambassadors of the way, we are called to resist the evils of segregation through acts of reconciliation. Acts of reconciliation require repentance, forgiveness, peace, justice, and sacrifice. Because we follow a God who has reconciled us to himself and who offers forgiveness freely, God's people are those who give themselves in love to one another and to the world in the freedom we have found in him. As we discussed in the previous chapter, we are called to make manifest the way from above, not only to a watching world, but to "rulers and authorities in the heavenly places" (Eph. 3:10). When Paul talks about making this way visible, he speaks of the church unveiling a deep mystery of the gospel that has been "hidden for ages in God who created all things" (Eph. 3:9): "This mystery is that the Gentiles are fellow heirs, members of the same body, and partakers of the promise in Christ Jesus through the gospel" (Eph. 3:6). When we embrace reconciled diversity as the family of God, we bear witness to God's way of power and stand against the world, the flesh, and the devil.

THE POWER OF NONDIVISIVE RESISTANCE

Our call to power in weakness against the powers of the world is a call to be light in the midst of darkness: "For at one time you were darkness, but now you are light in the Lord. Walk as children of light" (Eph. 5:8). The nonviolent resistance of Martin Luther King Jr. embodied this, seeking reconciliation in the face of suffering for the sake of making visible the invisible way of the kingdom. King's understanding of nonviolent resistance began with a refusal to hate the other person from the heart. Only after we refuse to hate can we resist nonviolently, turning to ways of peace and love that will expose the evil systems working through broken people. The focus was on exposing the evil embedded within the system, unmasking the brokenness of the system and its propensity for evil, and seeking to rescue both the abused *and* the abuser. This focus recognizes that oppressors, for however much they are willing agents of oppression, are also being dehumanized. Like the police officer who beat John Perkins and his companions, abusers are caught up in an evil that is undermining their humanity. By turning to hatred and domination, they give themselves to dehumanizing realities that only continue their demise. To love our enemies and pray for those who persecute us is to refuse to dehumanize and to engage in love—understanding that love unveils evil or else hardens hearts all the more.

Scripture calls us to nonviolent resistance, but because we live in the affluent West, we normally are not faced with violence in the church. Rather, we are faced with division: things like tribalism, factions, and church splits. In the household of faith, we must pursue resistance nondivisively against these realities. Resistance should entail some form of unmasking the powers in love, but it should be the kind of resistance that refuses division. In our culture, where people leave churches for nearly any possible reason, it is hard to understand how important unity has always been to Christian belief. Not only do we tolerate division; we harbor it and use it to fuel the juggernaut that is the evangelical industrial complex. To really enter into this reality, and to walk the way of nondivisive resistance, we must take on habits of the heart: patience, humility, honesty, and recollection. We stand before God as the forgiven. We stand as those who came with nothing yet received grace and mercy. We stand as those who were once enemies of God, but are now called beloved children (Rom. 5:10). Our brothers and sisters in Christ stand before God just as we do, and our calling to be united to them should guide the posture of our heart toward them.

Nondivisive resistance follows along the contours of MLK's call to nonviolent resistance. To be nonviolent, King refused to hate. Similarly, to seek reconciliation and love with generosity of heart, the church must refuse to be divisive. Paul declares to Titus:

> Remind them to be submissive to rulers and authorities, to be obedient, to be ready for every good work, to speak evil of no one, to avoid quarreling, to be gentle, and to show perfect courtesy toward all people. For we ourselves were once foolish, disobedient, led astray, slaves to various passions and pleasures, passing our days in malice and envy, hated by others and hating one another. . . . Avoid foolish controversies, genealogies, dissensions, and quarrels about the law, for they are unprofitable and worthless. As for a person who stirs up division, after warning him once and then twice, have nothing more to do with him, knowing that such a person is warped and sinful; he is self-condemned. (Titus 3:1–3, 9–11)

We need to distinguish something we have done in this book with what Paul is saying here. It can be easy to read passages like this and come to believe we shouldn't name evil in the church. But this is the very moment when we are supposed to name evil: "For what have I to do with judging outsiders? Is it not those inside the church whom you are to judge?" (1 Cor. 5:12). We are to level accurate and discerning judgments on what goes on in the church, but we are also to respond *Christianly* in these situations. Any Christian resistance to evil, even (especially!) evil in the church, will require a different kind of resistance than we see in the world. This is the resistance of love. Love is not undermined by naming the truth; love abstracted from truth is not love at all. We don't pass over truth for the sake of peace, but recognize that peace is found only in Christ, who is Truth. In other words, sometimes the loving thing to do is to speak truth and to speak it boldly. Abraham Kuyper challenges us, "When principles that run against your deepest convictions begin to win the day, then battle is your calling, and peace has become sin; you must, at the price of dearest peace, lay your convictions bare before friend and enemy, with all the fire of your faith."[4]

In our day and age, it is easy to find people who speak truth (at least what they think is truth) while rejecting love and thereby the way of Christ. They lay their convictions bare, while forgetting they are engaging the family of God. Some believe their function is to serve as God's arbiter of truth, doling out critique and personal aspersions to any who dare hold competing theological views. Others stand against those who embrace power to control, but seek to crush them with their words, verbally employing the very power they desire to resist. Some troll for the errors of others, not out of a desire to lovingly correct or reprove, but in order to create their own platform; they call themselves prophets, but they are self-aggrandizing charlatans. On the other side, we find those who refuse to speak critically for fear of offending others or being viewed as judgmental. Their avoidance of truth-telling is baptized by axioms such as "Nobody is perfect" or "Every church has its problems." They keep the peace at the cost of truth. Their commitment to love is properly primary, but ultimately the unity they seek to maintain is a façade.

Rarest, perhaps, are those who understand when to be silent and when to speak. The book of Proverbs calls us into discernment in this regard, giving us contradictory imperatives: "Answer not a fool according to his folly, lest you be like him yourself. Answer a fool according to his folly, lest he be wise in his own eyes" (Prov. 26:4–5).

At times we are called to be silent in the face of power, just as Jesus stood silent before Pilate's inquiry (Mark 15:5). Such silence is not passive acceptance, but a trusting in God's power and a subversive exposure of evil. At times we are called to speak hard truth, just as Jesus rebuked those who questioned him by saying, "You are of your father the devil, and your will is to do your father's desires" (John 8:44). In the face of evil, discernment is required. Whether in silence or in speech, we are called to stand with and for the truth against Satan, the father of lies.

What we need to see is an embrace of truth that is truly done in love—with compassion, grace, and generosity, seeking reconciliation and refusing to be divisive. This will look different in almost every situation because these kinds of actions are relationship- and context-specific. But we must search for that balance in order to unmask how the powers have infiltrated the church and the way the church handles disagreement—whether that disagreement is on an elder board or a blog. Perhaps the most obvious biblical example, so often ignored today, is of the weaker brother or sister in the faith. The person in Paul's example holds to a false view of meat sacrificed to idols, a view he holds because of his experience with idolatry before conversion (1 Cor. 8:7). Paul's first response is not to correct this person's ignorance (and it is ignorance), because Paul recognizes that the man's conscience has been tuned to his false belief. To correct him would be, in a sense, to ruin him. He would not be led into freedom but into a condemning conscience. Paul is more pastoral here, and would rather never eat meat again than wound a child in Christ (1 Cor. 8:13).

The heart forged in prayerful abiding and tempered by movements of generosity and reconciliation will be able to recognize nondivisive resistance as a feature of maturity. Others, no doubt, will interpret nondivisive resistance as a kind of weakness, or a failure to speak the truth. But as Jude remarks, "You must remember, beloved, the predictions of the apostles of our Lord Jesus Christ. They said to you, 'In the last time there will be scoffers, following their own ungodly passions. It is these who cause divisions, worldly people, devoid of the Spirit'" (Jude 17–19). In our day there are scoffers, and in our day there is much division. Even in the church, divisive actions can be valued and the weaker members can be ignored.

For instance, members of a church may resist any change in the culture, even though a change could make others feel more welcome. The goal becomes one's own comfort, and any attack on that is received as an attack on the faith. Once again, Jamin and I can recognize this in our own hearts, and we recall our own divisive actions. We have both sown division, seeking to be right or to win at the expense of others. Fueled by zeal and arrogance, and sometimes simple naivete, we have caused discord and fracture in the body of Christ. As teachers we have a propensity for wanting to be right, and such a desire can sometimes swallow up the pursuit of love. What might it look like in our age of social media outrage and accusation to speak the truth in love? What does this entail as we talk *at* others rather than being *with* them? How can our churches avoid serving themselves instead of caring for one another in generosity and humility? These are the questions we must hold as we seek to walk forward in the way from above.

CONCLUSION: LIVING THE WAY

JAMIN AND I HAVE COME A LONG WAY ON THIS JOURNEY. We have spent a good portion of the last five years traveling, thinking, praying, writing, deleting, talking, studying, and holding these things before the Lord. There is a weightiness to the questions of this book that we feel, even after writing. There is a sense in which the state of evangelical Christianity can seem so disheartening; and yet, amid such realities, we have learned not to lose heart. The church is always Christ's church, and not ours. The joy we saw on the faces of the people we interviewed came from decades of trusting that this is Christ's mission, Christ's church, and Christ's way, and it is ultimately not dependent on us. As such, our interviewees understood themselves as "fellow workers" with Christ (1 Cor. 3:9).

We have searched the Bible for guidance, embarked on a journey to seek embodied wisdom from sages, and then returned to see how the church and our own practices help form us in the way from above. But I fear that some may still mistakenly think that we are trying to undermine the importance of the individual's fortitude, skill, and work in the process. I have found, in my seminary teaching, that evangelicals have a tendency to push tough questions into a simple "either-or" paradigm. *Either* my action forms me completely, *or* my action does nothing. *Either* God is the one doing the work, *or* I am; and it cannot be both ways. But this is false. This is not how Christians throughout the ages have understood this dynamic, nor is it how Paul explains it when he claims, "Work out your own salvation with fear and trembling, for it is God who works in you, both to will and to work for his good pleasure" (Phil. 2:12–13).

As Jamin and I meditated upon power, the "from" and "for" features of power became important. Kingdom power is from God (through our abiding in Christ) and for love (as it is for God and his glory). In his missive to the Colossians, Paul encourages believers to work "not by way of eye-service, as people-pleasers, but with sincerity of heart, fearing the Lord. Whatever you do, work heartily, as for the Lord and not for men, knowing that from the Lord you will receive the inheritance as your reward. You are serving the Lord Christ" (Col. 3:22–24). Our work should be done for Christ, and therefore for love, just as it should be done through our abiding in him and his way. Similarly, Paul claims, "For no one can lay a foundation other than that which is laid, which is Jesus Christ. Now if anyone builds on the foundation with gold, silver, precious stones, wood, hay, straw—each one's work will become manifest, for the Day will disclose it, because it will be revealed by fire, and the fire will test what sort of work each one has done" (1 Cor. 3:11–13). This passage, in a nutshell, offers the overall message of this book. We are all doing work in the kingdom of God that has a source and a purpose. If our source is ourselves rather than God, it will be straw that is burned up by fire; if our purpose is other than God's purpose—love and his glory—then it too will burn. But only the last day will truly reveal these things. All of our work is sown either to the flesh or to the Spirit (Gal. 6:8), but we do not always see the fruit. This is why Paul adds, "Let us not grow weary of doing good, for in due season we will reap, if we do not give up" (Gal. 6:9).

Paul's call to "not give up" should be encouraging for those of us who seek to serve God according to his way. Paul assumes that faithfulness will lead us to question if any of our work matters or makes any ultimate difference, because Paul knows that the way of Christ runs contrary to the way of the world, the flesh, and the devil. Like silence and solitude, which can cause our hearts to run wild and our minds to feel restless and anxious, following Christ's way can reveal deep idolatries of the flesh. We assume faithfulness will "feel" a certain way, but what we often experience is ourselves and our own sin, and not the excitement we were looking for. We also tend to assume that faithfulness will bear fruit immediately, and when it doesn't, we begin to question our path. Do not grow weary. If we sow to the Spirit, we will reap in the Spirit.

POWER IN WEAKNESS FOR LOVE

Through the journey of the wilderness, Israel mistakenly believed that they left Egypt behind when they left the country. Then, amid the exposing struggle of the wilderness, their hearts were revealed to be like Pharaoh's, and they hardened their hearts against God. They did not become the kinds of people who could hear the Word, nor did they give themselves to ways of life that allowed them to walk with God. They were idolaters, and so like the idols themselves, they became people with eyes that could not see and ears that could not hear. They were becoming like the dead idols that looked alive but had no real life in them.

Today, we face a similar problem. It takes a certain kind of life to be a true listener of the Word of God. This does not happen at random, but demands that we give ourselves to the way of Christ. Unfortunately, we can neglect to consider how modern life and technology might hurt our ability to be listeners to the Word. We fail to consider how ways of living could hurt our ability to attend patiently to God's calling on our lives. We forget that influence and popularity are not intrinsically good. We do not notice that we are becoming like the idols in our lives, and that the rituals of God's family are boring and lack meaning for us. But this kind of numbing will always be the fruit of idolatry.

In our calling to be fruitful for the kingdom of God, we must discern the way of God (Eph. 5:10), so we must be the kinds of people who can discern this way (Heb. 5:11–14). The "from" and the "for" of our power need to align with God and his way, regardless of how savvy, sophisticated, or skilled we are. As we seek to thrive in whatever position the Lord has called us to, we can still seek to be skilled at what we do, as long as that skill is grounded in our abiding in Christ, and our purpose is oriented to God's calling to love. In this sense, our skill is like our unblemished lamb that we lay before the Lord in offering to him. Sacrifice was never a mechanistic reality. God wasn't waiting around for more dead animals. As the psalmist proclaims, "You do not delight in sacrifice, otherwise I would give it; You are not pleased with burnt offering. The sacrifices of God are a broken spirit; a broken and contrite heart, O God, You will not despise" (Ps. 51:16–17 NASB). Our sacrifice is, in part, the mode by which we can come before God in repentance, trust, and abiding. Our skill, therefore, is the way we present ourselves to the Lord, and is the vehicle by which we abide in Christ and serve him. The focus is always on God, and the sacrifice is our means to partake in his work and live in the freedom of his presence. The more skilled we become, however, the easier it is to seek power from within; and the more fruitful our power becomes, the easier it is to seek power for control and our own glory, rather than God's.

Power in weakness for love is power that bears fruit for the kingdom. Power in strength for control, used to achieve kingdom ends, will ultimately deceive us into thinking we're living in the way of Jesus, when in fact we are living in the way from below. This power is the power of straw; it is the power that seems invincible, and then one day just disappears. Power in weakness works the opposite way. Power in weakness appears to be powerless in the face of this world and it may even be denounced as foolish within the church itself. We must be prepared to face opposition, rejection, and mockery. We must be prepared to be ignored and passed over for the promotions of "powerful people." In these moments we ought to pray with Augustine: "Let the strong and mighty laugh at us, then, but let us weak and needy folk confess to you."[1]

THE TUNE OF OUR HEARTS

If we consider the prayerful heart that is tuned to the kingdom—living in generosity, reconciliation, and nondivisive resistance—then certain habits of heart and mind should become clear. For instance, many of the qualifications of an elder are relevant. An elder should be above reproach, relationally faithful, lacking arrogance or a quick temper. An elder is not a drunkard or "violent or greedy for gain," but is "hospitable, a lover of good, self-controlled, upright, holy, and disciplined" (Titus 1:7–8). Those who are unfit to be an elder are "insubordinate, empty talkers and deceivers," and they teach for "shameful gain" (Titus 1:10–11). These are not mere actions but postures and movements of the heart. To not be "quick-tempered" is not about having strong willpower, but about being the kind of person who does not explode in anger because his or her heart is tuned to love. Such a person's heart has embodied the call to be slow to speak, quick to listen, and slow to become angry (James 1:19). This way is the fruit of one who has sown in the Spirit and not sown to the flesh; it is the heart-texture of one who has rejected the quick-fix lies of the world.[2]

If we consider the person whose heart is recollected in prayerful abiding, who gives himself or herself to a generosity of spirit, seeks reconciliation, and refuses division, it becomes clear that Jesus is our model. Jesus, at times, did seek division (so he forces us into discernment about when divisiveness trumps our call to unity), but he also sought love across every boundary he confronted—whether Jew or Greek, slave or free, male or female—Jesus broke down barriers in love. But at the core of Jesus' action we see how detached he remained from the power systems of the world and how attached he was to the Father and his way of power. Jesus was grounded in an unhurried existence that allowed him to be present; to listen carefully and faithfully; to overflow in mercy, grace, and love; and to know his calling (and refuse to be seduced by callings that were not his, or callings not done according to his way). Jesus' heart was formed in abiding with his Father, in his times of silence and solitude seeking the Father's will, in his continued dependence and obedience, and, counterintuitively, in his suffering. The author of Hebrews writes, "In the days of his flesh, Jesus offered up prayers and supplications, with loud cries and tears, to him who was able to save him from death, and he was heard because of his reverence. Although he was a son, he learned obedience through what he suffered" (Heb. 5:7–8). In the wilderness, we discover that we too learn obedience through suffering, and that if we embrace the way from above and its movement of heart and life, we will suffer in the very place we don't expect—in the church.

SUFFERING ON THE WAY

As we journey through this present evil age, faithful living will entail suffering. Suffering is assumed on every page of Scripture. The question is not *if* we will suffer, but *how* we will suffer (and if our suffering will be meaningful). When we focus on what God can offer us, what the church can do for us, and how meaningful the Christian life can feel to us, suffering does not seem to have a place in our story. However, to reject the reality of suffering is just that: a rejection of reality. It is also a refusal to embrace another means by which God invites us ever deeper into his way of love. A rejection of suffering is a rejection of weakness and vulnerability in relationship with God. To reject suffering is to reject the comfort God provides within our suffering, and to reject the suffering we share with the entire body of Christ (2 Cor. 1:3–7). Ultimately, to reject suffering is a subtle acceptance of a vision of the Christian life without the cross; it is an embrace of the way from below.

In his letter to the Philippians, Paul writes, "For it has been granted to you that for the sake of Christ you should not only believe in him but also suffer for his sake, engaged in the same conflict that you saw I had and now hear that I still have" (Phil. 1:29–30). Whereas the system of the world seeks to destroy suffering at all cost—often turning to avoidance and numbing as suitable solutions—the way of Christ entails an acceptance of suffering for *his* sake. The Christian call is to witness to the way of life found in Christ, but this is not another plan for thriving, as if suffering in itself is somehow fruitful for human flourishing. Rather, as Christians, our suffering is a suffering *in* Christ, *with* Christ, and in anticipation of Christ's return. Therefore, Peter admonishes, "Beloved, do not be surprised at the fiery trial when it comes upon you to test you, as though something strange were happening to you. But rejoice insofar as you share Christ's sufferings, that you may also rejoice and be glad when his glory is revealed" (1 Peter 4:12–13). Likewise, Peter reminds his audience that they should not be suffering on behalf of foolishness, but on behalf of wisdom. Suffering because of one's poor choices in life is not virtuous, but suffering for Christ's sake is accepting the will of God as a faithful servant. In Peter's words, "For this is the will of God, that by doing good you should put to silence the ignorance of foolish people. Live as people who are free, not using your freedom as a cover-up for evil, but living as servants of God"; "Therefore let those who suffer according to God's will entrust their souls to a faithful Creator while doing good" (1 Peter 2:15–16; 4:19). Suffering according to God's will is suffering for doing good in the face of evil—it is living according to the way from above when the way from below is crouching at your door.

Every sage along our journey spoke of the experience of suffering in their lives. John Perkins embraced God's way of power and returned to the very system of oppression and dehumanization he had known growing up because he was called to unmask its evil. Marva Dawn has a laundry list of physical maladies that seem unbearable to live with, yet she continues to travel and speak because she believes the Lord has given her a voice within her suffering. James Houston experienced the loneliness of downward mobility, accepting God's call to start a school for "mere Christians" that seemed foolish in light of worldly wisdom. Jean Vanier gave his life to people with extreme disabilities, and was exposed to the deep anger of his heart because Jesus called him to love his neighbor as himself. Each person, in light of his or her unique calling and circumstances, accepted the call to suffer for Christ's sake, and all of them revealed how their suffering was used by God to anchor their hearts ever more into his way of love. The Christian's embrace of suffering in Christ is perhaps the most powerful resistance to the way of evil—a form of resistance that continues on most vividly in the witness of martyrs.[3]

To a much lesser degree, when we accept the suffering we experience in Christ, we unveil a different way in the world. This does not mean that we go looking for suffering, nor does it mean that we ignore our call to stand against abuse. We are the people who care for those who are under abuse, who are fragile, and who are exposed to evils. But it means that we know that suffering is a reality of the Christian life, and that our primary emphasis should not be avoiding it at all cost.

All people suffer. There is no way out of that, no matter how hard we try to overcome, medicate, or avoid our suffering. But only Christians can suffer with Christ. When we are confronted with suffering, we can choose to receive it in the Spirit or in the flesh (Gal. 6:8). In both ways, we will immediately cry out for God to take the suffering away, and God may do so. But our hearts are truly exposed when God's response mirrors his word to Paul in 2 Corinthians: "My grace is sufficient for you, for my power is made perfect in weakness" (12:9). If we reject God's call to enter into our weakness, we are living according to the flesh. But if we accept the way from above, Paul's words will become our own: "Therefore I will boast all the more gladly of my weaknesses, so that the power of Christ may rest upon me" (2 Cor. 12:9).

To walk in the way from above we need to hold fast to the words of Jesus: "Blessed are the poor in spirit. . . . Blessed are those who mourn. . . . Blessed are the meek. . . . Blessed are those who hunger and thirst for righteousness. . . . Blessed are the merciful. . . . Blessed are the pure in heart. . . . Blessed are the peacemakers" (Matt. 5:3–9). We who embrace power in weakness for love in the face of suffering, shame, and ridicule are those who are blessed. We cling to the truth that an embrace of kingdom power, if we have the courage, will unveil the freedom known in Christ. Power in weakness is freedom because it is a call to find our all in God, and in so doing, to discover our true mission in the world in Christ. It is in Christ, and in him alone, that we find life. Therefore it is in Christ, and in him alone, that we come to understand the Christian nature of power. So now, we do not live by sight, but we live by faith, trusting that this path is the weighty way of the kingdom.

"There are two ways, one of life and one of death, and there is a great difference between these two ways."

—*The Didache*, CIRCA 150 CE

"Two loves have made two cities. Love of self, even to the point of contempt for God, made the earthly city, and love of God, even to the point of contempt for self, made the heavenly city. Thus the former glories in itself, and the latter glories in the Lord. The former seeks its glory from men, but the latter finds its highest glory in God. . . . In the former the lust for domination dominates both its princes and the nations that it subjugates; in the latter both leaders and followers serve one another in love. . . . The former loves its own strength, displayed in its men of power; the latter says to its God, *I love you*, O LORD, *my strength* [Ps. 18:1]."

—SAINT AUGUSTINE

"That the zeal for God's honor is also a dangerous passion, that the Christian must bring with him the courage to swim against the tide instead of with it . . . and accept a good deal of loneliness, will perhaps be nowhere so clear and palpable as in the church, where he would so much like things to be different. Yet he cannot and he will not refuse to take this risk and pay this price . . . he belongs where the reformation of the church is underway or will again be underway."

—KARL BARTH

"Do not desire to be strong, powerful, honored, and respected, but let God alone be your strength, your fame, and your honor."

—DIETRICH BONHOEFFER

"What makes the temptation of power so seemingly irresistible? Maybe it is that power offers an easy substitute for the hard task of love. It seems easier to be God than to love God, easier to control people than to love people, easier to own life than to love life."

—HENRI NOUWEN

INTERVIEWEE READING LIST

AN ABRIDGED LIST OF BOOKS FROM OUR INTERVIEWEES
that are most relevant to the topics found in this book:

Marva Dawn

¤ *Joy in Our Weakness: A Gift of Hope from the Book of
Revelation* (Grand Rapids: Eerdmans, 2002).
¤ *Powers, Weakness, and the Tabernacling of God* (Grand
Rapids: Eerdmans, 2001).

Marva Dawn with Eugene Peterson

¤ *The Unnecessary Pastor: Rediscovering the Call* (Grand
Rapids: Eerdmans, 1999).

James Houston

¤ *Joyful Exiles: Life in Christ on the Dangerous Edge of Things*
(Downers Grove, IL: IVP, 2006).
¤ *The Mentored Life: From Individualism to Personhood*
(Vancouver: Regent College Publishing, 2011).
¤ *A Vision for the Aging Church: Renewing Ministry for and by
Seniors* (Downers Grove, IL: IVP Academic, 2011).

J. I. Packer

¤ *Keep in Step with the Spirit: Finding Fullness in Our Walk with God* (Grand Rapids: Baker, 2005).
¤ *Weakness Is the Way: Life with Christ Our Strength* (Wheaton, IL: Crossway, 2013).

John Perkins

¤ *Let Justice Roll Down* (Grand Rapids: Baker, 1976).
¤ *With Justice for All: A Strategy for Community Development* (Ventura, CA: Regal, 1982).

Eugene Peterson

¤ *The Contemplative Pastor: Returning to the Art of Spiritual Direction* (Carol Stream, IL: Word, 1989).
¤ *The Pastor: A Memoir* (San Francisco: HarperOne, 2011).
¤ *Working the Angles: The Shape of Pastoral Integrity* (Grand Rapids: Eerdmans, 1987).

Jean Vanier

¤ *Community and Growth* (New York: Paulist, 1989).
¤ *From Brokenness to Community* (New York: Paulist, 1992).

Dallas Willard

¤ *The Divine Conspiracy: Rediscovering Our Hidden Life in God* (San Francisco: HarperSanFrancisco, 1998).
¤ *The Divine Conspiracy Continued: Fulfilling God's Kingdom on Earth*, cowritten with Gary Black Jr. (New York: HarperOne, 2014).

ACKNOWLEDGMENTS

THIS BOOK TOOK US ON AN UNEXPECTED AND LONG journey. Along the way many people have encouraged, exhorted, challenged, and blessed us immeasurably. To each of our interviewees: your encouragement, candor, and love for us was profound. Our time with you was deeply impactful, and continues to bear fruit in our lives. To our agent Jenni Burke, we're so glad you are on this journey with us! Your unseen work does not go unnoticed by us and we love having you in our corner. Joel Miller (who first signed this book and was always excited about it), your initial enthusiasm helped us bring this book to completion, which we deeply appreciate. Webb Younce, we appreciate you stepping in and carrying the editorial heavy-lifting for this project. Thank you for your encouragement, guidance, and editorial direction. The support of our respective institutions, Biola University and Mission Hills Church, in particular the Institute of Spiritual Formation at Talbot School of Theology, whose guidance, support, and love of us both has been rich. The office workers at the institute, Tasha Austin, Paul Rheingans, and Robbie Goforth, in one way or another served this project and for that help we are grateful.

We have also been blessed by friends who have been willing to read for us, critique, question, and push us on these topics in various ways. In particular, we received incredibly helpful feedback from Bob Mehaffey, Sam Paschall, Nick Kinnier, Joshua

Butler, Nish Wciseth, and Ty Kieser. To my (Jamin's) companions in "The Writer's Room," you know who you are and you know how much your listening ears, giving hearts, and vocal encouragement helped me in the writing of this book.

We, of course, cannot put into words how much our families have supported us in this endeavor, particularly our wives, Kelli and Kristin. Your encouragement, editing, and companionship on this journey means more than you know and certainly more than we can express. The way from above is more than just a concept for this book, but is our calling as families to bear witness to Christ in this world. Our wrestling through the ideas of power in weakness was more than just conceptual, but entailed (and continues to entail) wrestling in discernment concerning the call on our lives. Because of this, we were not alone in our struggle through these topics, and your steadfast hope for us throughout has been a blessing. Thank you both for all that you took on to allow us to travel, write, and research this book. You both are such gifts to us.

ABOUT THE AUTHORS

JAMIN GOGGIN SERVES AS A PASTOR AT MISSION HILLS Church in San Marcos, California. Jamin speaks and writes from the depths of his own journey, seeking to invite others into the beauty and goodness of life with God. His primary areas of interest are spiritual formation, theology, pastoral ministry, and church life. He is the coauthor of *Beloved Dust: Drawing Close to God by Discovering the Truth About Yourself.* Jamin holds a master's degree in New Testament Studies and a master's degree in Spiritual Formation and Soul Care. Jamin and his family live in Escondido, California.

KYLE STROBEL SERVES AS AN ASSISTANT PROFESSOR OF spiritual theology and formation at Talbot School of Theology, Biola University, and on the preaching team at Redeemer Church, La Mirada, California. Kyle speaks broadly on issues pertaining to spiritual formation, theology, and the life of the church. Kyle holds a BA in Biblical Studies, master's degrees in Philosophy of Religion and Ethics as well as New Testament Studies, and a PhD in Systematic Theology. He is the author of *Formed for the Glory of God: Learning from the Spiritual Practices of Jonathan Edwards* and coauthor of *Beloved Dust: Drawing Close to God by Discovering the Truth About Yourself.* Kyle and his family live in Fullerton, California.

NOTES

CHAPTER 1: THE WAYS OF POWER

1. For further exploration of recent discussions on power, see *Playing God: Redeeming the Gift of Power* by Andy Crouch (Downers Grove, IL: IVP Books, 2013) and *To Change the World: The Irony, Tragedy, and Possibility of Christianity in the Late Modern World* by James Davison Hunter (Oxford: Oxford University Press, 2010).

2. The words of Bonhoeffer grip us here: "God allows himself to be edged out of the world and on to the cross. God is weak and powerless in the world and that is exactly the way, the only way, in which he can be with us and help us." Dietrich Bonhoeffer, *Letters and Papers from Prison*, quoted in Donald G. Bloesch, *God the Almighty* (Downers Grove, IL: InterVarsity Press, 1995), 105.

3. J. R. R. Tolkien, *The Fellowship of the Ring* (New York: Mariner, 2012), 67–68.

4. "Denethor looked indeed much more like a great wizard than Gandalf did, more kingly, beautiful, and powerful; and older. Yet by a sense other than sight Pippin perceived that Gandalf had the greater power and the deeper wisdom, and a majesty that was veiled." J. R. R. Tolkien, *The Return of the King* (New York: Del Rey, 2012), 15.

5. Martin Luther King Jr., *A Call to Conscience: The Landmark Speeches of Dr. Martin Luther King, Jr.*, ed. Clayborne Carson and Kris Shepard (New York: Warner Books, 2001), 186. This speech

can also be heard on YouTube: https://www.youtube.com/watch
?v=UouEVThoios&feature=related.

6. It is true that people living in an antithetical way to Christ can
still bear fruit for the kingdom, but they are bearing fruit that is
foreign to them. If we bear external fruit but lack the internal fruit,
we are partaking in God's work as aliens to the outcome. God can
achieve his kingdom ends through us, and we can fail to be "fellow
workers" with him in the process (1 Cor. 3:9). This fruit may come
from us, but in a very real sense it is not *our* fruit.

7. A. W. Tozer, *Born After Midnight* (Camp Hill, PA: WingSpread,
2008), 27.

8. Søren Kierkegaard, *Provocations: Spiritual Writings of Kierkegaard*
(Walden, NY: Plough, 2014), 225.

9. In his book *Kingdom Conspiracy: Returning to the Radical Mission
of the Local Church* (Grand Rapids: Brazos, 2014), Scot McKnight
articulates a problem that has become an epidemic on a popular
level in the church. We assume the church is powerless, so we turn
to entities outside of the church, and then seek to Christianize
them to give them eternal significance. This is particularly easy
with a notion like *kingdom*, which is a term we can readily employ
for whatever we want. Ultimately, it is the church that the gates
of hell will not prevail against, and not our programs to create
cultures of goodness.

10. Karl Barth, *Church Dogmatics I.I: The Doctrine of the Word of
God*, ed. G. W. Bromiley and T. F. Torrance, trans. G. W. Bromiley
(Peabody, MA: Hendrickson, 2010), 3.

11. In keeping with Cassian and Germanus's journey in *The
Conferences* to seek out the wisdom of the desert, now Jamin and
I, two friends, seek out wisdom from those who have embraced
humility, grace, and the way of Jesus in this world.

12. All interviews have been edited for clarity, conciseness, and content.

CHAPTER 2: POWER IN WEAKNESS

1. Skye Jethani originally coined this term in a blog post titled "The Evangelical Industry Complex & Rise of Celebrity Pastors," that you can find here: http://skyejethani.com/the-evangelical-industrial-complex-the-rise-of-celebrity-pastors.

2. This is not to somehow limit the questions concerning power to Corinth. Power is a fallen-human issue first and foremost, but in the New Testament we see this play itself out in much of Jesus' and Paul's ministries specifically. Musing on Jesus' call not to "lord it over" others, Scot McKnight claims, "Roman politics is about power and dominion and might and force and coercion and the sword. The politics of Jesus is about sacrificial love for the other *even if that means death from the sword.* Lording it over others is the way of Rome; serving others is the way of Jesus." Scot McKnight, *Kingdom Conspiracy: Returning to the Radical Mission of the Local Church* (Grand Rapids: Brazos, 2014), 61, emphasis in original.

3. D. A. Carson and Douglas J. Moo, *An Introduction to the New Testament* (Grand Rapids: Zondervan, 2005), 420.

4. David E. Garland, *1 Corinthians*, Baker Exegetical Commentary on the New Testament (Grand Rapids: Baker Academic, 2003), 2.

5. Timothy B. Savage, *Power Through Weakness: Paul's Understanding of the Christian Ministry in 2 Corinthians* (Cambridge: Cambridge UP, 2004), 41.

6. Our culture loathes weakness. It is to be avoided at all costs. We have completely bought into Nietzsche's formula: "I teach the No to all that makes weak—that exhausts. I teach the Yes to all that strengthens, that stores up strength, that justifies the feeling of strength." We say no to weakness and yes to strength. The idea that weakness could be a good, let alone an accepted reality, is antithetical to our vision for happiness, health, and success. As Nietzsche states, "Everything done in weakness fails." Friedrich

Nietzsche, *The Will to Power*, ed. Walter Kaufmann (New York: Vintage, 1967), 28, 33.

7. N. T. Wright underscores this point nicely: "In contrast to the Corinthians' apparent expectations that he present himself as a fine, upstanding, noble, heroic figure, Paul insists as a matter of symbolic praxis that that is entirely the wrong way round. Exactly in line with the redefinition of power and authority in Mark 10:25–45, Paul believes that apostolic life consists not only in *telling* people *about* the dying and rising of the Messiah, but also in going through the process oneself." N. T. Wright, *Paul and the Faithfulness of God: Book I* (Minneapolis: Fortress, 2013), 433.

8. Our friend Joe Hellerman draws a fascinating biblical parallel between Paul and Silas's actions in Acts 16 and the description of Jesus' humble and sacrificial incarnation in Philippians 2. The parallels vividly highlight Paul's following of Christ in his way of weakness. Hellerman notes that in the scene of turmoil, opposition, and imprisonment that Paul and Silas face in Philippi, we encounter vivid imitation of Christ. Paul and Silas "refused to exploit their Roman citizenship," just as in Philippians 2 we are told Jesus "did not regard equality with God as something to be exploited" (v. 6). In Acts 16 we see Paul and Silas "willingly suffered the humiliation of flogging and imprisonment at the hands of Roman magistrates" (vv. 19–23). This echoes Philippians 2, which tells us Christ "willingly suffered the humiliation of crucifixion at the hands of a Roman magistrate" (v. 8). Finally we read in Acts 16 that Paul and Silas are "vindicated by a sudden status reversal" in which their "citizen status is recognized" and their "oppressors are put to shame" (vv. 35–39). This follows what we find in Philippians 2, which tells us Christ was "vindicated by a sudden status reversal" and he is met with recognition of his "divine lordship" as "every knee will bow" (vv. 9–11). Joseph H. Hellerman, *Embracing Shared Ministry: Power and Status in the Early Church and Why It Matters Today* (Grand Rapids: Kregel, 2013), 116.

9. This is the theme we developed in our book *Beloved Dust: Drawing Close to God by Discovering the Truth About Yourself* (Nashville: Thomas Nelson, 2014).

10. John Calvin, *Calvin's Commentaries* vol. 20, *1 Corinthians, 2 Corinthians* (Grand Rapids: Baker, 2003), 378–79.

Chapter 3: Becoming Powerful

1. We take this phrase from Eugene Peterson's book *A Long Obedience in the Same Direction: Discipleship in an Instant Society* (Downers Grove, IL: InterVarsity Press, 2000).

2. See James M. Houston and Michael Parker, *A Vision for the Aging Church: Renewing Ministry for and by Seniors* (Downers Grove, IL: IVP Academic, 2011).

3. This phrase comes from the title of a book that James Houston loves. Stephen Neill, *A Genuinely Human Existence* (Garden City, NY: Doubleday, 1959).

4. G. K. Chesterton, *What's Wrong with the World* (San Francisco: Ignatius, 1994), 37.

5. C. S. Lewis, *The Great Divorce* (New York: HarperSanFrancisco, 1946), 21.

6. Ibid., 25.

7. For this material on pornography, two key books (among many) come to mind. From a Christian point of view, see William M. Struthers, *Wired for Intimacy: How Pornography Hijacks the Male Brain* (Downers Grove, IL: IVP Books, 2009); and for a secular but equally fascinating proposal, see Philip G. Zimbardo and Nikita Duncan, *The Demise of Guys: Why Boys Are Struggling and What We Can Do About It* (Amazon Digital Services, 2012).

Chapter 4: Standing Against the Powers

1. Brené Brown has an interesting take on the rise of what we call "narcissism," claiming that it is the "shame-based fear of being

ordinary." This seems particularly prevalent among pastors. There is an industry that weaves together the notion of faithfulness with being extraordinary that seems particularly devastating for the pastor. Add to that the relative ease with which we can judge ourselves and our ministry based on superficial realities such as influence and numbers of people, and it isn't surprising that there are so many pastors who fit into this category. See Brené Brown, *Daring Greatly: How the Courage to Be Vulnerable Transforms the Way We Live, Love, Parent, and Lead* (New York: Gotham, 2012), 22.

2. Bernard of Clairvaux, *De consideratione ad Eugenium pap am*, 3.1.2, as quoted in Reinhard Feldmeier, *Power Service Humility: A New Testament Ethic* (Waco, TX: Baylor UP, 2014), 1.

3. The literature on powers and principalities is diverse. For a general overview and incredibly helpful and penetrating analysis, we suggest Robert Ewusie Moses, *Practices of Power: Revisiting the Principalities and Powers in the Pauline Letters* (Minneapolis: Fortress, 2014). Not only does Moses provide an overview of what he sees as the four major views on the topic, but he also advances the discussion with a particularly helpful focus on the practices of power. We owe Moses this insight for our own turn to the practices in the latter chapters of the book. Clint Arnold, furthermore, does an excellent job of unpacking the historical issues behind the biblical text, particularly in Paul's letters, and highlighting the demonic and syncretistic worldview that this language comes from. See his works *Power and Magic: The Concept of Power in Ephesians* (Eugene, OR: Wipf and Stock, 2001) and *Powers of Darkness: Principalities and Powers in Paul's Letters* (Downers Grove, IL: InterVarsity Press, 1992). For a more theological take on the principalities and powers, through an engagement with Karl Barth and John Howard Yoder, see Scott Thomas Prather, *Christ, Power and Mammon: Karl Barth and John Howard Yoder in Dialogue* (New York: Bloomsbury T&T Clark, 2013). Prather's account is more than a historical

reconstruction but is a work of theological ethics seeking to give an account of how the powers work to dominate in our society. Reinhard Feldmeier's *Power Service Humility: A New Testament Ethic* is another helpful starting place from a New Testament scholar. There is a lot of helpful exegetical work here, and it is a good starting place to think about the powers and their relationship to the construction of a Christian ethic. Last, any discussion of the powers and principalities has to engage the work of Walter Wink. Wink's four-volume work is the most robust project undertaken on the principalities and powers (We're including within this his edited volume *Peace Is the Way: Writings on Nonviolence from the Fellowship of Reconciliation* [New York: Orbis, 2000]). The bulk of the work is found in his trilogy: *Naming the Powers: The Language of Power in the New Testament* (Minneapolis: Fortress, 1984); *Unmasking the Powers: The Invisible Forces That Determine Human Existence* (Minneapolis: Fortress, 1986); and *Engaging the Powers: Discernment and Resistance in a World of Domination* (Minneapolis: Fortress, 1992). Each of these works differs in scope and theology, often radically, but they all serve to highlight key features of the biblical text that are easy to ignore. Along with Marva's work, particularly her *Powers, Weakness, and the Tabernacling of God* (Grand Rapids: Eerdmans, 2001), our view would be closest to Moses' in his *Practices of Power*. That point should not take away from how profoundly enlightening and important these other works are (and were for us in general). One book that didn't influence our writing much, simply because we did not have access to it, was Richard Beck's, *Reviving Old Scratch: Demons and the Devil for Doubters and the Disenchanted* (Minneapolis: Fortress, 2016). There is remarkable kinship, in many key areas, between what we are doing and what Richard is doing (even though there are several key differences as well). As we finalized this manuscript, he was kind enough to send along his book for our perusal.

4. Jacque Ellul, who informed much of Marva's thinking on these things, speaks cogently into the danger of the church propagating the way from below. He states, "The whole Bible tells us that these people in the world are enslaved by the world. They belong to it. They are the slaves of political, economic and intellectual forces. The Church is there to proclaim and to bring them freedom. But if she is an agent of those forces, and shares in them herself, she cannot be for people at all. If she justifies the works of the world, she is in no position to witness, on people's behalf, to the justification in Christ. She becomes what she always tends to become: one of the powers of the world." See Jacque Ellul, *False Presence of the Kingdom*, trans. C. Edward Hopkin (New York: Seabury, 1972), 39.

5. C. S. Lewis, *The Screwtape Letters* (New York: HarperOne, 1942), 32.

6. In recent years New Testament studies have been flush with discussion of "empire criticism." According to McKnight and Modica, empire criticism "refers to developing an eye and ear for the presence of Rome and the worship of the emperor in the lines and between the lines of New Testament writings." We would agree with the trajectory of argument found in McKnight and Modica's book that empire criticism is over-read into the New Testament text. It is not a governing agenda of the text. However, this does not negate the reality, for example, that claims of Jesus' lordship and his identity as the Son of God are clear affronts to Caesar's power and divine status. In relation to our argument in this book, we would contend that the Empire represents one example of a worldly power that is caught up in the way from below, and thus is antithetical to Jesus' kingdom. *Jesus Is Lord, Caesar Is Not: Evaluating Empire in New Testament Studies*, ed. Scot McKnight and Joseph B. Modica (Downers Grove, IL: IVP Academic, 2013), 16.

7. While we would not agree with his use of "mythological" here, Feldmeier's point still remains helpful: "As we have shown, it is possible to read the entire New Testament as the story of a power struggle between a destructive autonomous power that is called mythologically the devil, anthropologically the flesh, and theologically sin, on the one hand, and the good news of the rule of God, on the other hand, which does good to its counterpart, saves, redeems, builds up, endows with gifts, and is thus perfected as a 'spiritual' empowering power in the weak." Feldmeier, *Power Service Humility*, 95.

8. Kate Shellnutt and Morgan Lee, "Mark Driscoll Resigns from Mars Hill," *Christianity Today*, October 15, 2014, http://www.christianitytoday.com/ct/2014/october-web-only/mark-driscoll-resigns-from-mars-hill.html.

9. John Ortberg, "When a Pastor Resigns Abruptly: The Snare of Smugness and Fuzzy Immorality," *Christianity Today*, October 16, 2014, http://www.christianitytoday.com/parse/2014/october/when-pastor-resigns-abruptly.html.

10. Os Guiness, *The Gravedigger File* (Downer's Grove, IL: InterVarsity Press, 1983), 15.

11. Moses, *Practices of Power*, 201.

12. Ibid.

13. Reinhard Feldmeier states, "Hidden in the lowliness of the crucified Jesus, the rule of God has dawned. A Changeover of power has occurred through his exaltation, and the risen Jesus indicates this when he says that all power in heaven and on earth has been handed over to him. In their union with Christ, those who follow him already share in this new reality." Feldmeier, *Power Service Humility*, 9. See also Michael J. Gorman, *Cruciformity: Paul's Narrative Spirituality of the Cross* (Grand Rapids: Eerdmans, 2001).

Chapter 5: The Power of Love

1. J. R. R. Tolkien, *The Fellowship of the Ring* (New York: Mariner, 2012), 82.
2. Philip Cushman, *Constructing the Self, Constructing America: A Cultural History of Psychotherapy* (Boston: Da Capo, 1995), 43.
3. Ibid., 41–52.
4. For example, consider the song "Dixie." Ibid., 48.
5. Miroslav Volf, *Exclusion and Embrace: A Theological Exploration of Identity, Otherness, and Reconciliation* (Nashville: Abingdon, 1996), 36.
6. Martin Luther King Jr., *The Papers of Martin Luther King, Jr.*, vol. 5, *Threshold of a New Decade, January 1959–December 1960*, ed. Clayborne Carson (Berkeley: University of California Press, 2005), 521.
7. Ibid., 24.
8. "Martin Luther King, Jr.–On Love and Nonviolence," YouTube video, 2:03, posted by mrholtshistory. https://www.youtube.com/watch?v=EnoH2psiDhY.
9. Martin Luther King Jr., *The Papers of Martin Luther King, Jr.*, vol. 5, 269.
10. Donald G. Bloesch, *Jesus Christ: Savior and Lord* (Downers Grove, IL: InterVarsity, 1997), 227.
11. Martin Luther King Jr., *The Papers of Martin Luther King, Jr.*, vol. 5, 269.
12. Ibid., 124–25.
13. Ibid., 521.
14. Martin Luther King Jr., *The Papers of Martin Luther King, Jr.*, vol. 4, *Symbol of the Movement, January 1957–December 1958*, ed. Clayborne Carson (Berkeley: University of California Press, 2000), 105.
15. Ibid., 213. Cf. Matt. 5:44; Matt. 26:52; and Luke 6:27–28.
16. For the full story, see John M. Perkins, *Let Justice Roll Down* (Grand Rapids: Baker, 1976), 147–58.
17. Ibid., 158.
18. Ibid.

19. John Perkins, *With Justice for All: A Strategy for Community Development* (Ventura, CA: Regal, 1982), 107–8.

20. 2 Cor. 12:9.

21. 2 Cor. 5:19.

22. Wendell Berry, *The Hidden Wound* (New York: North Point, 1989), 16.

23. We owe this reflection to Christena Cleveland's insights. Christena Cleveland, "Urban Church Plantations," *ChristenaCleveland.com*, March 18, 2014, http://www.christenacleveland.com/blogarchive /2014/03/urban-church-plantations?rq=urban%20church%20 plantations.

24. Ibid.

25. This phrase is the title of a book, *Love Alone Is Credible* by Hans Urs von Balthasar (San Francisco: Ignatius, 2004).

26. Andy Crouch, *Playing God* (Downers Grove, IL: InterVarsity Press, 2013), 201.

Chapter 6: Unexpected Power

1. Fyodor Dostoyevsky, *The Brothers Karamazov* (New York: Farrar, Straus and Giroux, 2002), 58.

2. Brené Brown argues that our culture has given rise to numbing at a dangerous level, focusing on shame, anxiety, and disconnection as three ways we numb. "Shame enters for those of us who experience anxiety because not only are we feeling fearful, out of control, and incapable of managing our increasingly demanding lives, but eventually our anxiety is compounded and made unbearable by our belief that if we were just smarter, stronger, or better, we'd be able to handle everything. Numbing here becomes a way to take the edge off of both instability and inadequacy." Similarly, "Feeling disconnected can be a normal part of life and relationships, but when coupled with the shame of believing that we're disconnected because we're not worthy of connection, it creates a pain that we want to numb." Brené Brown, *Daring Greatly: How the Courage to Be*

Vulnerable Transforms the Way We Live, Love, Parent, and Lead (New York: Gotham, 2012), 138–39.

3. Also in *Daring Greatly*, Brené Brown talks a great deal about vulnerability, and her insights are genuinely profound, but she often does so in contrast to weakness. For instance, she states, "The perception that vulnerability is weakness is the most widely accepted myth about vulnerability *and* the most dangerous. . . . To feel is to be vulnerable. To believe vulnerability is weakness is to believe that feeling is weakness" (33) This is more complicated than an endnote can handle, but with how popular and influential her work is, it is important to make a comment or two here. First, Brown is a social scientist whose work is always placed within a larger conversation that broadly assumes a general anthropology. Second, though Brown is a Christian, her work as a social scientist is not theological work. In other words, she is allowing her research to speak critically into an ongoing conversation, but it is not a conversation that would readily allow for theological assumptions to reign. As a theologian, I (Kyle) can readily employ her work, but I need to do so within a theological anthropology. On Brown's view, weakness is just that; it is weak. There is no power on the other side of weakness, not even kingdom power. But with her study of vulnerability, there is some kind of power on the other side. When one embraces and goes through vulnerability, one finds "love, belonging, joy, courage, empathy, and creativity" (34). Jesus' claim that if one tries to save their life they will lose it seems to have real impact even in everyday relationships outside of the body of Christ. But in our view, weakness in Christ does not beget weakness. Weakness in Christ leads to kingdom power, even though kingdom power will be seen as foolish and weak to the world.

4. J. Ramsey Michaels, "Going to Heaven with Jesus: From 1 Peter to *Pilgrim's Progress*," in *Patterns of Discipleship in the New Testament*, ed. Richard N. Longenecker (Grand Rapids: Eerdmans, 1996), 267.

5. Dietrich Bonhoeffer, *Life Together* (New York: Harper & Row, 1954), 30.

6. Brené Brown makes a similar point about vulnerability: "Vulnerability without boundaries leads to disconnection, distrust, and disengagement.... Vulnerability is bankrupt on its own terms when people move from *being* vulnerable to *using* vulnerability to deal with unmet needs, get attention, or engage in the shock-and-awe behaviors that are so commonplace in today's culture." Brown, *Daring Greatly*, 46.

7. Dietrich Bonhoeffer, *Dietrich Bonhoeffer Works*, vol. 5, *Life Together* (Minneapolis: Fortress Press, 1996), 95.

8. Jean Vanier, *Community and Growth* (New York: Paulist, 1989), 29–30.

9. We are called, in the words of Bonhoeffer to "genuine Christian community." Bonhoeffer, *Life Together* (New York: Harper & Row, 1954), 39.

10. Henri Nouwen, *The Selfless Way of Christ: Downward Mobility and the Spiritual Life* (Maryknoll, NY: Orbis, 2007), 29.

11. Ibid., 31.

Chapter 7: The Power of the Lamb

1. Eugene Peterson's four key books on pastoral theology are *Working the Angles* (Grand Rapids: Eerdmans, 1989); *The Contemplative Pastor* (Eerdmans, 1993); *Five Smooth Stones for Pastoral Work* (Eerdmans, 1992); and *Under the Unpredictable Plant* (Eerdmans, 1994).

2. Peterson, *Working the Angles: The Shape of Pastoral Integrity* (Grand Rapids: Eerdmans, 1987), 1.

3. Peterson, *The Pastor: A Memoir* (San Fransisco: HarperOne, 2011).

4. Ibid., 156.

5. Ibid., 157.

6. Peterson, *Reversed Thunder: The Revelation of John and the Praying Imagination* (San Francisco: HarperCollins, 1988), 132–33.

7. See the chapter entitled "New York: Pastor John of Patmos" in *The*

Pastor to hear how Revelation and Saint John informed Eugene early in his calling.

8. Martin Luther states, "For Christ did not establish and institute the ministry of proclamation to provide us with money, property, popularity, honor, or friendship, nor to let us seek our own advantage through it; but to have us publish the truth freely and openly, rebuke evil, and announce what pertains to the advantage, health, and salvation of souls." Martin Luther, *Luther's Works*, vol. 21, *Sermon on the Mount and the Magnificat*, ed. Jaroslav Pelikan (St. Louis: Concordia, 1956), 9.

9. Peterson, *The Pastor*, 5.

10. Peterson, *The Contemplative Pastor*, 131.

11. Peterson, *The Pastor*, 5.

12. The sixteenth-century Puritan writer William Perkins states, "One in ten may be a good lawyer; one in twenty a good physician; one in a hundred may be a good man; but a good minister is one in a thousand." William Perkins, *The Art of Prophesying and the Calling of the Ministry* (Carlisle, PA: Puritan Paperbacks / Banner of Truth, 1995), 102.

Chapter 8: The Power of Faithfulness

1. In the words of Søren Kierkegaard, we want the genius. "A genius," says Kierkegaard, "is evaluated purely esthetically according to what his content, his specific gravity, is found to be." Kierkegaard has some sobering words regarding the consequence of this approach to leadership in the kingdom. He states, "When the sphere of the paradoxical-religious is now abolished or is explained back into the esthetic, an apostle becomes neither more nor less than a genius, and then good night to Christianity." Søren Kierkegaard, *Without Authority*, ed. and trans. Howard V. Hong and Edna H. Hong (Princeton, NJ: Princeton UP, 1997), 96, 95.

2. Henri Nouwen's reflections are interesting when considering toxic

leadership. He states, "One thing is clear to me: the temptation of power is greatest when intimacy is a threat. Much Christian leadership is exercised by people who do not know how to develop healthy, intimate relationships and have opted for power and control instead. Many Christian empire-builders have been people unable to give and receive love." Henri J. M. Nouwen, *In the Name of Jesus* (New York: Crossroad, 2001), 60.

3. These ideas are inspired by many of Jean Lipman-Blumen's behavioral traits of toxic leaders. Jean Lipman-Blumen, *The Allure of the Toxic Leader* (New York: Oxford UP, 2005), 19–20.

4. Jean Vanier, *Signs: Seven Words of Hope* (Mahway, NJ: Paulist, 2013), 64.

5. Lipman-Blumen, *Allure of the Toxic Leader*, 29.

6. The words of Saint Augustine are instructive on this point. He states, "What the demons have, then, is knowledge without love, and, as a result, they are so puffed up, so proud, that they have made every effort to get for themselves the divine honors and religious service that they know full well is due only to the true God. And they are still doing this now, as much as they can and with whomever they can. Over against the pride of the demons, by which mankind has deservedly been held captive, there stands, in contrast, the humility of God, made known in Christ. But human souls, puffed up with the uncleanness of pride, know nothing of the power of his humility. They are like the demons in pride but not in knowledge." Saint Augustine, *The City of God*, books 1–10, trans. William Babcock (Hyde Park, NY: New City, 2012), 299.

7. Jer. 45:5 KJV.

8. Luke 9:46–48.

9. Dallas Willard, *The Great Omission: Reclaiming Jesus's Essential Teachings on Discipleship* (New York: HarperCollins, 2006), 60.

10. Dallas Willard, *The Divine Conspiracy: Rediscovering Our Hidden Life in God* (San Francisco: HarperSanFrancisco, 1998), 48.

11. Ibid., 48–49.
12. Ibid., 88.

CHAPTER 9: WALKING IN THE WILDERNESS

1. In his book *Kingdom Conspiracy* (Grand Rapids: Brazos, 2014), Scot McKnight rightly argues that many Christians today have come to see the real "action" of God as what goes on outside the church, in something we tend to call "the kingdom." McKnight shows how recent attempts to articulate the notion of "kingdom" tend to be misguided biblically because they abstract the notion of God's reign from the fundamental notions of God's people, God as king, and a specific place or space with boundaries that make up God's kingdom.

2. Scot McKnight helpfully adds, "Put differently, *opposing the principalities and powers manifests itself first and foremost in a local church unaffected and uninfected by the evil systems of this world.*" Scot McKnight, *Kingdom Conspiracy*, 157, emphasis in original.

3. This is also what Douglas Moo argues in his commentary on Romans. See Douglas J. Moo, *The Epistles to the Romans* (Grand Rapids: Eerdmans, 1996), 384 n. 169.

4. The point here is not to say that Jesus somehow failed to deal with sin. Far from it. Rather, there is a parallel reality in what happened with the flood and what happens in baptism. Our sin is dealt with in Christ, even the roots of it, but sin still remains. That is the reality we must face in the Christian life.

5. William Willimon, "Preaching," in *Sanctified by Grace: A Theology of the Christian Life*, ed. Kent Eilers and Kyle C. Strobel (London: Bloomsbury T&T Clark, 2014), 223.

6. Mark A. Seifrid, *The Second Letter to the Corinthians*, Pillar New Testament Commentary (Grand Rapids: Eerdmans, 2014), 84–86.

7. Ibid., 85–86.

8. Walter Brueggemann claims, "Sabbath is the regular, disciplined, visible, concrete yes to the neighborly reality of the community

beloved by God." Walter Brueggemann, *Sabbath as Resistance: Saying No to the Culture of Now* (Louisville: Westminster John Knox, 2014), 87.

9. Ibid., 21.

Chapter 10: The Way of Resistance

1. I am taking this emphasis from Sarah Coakley. She continues, "What is sure, however, is that engaging in any such regular and repeated 'waiting on the divine' will involve great personal commitment and (apparently) great personal risk . . . whilst risky, this practice is profoundly transformative . . . for it is a feature of the *special* 'self-effacement' of this gentle space-making—this yielding to divine power which is no worldly power—that it marks one's willed engagement in the pattern of cross and resurrection, one's deeper rooting and grafting into the 'body of Christ' . . . as a 'hidden self-emptying of the heart.'" Sarah Coakley, *Powers and Submissions: Spirituality, Gender and Philosophy* (Malden, MA: Blackwell, 2002), 34–35.

2. John William Fletcher, *The Whole Works of the Rev. John Fletcher* (London: S. Thorne, 1835), 460.

3. Interestingly, this emphasis on homogeneity is an intentional strategy in North American evangelicalism. In many ways it finds its genesis in a book written by Donald McGavern in the 1970s titled *Understanding Church Growth*. In this book McGavern applied his "homogeneous unit principle" to church growth in the United States. In the words of David Wells, "His is the very simple observation that birds of a feather like to flock together" (David F. Wells, *Above All Earthly Pow'rs: Christ in a Postmodern World* (Grand Rapids: Eerdman's, 2005, 288). As McGavern's principle caught the attention of North American pastors, it was employed as a strategy for church growth. David Wells argues that we see the homogeneous unit principle being employed quite clearly in the strategies of church planters and pastors over the past few decades.

Pastors are intentionally pursuing "target audiences" and seeking to create environments that are comfortable, safe, and familiar for particular groups of people. He states, "These churches, as a consequence, are typically suburban, overwhelmingly white, middle class, and deliberately shaped for well-off, well-educated Boomers, though some churches are now moving on to the niche occupied by the Xers. These are the birds of a feather that are flocking together" (ibid., 289).

4. This is one of those famous historical quotes that everyone uses without offering any link to the actual quote itself! It is probably a loose translation of Kuyper from his "*A Fata Morgana*," published in *The Methodist Quarterly Review*, trans. Rev. John Hendrick (New York: Phillips & Hunt, 1906), 187.

CONCLUSION

1. Saint Augustine, *The Confessions*, 2nd ed. (Hyde Park, NY: New City, 1997), 93.

2. "It was at the beginning that God blessed the human creatures and said to them, 'Be fruitful.' The God who gave the blessing and invited fruitfulness is the Lord of the Sabbath. It requires Sabbath to bear the fruits of God's kingdom. Those who refuse Sabbath produce only sour grapes, the grapes of wrath and violence and envy and, finally, death. Sabbath is a refusal of the grapes of wrath, an embrace of good fruits of life and joy, of praise and *shalom*." Walter Brueggemann, *Sabbath as Resistance: Saying No to the Culture of Now* (Louisville: Westminster John Knox, 2014), 57.

3. New Testament scholar Richard Bauckham adds thoughtful reflection on this point in his insightful work on the theology of Revelation. In reflecting on the believer's participation in Christ's victory over Satan in Revelation 12:11, Bauckham states, "The whole verse requires that the reference to 'the blood of the Lamb' is not purely to Christ's death but to the deaths of the Christian

NOTES

martyrs, who, following Christ's example, bear witness even at the cost of their lives. But this witness even as far as death does not have an independent value of its own. Its value depends on its being a continuation of his witness. So it is by the Lamb's blood that they conquer. Their deaths defeat Satan only by participating in the victory the Lamb won over Satan by his death." Richard Bauckham, *The Theology of the Book of Revelation* (Cambridge: Cambridge UP, 1993), 75–76.